TROLLEY
TO THE PAST

A Brief History and Companion to the Operating Trolley Museums
of North America

Interurbans Special 85

by Andrew D. Young

INTERURBAN PRESS
Glendale, California

First Printing: Summer 1983
ISBN 0-916374-56-4
Printed and bound in the United States of America.

Published by
INTERURBAN PRESS
P. O. Box 6444
Glendale, California 91205

FRONT COVER PHOTO: Winterfest 1981 at the Connecticut Electric
Railway. Connecticut Company #1326 and (behind) ex-Springfield
Street Railway, later Montreal Tramway #2056 await rides under
Christmas lights.   *Wendell O. Chantry*

BACK COVER PHOTO (TOP): Ex-Illinois Terminal Class B locomotive
#1565 runs "light" on the main line of the Illinois Railway Museum,
bringing to mind the halcyon days of the interurban era.   *A. D. Young*

BACK COVER PHOTO (BOTTOM): Thirty years ago, in October 1953,
little four-wheel open-bench car #34 from Lynchburg, Virginia, poses
among the vivid Fall colors at the Branford Electric Railway. The gentlemen in overalls at left is the late E. Jay Quinby, a founder of the Electric
Railroaders' Association and a longtime museum supporter.
                                          A. D. Young Collection

FRONTISPIECE: The past comes alive at the operating trolley
museums. This Dallas, Texas, car is a typical Stone & Webster Corporation car of the early 'teens. This engineering firm, very much in business
today, seventy years ago had over two dozen street railway properties
in small and medium-sized towns and cities and evolved some very
attractive standard designs of streetcars to run their services. In later
years it was Stone & Webster's requirements which led to the development of the single-truck Birney Safety car, a lightweight, one-man-
operated vehicle. #434 holds forth on the Seashore Trolley Museum's
main line near Kennebunkport, Maine.   *Seashore Trolley Museum*

Preface

IN RECENT YEARS, a new kind of museum has made its appearance on the American scene. It is a museum quite unlike its predecessors, with few roped-off areas, no intimidating marble floors or pillars, and no grim-faced, uniformed guards. Rather it is a place of color, of movement, and of abiding interest. It is the operating trolley museum, specializing in the collection and the running of that almost wholly American invention, the electric trolley car.

In the years since 1945, the electric trolley has been in danger of becoming as much a relic of long-ago America as suits of armor are relics of long-ago Europe. Visitors have been flocking to trolley museums as much from nostalgia for a half-forgotten past as they are out of plain curiosity. But once they get there, they find no aura of hushed reverence, the usual reaction of museum visitors to the embalmed relics of a bygone age. On the contrary, the exhibits are alive and going about their business just as they always did when in regular service. They are brightly, not to say gaudily, painted and give an air of cheery informality. The typical trolley museum, therefore, is a place where kids and parents can have fun while learning and living in the past. That can't always be said about more traditional museums.

The most astonishing fact behind the movement which spawned the institutions examined in this book is that it came into existence through the vision, determination and dogged persistence of very small groups of highly motivated people. They had no formalized training in the art and science of museum curatorship, no precedent to guide them and little money to sustain them. Yet the problems they have overcome are monumental. How would *you* set about preserving a vehicle weighing between 10 and 110 tons, anywhere from 20 to 75 feet long, much less restore it to "as new" condition and then put it into safe operating trim to haul fare-paying passengers on a regular schedule?

This book will show a little of how these people did exactly those things, by telling something about the beginnings of the amateur trolley museum movement, the creation of the museums and the gradual winning over of the skeptical professionals. For the professionals are being won over. The amateur trolley museum movement has shown conclusively that its particular approach to museum creation and display can produce viable institutions, and its success has given the orthodox museum profession an infinitely broader perspective on how to preserve our industrial past in a way that can speak directly to all the senses of today's visitor.

In short, they have brought the past back to life by successfully operating their exhibits in conditions which closely match those one could have found in real life. That can be seen in the photographs, which taken together show the high quality of the work done by these amateurs over the years in preserving something of the heritage of the electric trolley car.

This is not intended to be a complete history of the trolley museum movement and its constituent member institutions. That is a story which remains to be told by others. But it is my intention to provide the reader and the museum visitor with a companion and guide to the places they have seen and enjoyed. It is for you to say whether I have succeeded.

A NOTE ON THE ROSTERS

The rosters accompanying the text are at best tentative. No museum has yet published a 100 percent satisfactory roster that accounts for the car's full history, its technical specifications and measurements, and its subsequent wanderings to different owners, if such occurred. Moreover, many of the rosters do not agree even in terminology used to describe car types or function. Nor yet does there seem to be much consistency in listing a car by its current paint scheme and lettering, so that what is described as car X from city Y might be masquerading in the colors of car A of city B. Since no book of this sort has been published before, with rosters accompanying each museum description, I ask for your indulgence over mistakes which may have been made and request that corrections be sent in care of the publisher.

Acknowledgements

THE IMMEDIATE inspiration for this book was a series of ongoing articles on North American trolley museums written by the author for publication in England's *Modern Tramway* magazine. These began in the early 1970s as a part of its lively "Museum Notes" monthly column, which surveys the trolley museum scene worldwide. But my connection with the museum movement goes back much further. As a teenager, I was involved as a humble worker in a number of British museum projects until compelled to concentrate on the more pressing need to complete an education. From that background grew my interest in the parallel American museum experience, the more so once I came to live in the U.S.A.

In England, John H. Price read and commented on the draft manuscript, and my thanks go to him. John Price's contributions to the study and preservation of trolleys in England (and elsewhere) are legion. It is in great measure due to his knowledge and historical perspective that the National Tramway Museum of England is the world influence it is in the trolley museum movement. In addition he has been active in the affairs of many other British trolley museum projects, not to mention other operations with no trolley connections. Moreover, as Historical Features Editor of *Modern Tramway*, Mr. Price has encouraged many reluctant writers (myself included) to contribute major historical pieces to *Modern Tramway* which otherwise might have remained unwritten. Not the least important of his activities has been his overall stewardship of the "Museum Notes" column of *Modern Tramway*, the only one of its kind in the English-speaking world, which has now been going for over 20 years.

Also in England, A. Keith Terry, Barry Spencer and his cousin Richard, Rowland Wilks, Roy Wardroper, Ian Dougill, Colin Heaton, Alex Brown, Dr. Mike Harrison, David Higgins, Bernard Donald, Brian Parkin and Jim Soper, together with other members past and present of the Leeds Transport Historical Society and the Tramway Museum Society, remain friends whom I manage to see all too seldom. I thank them for the good times we had together "tramming" in England, Scotland and Wales, in the museums, at Middleton, and in the still-operating tramway towns of Europe.

In the U.S. and Canada I want to thank the very many individuals connected with the museums who helped with the research, checked and corrected the entries and helped with the project, but first I want to acknowledge the assistance given by museum members of the Association of Railway Museums.

I particularly want to thank William J. Clouser of St. Louis, Mo., and of course Mac Sebree and Jim Walker of Interurban Press for their critical comments and suggestions. In addition, my thanks is due the following ladies and gentlemen for their time, either at the museums, through conversation or correspondence, or as knowledgeable friends, happy to help a transplanted "Brit" through the multitude of pitfalls separating my first general impressions of the movement from the actual facts. I hope they get some pleasure from the book. They are: Clyde L. Anderson, Edward Anderson, Paul Averdung, Wilson Bates, Paul Bettman, J.C. Boykin, F. Travers Burgess, W.J. Campbell, Dr. Harold E. Cox, R.R. Clark, Paul V. Class, the late George Crook, Henry Elsner, Kevin T. Farrell, Gordon Frederick, Mark Goldfeder, Don Haeussermann, Bill Heger, Robert Hepp, Paul Hinchey, D. Horachek, Bill Hoss, Dr. Al Howe, Russell E. Jackson, David Jobe, Jim Johnson, Nick Kallas, Edwin Klasky, Tom Konieczny, Jim Kottkamp, Allan Koplar, F. Axtell Kramer, R.T. Lane, Wayne Laepple, Michael Lennon, Steven Marx, John McInnes, George Metz, D. Ben Minnich, Roy Nelson, David Neubauer, David Norman, Bill Olsen, K.A. Pearson, Bill Peters, Alex Pollock, Tolbert Prowell, Cheryl Richardson, K.H. Rucker, Theodore Santarelli, Vernon J. Sappers, Jack Schramm, Joan Seegmiller, David Steinberg, Donna and Bob Trebing, Willard B. Thomas, John Thomsen, Rod Varney, Dave Wright and William Wood.

Finally, my thanks to my wife Evelyn, my mother and my mother-in-law who over the years have joined me in my visits to many of the museums in this book. They were delighted with what they saw and are convinced my son Joshua is about to follow in his father's footsteps and that my son Benjamin will do so in his turn.

A.D. Young
Maryland Heights, Missouri
April, 1983

Table of Contents

COLOR

A scene much like that of a trolley station in a small city has been re-created at the ORANGE EMPIRE RAILWAY MUSEUM, Perris, California. One of its newest exhibits, Los Angeles Transit Lines #3165 (built in 1948), will soon take on passengers for a trip on the museum's one-half-mile "loop" line.

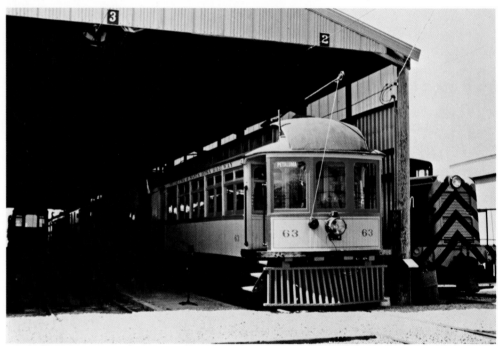

Petaluma & Santa Rosa #63, sitting in Car House No. 1 at the CALIFORNIA RAILWAY MUSEUM, Rio Vista Junction, California, is a fine example of "resurrection." Its body, located in use as a shed in an orchard, was combined with mechanical and electrical components, then renewed inside and out, and it now delights visitors as an operating interurban car.

This view looks west along the double-track portion of the BRANFORD TROLLEY MUSEUM, East Haven, Connecticut. Building B2 (see on locator map in the museum's listing) at left, is one of the museum's early carbarns. Connecticut Company parlor car #500, approaching at center right, is furnished with wicker chairs and is one of Branford's premier exhibits.

ALBUM

Connecticut Company #840 stands at the entrance to the CONNECTICUT ELECTRIC RAILWAY, near Warehouse Point, Connecticut, which operates a number of the vintage vehicles. Open-bench trolley travel, once a popular summer pastime in New England, is still a delightful experience at many of the trolley museums.

THE FOX RIVER LINE, South Elgin, Illinois, operates its collection over a portion of a former interurban railway. Chicago, Aurora & Elgin arch-window interurban #316 is returning from the outer portion of the line. It passes an open-bench trolley brought to the museum from Brazil.

The vast streetcar network of Chicago is represented by Chicago Surface Lines #144, carrying a full load along the main line at the ILLINOIS RAILWAY MUSEUM, Union, Illinois. This museum conducts one of the most comprehensive operations of any of those included in this book; not only trolleys, interurbans and trolley buses, but steam locomotive-hauled passenger trains.

If you come to the annual Old Threshers Reunion at Mt. Pleasant, Iowa, you can partake of trolley rides while enjoying the display of operating steam and internal combustion tractors and stationary farm machinery. The MIDWEST ELECTRIC RAILWAY collection includes this Waterloo, Cedar Falls & Northern city streetcar.

The SEASHORE TROLLEY MUSEUM, Kennebunkport, Maine, has not only an operating railway, but also extensive visitor facilities including this display barn. Among its earliest acquisitions, and most nicely restored exhibits, is Manchester & Nashua Street Railway interurban #38. The grillwork at far right belongs to another prized car, the City of Manchester (see photos in the museum's listing).

Located not far from downtown, the BALTIMORE STREETCAR MUSEUM displays and operates a collection of streetcars from that city's system from earliest electrics to streamliners. Examples of both eras, #3651 and PCC #7407, are seen in this view in front of the museum's carbarn.   *Jim Walker*

Representative cars from Washington, D.C., streetcar system have been collected by the NATIONAL CAPITAL TROLLEY MUSEUM, Wheaton, Maryland. Capital Transit Co. PCC streamliner #1101 stands at the museum loading platform. The museum also operates an interesting selection of European tramcars.

One of the former Lisbon, Portugal, deck-roof streetcars that were brought to America for use on the DETROIT CITIZENS RAILWAY, runs against traffic along a main thoroughfare toward the carbarn terminal. Since its opening in 1976, the tourist-oriented line has become a favorite with convention-goers and visitors to the riverfront area.   *Jim Walker*

Twin Cities Rapid Transit #1300, one of the large fleet of streetcars which once served Minneapolis, once again carries passengers between Lake Harriet and Lake Calhoun on a revived section of the Como-Harriet route under the aegis of the MINNESOTA TRANSPORTATION MUSEUM. It has just arrived at the Lake Calhoun terminus.   *Jim Walker*

This route, through lawns and homes in a mobile home park, is traversed by Chicago, Aurora & Elgin interurban #319 at TROLLEYVILLE, U.S.A., Olmsted Falls, Ohio. This trolley operation was built through the efforts of the late Gerald E. Brookins.

Unable to acquire a complete Columbus streetcar when the system was converted to buses, the OHIO RAILWAY MUSEUM, Worthington, Ohio, later found the body of Columbus Railway, Light & Power #703 and brought it back to life with trucks, motors and other equipment gathered from other areas.

Johnstown Traction Co. double-truck Birney Safety Car #311 carries visitors at the SHADE GAP ELECTRIC RAILWAY operation at Orbisonia, Pennsylvania. The electric railway shares a common site with the East Broad Top, a steam-operated tourist railway.

Broad-gauge trolleys from both ends of Pennsylvania operate at the ARDEN TROLLEY MUSEUM, Washington, Pennsylvania. At left is center-door suburban car #66 from the Red Arrow system of Philadelphia, and Pittsburgh Railways #3756 heads north on the Arden Mines Extension. The museum's line is built to the broad (5′2½″) track gauge of most systems in the Commonwealth.

Chicago, North Shore & Milwaukee #757, one of the cars preserved by the EAST TROY TROLLEY MUSEUM'S sponsoring organization, rolls along the outer section of the former Milwaukee Transport interurban line to the village of East Troy, Wisconsin. The village retained this portion for freight switching and the museum provides passenger service.

Traveling through the woods of Ontario in autumn is a real treat, especially on a trolley car. Included in the collection of the HALTON COUNTY RADIAL RAILWAY, near Rockwood, is #327, a replica of an early open electric car built by the Toronto Transportation Commission some years ago.

PART 1: The Movement

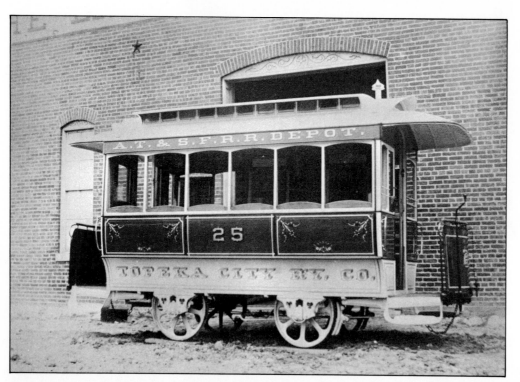

In the 1880s, the horse car was king of local transit. Its lack of physical amenities such as heat, ventilation and space were compensated for by the care lavished on the car's external appearance, as with Topeka, Kan. #25 (LEFT) here seen at its birthplace, St. Louis's Laclede Car Co. in the mid-1880s. *Author's Collection*

A set of both open and closed equipment was necessary in the 1880s and for many years afterwards for fair and foul weather operations. Two horse cars (BELOW) from Kansas City's *Metropolitan Street Railway* are outside the Laclede Car Co. in the mid-1880s. *Author's Collection*

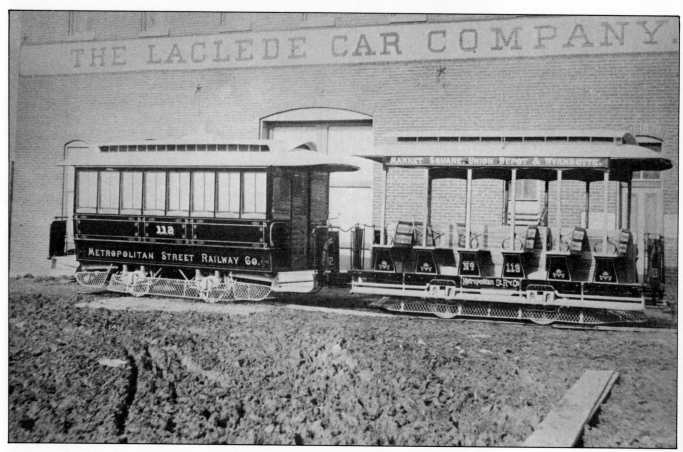

Chapter 1

A Passing Transport Era

THERE'S BEEN nothing quite like the electric trolley car in the history of North America. Its impact on domestic life was swift and stupendous. In the 30 years before 1917, almost nothing stood in its way. Without the electric trolley, urban life on this continent hardly seemed worth living. From the largest city to the smallest town, communities struggled mightily to get services started and, once they had begun, moved heaven and earth to get them improved and extended. Why? Because in that pre-auto age the installation of an electric trolley system within a community overnight made the movement of large numbers over short distances not just possible for the first time in man's history, but utterly simple and cheap. The coming of the electric trolley opened up possibilities for the amelioration of overcrowded conditions and an enrichment of urban life for the masses that then seemed to be limitless.

The electric trolley astounded contemporary observers with its power. It seemed to touch and improve all lives equally in the most approved democratic fashion. Many indeed professed to see a mystical, perhaps divinely guided quality to the trolley's relentless progress across the continent on what all were agreed was its civilizing mission. Some said it was no less than a miracle.

Certainly, the enrichment of urban life the trolley made possible was tangible enough, but philanthropy was not the motive of those who brought the trolley to the people. On the contrary, those who promoted, financed and operated electric trolley systems were in it primarily for the money. In an age which looked on such activities with a less jaundiced eye than our own, their appetite for quick and large profits was undisguised. It was the primary reason for entering the trolley business. But if in the rush to make their millions, the promoters' activities happened to realize the fondest aspirations of the citizenry, well, that was just dandy. It was proof of the civic morality of the profit motive and *laissez-faire* business practices.

For no one argued that one of the side benefits of a profitable trolley company's service to the public was civic progress. That progress was undeniable and it was swift; almost as swift as the trolley as it spread across the country. These, after all, were the days when North America had finally turned its back on its frontier, seeing its future lying instead with the rapidly growing cities and their industries. Many felt civilized life to be possible only in urban areas, and it was the trolley companies in seemingly casual fashion which emphasized that point of view as they became agents of city growth

The early electric cars, too, were elaborately finished. *Birmingham Railway and Electric* #41 is seen at the Avondale line on October 30, 1891, the first day of electric service. *Edwin J. Klasky Collection*

(largely unplanned) in and around the areas they served. Lines were built to serve every existing suburb and every possible city amenity. Parks, lakes, botanical gardens, downtown shopping areas, railway stations, factories, beaches, ball parks and cemeteries were all served. And where such amenities didn't exist, a go-ahead trolley company would build its own. A whole raft of attractions and activities were owned or sponsored by trolley companies, from baseball teams to moonlight car parties. But the most common and the most spectacular of trolley enterprises was the trolley park.

Eighty years ago, the trolley park was a familiar part of city life. It was usually a high-tone amusement park built by the company, invariably miles from anywhere, accessible only by way of the company's trolley line, custom-built to serve it. The parks' attractions were many, and appealed to the multitudes: boating, fishing, calliopes, food, fireworks, parades, good bands and, in the best of all, high-class vaudeville. For years the parks and the lines built to serve them were money spinners for the trolley companies.

Wherever the trolley went, the builder quickly followed. Frequently the trolley company itself was heavily into real estate. It was common practise to buy huge lots in virgin territory, lay tracks adjacent to them, and then quickly resell the lots for building purposes. This ensured an immediate profit and, of course, guaranteed that in the near future the trolleys would carry many new passengers between their gleaming sub-

urban homes and the city. Lines thus fanned out in every direction, leaving the seeds of future suburban sprawl in their wake as vacant tracts on their line of route were covered with new buildings further and further away from the downtown core. In this way, huge sections of the continent's rapidly growing cities were shaped by the facilities the electric trolley provided. For more than 30 years the electric trolley was absolute master of urban transit and the chosen instrument of city growth.

Much of the trolley's immediate acceptance had to do with its cheerfully opulent "dress." The handsome finish and bright colors of the electric trolley were a novelty, and in the 1890s many companies openly stated that spending good money on a handsome finish was the best way to attract otherwise skeptical passengers to sample the amenities offered by the new electric car. Trolleys were luxuriously equipped in many respects during the '90s, some with costly rare woods, others with Wilton carpets, window shades of Russian leather, and a multitude of fittings in polished brass. There were even cut glass shades around the electric lights on some cars. Electric lighting was a rarity in the 1890s in most homes and public buildings, and not universal even at the end of World War I. But it was available to anyone for the price of a trolley ride.

Most important of all, the electric trolley was unbelievably swift in an age which measured transit speed and efficiency solely in terms of the horse. The trolley was quiet, clean, cheap, convenient and comfortable;

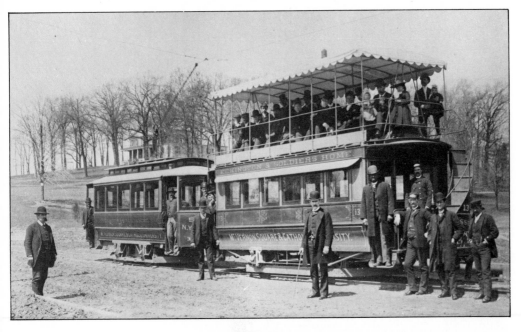

Though woefully underpowered and at first somewhat unreliable, the early electric cars were so much an improvement over the horse cars they replaced that operators thought nothing of hanging an extra trailer or two behind, packed with people ready for a pleasure trip to the suburbs. This is one of Washington, D.C.'s first electric lines, the *Eckington and Soldiers' Home,* with car #5 and double-deck trailer #13, around 1895. A few American cities even had powered double-deck cars. *Author's Collection*

The cable car, while never very extensive in its proliferation, was a reliable and accepted method of mechanical traction in the continent's larger cities. It did not, however, survive the coming of the electric trolley. This Portland, Oregon, cable car was built at the same time as the cable line in 1890, but the line itself survived only until 1896, when it was wholly replaced by electricity, save for a small stretch of fearsome grade, which survived until 1904. Car #2 meets two electrics (ex-cable cars themselves) at Junction Point (the corner of Chapman and Jefferson) in 1896.

William J. Clouser Collection

an unbeatable combination. Not surprisingly, it was used by all social classes from the very first, quickly becoming an integral part of life's fabric and a familiar, almost intimate, friend to the urban dweller.

Because the cars were so quickly accepted by the public, the electric trolley did much to demonstrate the safety of electric power in everyday use. Electricity was the wonder of the age, yet other than those connected with the burgeoning electrical industry, people were ignorant of its nature and scared of its power. The telephone and the electric light were the only large-scale applications for electricity perfected before the electric trolley, and those items were luxuries for the very rich. Many felt electricity was best kept under lock and key in the laboratory. But, going about its

appointed duties without fuss, the electric trolley changed those attitudes, breaking down fear and prejudice. By 1900 (some would argue even before that date) the trolley had become a robust and reliable machine of docile mien, as even the most casual observer could not fail to see. One man, with a twirl of his wrist, could start, stop and vary the car's speed with an ease utterly unknown to any other form of animal or mechanical traction, and he could do it without compromising anyone's safety.

It was not long, therefore, before the trolley spread beyond the city and its suburbs. In those pre-auto days, few roads were adequate for sustained all-weather use, and short-distance travel from most farms or villages to a railhead, county seat or city, could be fraught with difficulty. Interstate links by rail and water were well developed by this time, but short-distance intrastate transport was not. It was the electric trolley which first held out promise of solving this problem. At the turn of the century, with the city trolley seemingly perfected, electric rail lines suddenly leaped beyond city limits to connect whole strings of small or medium-sized towns with a county seat or a big town.

The interurbans (as they quickly became known) could provide fast, clean, electric passenger service over distances and through areas the steam railroads either could not or would not cover. The new cars were nearly as big and certainly as comfortable as a steam railroad car, and often more impressive with the typical plate glass windows and art glass characteristic of the time.

The electric interurbans also could provide quick same-day freight service for less-than-carload perishables, and the economic stimulus given rural areas by the coming of an interurban was very real. Typical was the quick development of large-scale commercial growing enterprises (later known as truck farms) which were able to use the interurban to ship fresh fruit, vegetables, meat and dairy produce to market in neighboring towns up to 60 miles away, without risk of spoilage.

For those few heady years before the coming of the motor truck and the paved road, the interurban was perceived as the tool by which rural North America might finally be tamed, developed and civilized. The swift service of the interurban constituted a rural transportation revolution of great magnitude, in some ways of far greater importance than the coming of steam railroad 50 years back. Indeed, during 1904, one interurban manufacturer boldly stated that the entire western U.S.A., considered undeveloped frontier land before 1890, would in a matter of years be "honeycombed with interurban lines, enabling one to travel from village to village, city to city and state to state." In due course, this seemingly wild boast became close to the truth in many western and midwestern states. California, Indiana, Illinois, Iowa, Michigan, Ohio, Pennsylvania, Utah and Wisconsin ultimately had some of the best-developed and longest-lived interurban networks, serving a large proportion of their states' inhabitants. In addition, upstate New York, parts of New Jersey and northern Oregon, together with western British Columbia, eastern Ontario and parts of Quebec in Canada, possessed well-developed networks. Moreover, for decades the New England states of Connecticut, Maine and Massachusetts (and to a lesser extent Rhode Island and southeastern New Hampshire) were thoroughly laced with innumerable rural trolley lines—not built to interurban standards, but nonetheless serving to connect cities and towns.

The large-scale construction of electric trolley and interurban lines was the impetus needed to lift the electrical manufacturing industry out of the laboratory and into the marketplace, becoming as it did so the basic

industry it is today. Many firms now manufacturing or supplying electrical products, from light bulbs to generators and switchgear, got their first commercial breaks from the electric trolley. Mighty General Electric, for example, was formed in 1892 as a result of a merger between early trolley supply companies. In some places the trolley company itself was the first commercial supplier of domestic and industrial current to its area and many times was the largest local producer of electricity. The interurbans followed their city cousins' example in the countryside they served. Southeastern Wisconsin is a good example of a region where rural electrification came early, solely as the result of good interurban railway penetration.

Not surprisingly, then, there was a rush to invest in the electric trolley. Between 1887 and 1907, trolley securities were the hottest properties on the market, almost all lucrative investments of blue chip quality. This was largely as a result of the trolley's immunity to cyclical economic fluctuations. In those 20 years, the trolley industry did not cease to grow. The country had recessions, but the trolley industry did not. As a result, the "days of '49" lived again in the gold-rush fever trolley stock seemed to induce. Growth and yield were exceptional—if you picked the right companies—and for those that owned enough of them, the power they conferred in financial circles was formidable. Would-be financiers, unable to make their killings in the robber baron-dominated railroad securities market, turned instead to building up similar empires in trolley and interurban securities, empires which came and went astonishingly quickly. For the average investor, trolley securities provided an income-producing haven for his money. Purchase of selected trolley stocks was often advised to round out the portfolios of widows and orphans in need of high income at low risk.

Those more interested in securities speculation went out of their way to outshine their already legendary railroad contemporaries in the outrageousness of their deals and the flamboyance of their style of living. In doing so, they began to tarnish the electric trolley's hitherto unsullied reputation. While no one ever outdid the Morgans, Goulds and Harrimans of the railroad empires, the audacity and panache with which the trolley magnates conducted their affairs was fully in keeping with the standards set by those gentlemen.

There was Charles Tyson Yerkes, thinly disguised as Frank Algernon Cowperwood by Theodore Dreiser in his blistering expose of the breed in a book entitled *The Titan*. Yerkes gained and lost a vast traction empire in Chicago during the '80s and '90s before moving on to London and the successful financing of that city's still-operating tube network.

There was Henry Huntington, nephew of the Southern Pacific's Collis P. Huntington, whose large collection of trolley and interurban companies were the roots of the huge Pacific Electric system and the comprehensive Los Angeles Railway. The former operation in the first 20 years of this century almost single-handedly created the Los Angeles area as we know it today. When Huntington sold all his interests in Pacific Electric, much of the money he received in exchange was showered on the Huntington Library, today perhaps the western U.S.A.'s single most important cultural institution.

And there was John I. Beggs, who for three decades shaped the transport destinies of countless communities in Wisconsin and Missouri through the great new corporate device known as the holding company. Beggs was in fact a director and major stockholder in the North American Company, the first successful holding company in the country. Beggs was the first of his breed in the traction industry, the first "corporate man" and his interests on behalf of North American stretched far beyond traction to encompass electrical supply and other utilities. But in style, he was even more of a traction "robber baron" than the others.

His fortune was firmly based upon successful trolley operation, and he differed from his contemporaries in the business only that he continually preached the gospel of honest accounting to his less scrupulous brethren. Moreover, he took the precaution of heeding his own advice. Consequently his companies were among the best run in the U.S. (particularly the TMER&L in Milwaukee) and he died in 1925 worth some $30 million, probably the only trolley man of his generation to both keep and augment his fortune. When probate was finally settled in 1930, his estate had appreciated in value to $54 million!

So long as trolley securities were synonymous with high yield, sound financial management of day-to-day corporate activities in the average trolley company had a habit of taking second place to a frenzied game of musical chairs played by the speculators seeking to buy and sell stock. It took no great leap of the imagination to see that electric trolley companies could make money faster than the U.S. Mint and soon a host of parasites began to latch onto the money machine; ranging from over-greedy cities, and corrupt city legislators, to former snake-oil salesmen. Soon fledgling trolley companies began to be overburdened with watered stock issued by their promoters, saddled with onerous franchises by the communities they were to serve and pledged to return large and regular dividends to stockholders. Frequently a company would have these obligations on its head before ever a wheel was turned in public service!

The whole of this burden was heaped upon the industry on the not unreasonable assumption that large profits were automatically assured no matter how weighty the obligations on the company. The trolley, after all, had a total monopoly of short-distance urban transit; a commodity in monumental demand. But, with so many companies assuming financial burdens of that nature, profitability was *not* always guaranteed, even on the largest of consolidated city systems. And too many companies made the unpardonable error of paying stockholder dividends without fail every quarter, even if it meant paying them out of capital—the high road to ruin.

In such a situation, those operating the trolleys were

By 1900, the electric trolley was an accepted part of daily life. It carried people to and from their work, delivered their packages, collected their freight, picked up fresh milk and fruit from the farmer for shipment to city markets, took the people on pleasure trips in open cars, to the hospital in ambulance cars and to the grave in funeral cars. And in some cities, they delivered the mail! *Chicago Union Traction #8 and its crew (LEFT) are seen in 1899.*
Edwin J. Klasky Collection

(ABOVE) Immediately recognizable as classic early wooden interurban cars, these three units of the *Puget Sound Electric Railway* are at Meredith in Washington's White River Valley, early in 1903. Motor #500 is towing trailers #513 and 519. The line used third-rail current collection between towns, and overhead collection elsewhere; this required fencing of the rural sections for safety. Third-rail pickup on interurban lines was not the industry norm but was not rare, and examples of this could be seen in the Chicago area as late as 1963. The white glass in each car indicates the location of the lavatories, thought by many to be the crucial identification tag of a true interurban car as opposed to a high-speed suburban trolley. The undeveloped nature of the countryside is typical of the early years of interurbans; the line served small towns and villages. The coming of the paved roads was fatal to the PSR. It entered bankruptcy in 1927 and the last train ran in 1928.
Edwin J. Klasky Collection

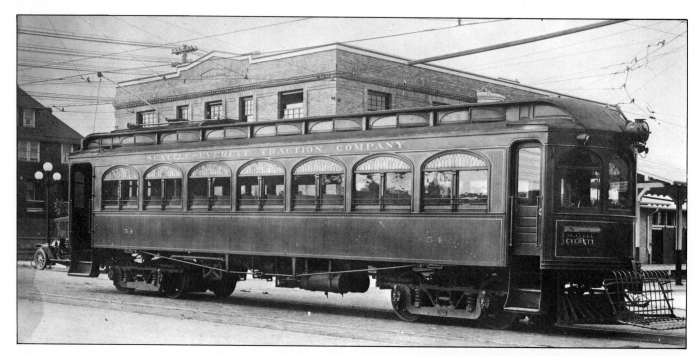

(ABOVE) Between 1903 and 1910, the interurban networks came into full flower with their clean speedy passenger services, extensive freight services and beautifully got up cars. Imposing *Seattle-Everett Traction Co.* #54 prepares to leave on a trip in 1910. Noteworthy classic interurban car features include the full railroad roof, the arched art-glass upper window sash, the high narrow entrances, the huge arc headlight hung above the motorman's window and the heavy-duty, high-speed trucks, which with the powerful motors could give a wooden interurban a top speed in excess of 60 mph. The elaborate Providence fender at the car's front was not normal interurban equipment and may have been fitted to comply with a local city ordinance. Though the interurban car is seen here in its heyday, nemesis is already at hand; there is a parked automobile at the very left of the picture.
Edwin J. Klasky Collection

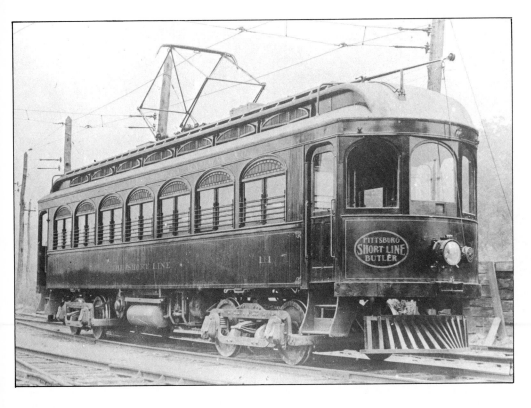

(LEFT) Riding high on large wheels, this handsome wooden interurban of the Short Line between Pittsburgh and Butler, Penna., weighed nearly 38 tons. The use of pantographs on interurban lines was not widespread, and not even universal on this line, which used trolley poles to collect current on city streets.
Edwin J. Klasky Collection

between a rock and a hard place, for if dividends were not paid frequently, the whizz-fizz image of the business which kept investors interested would quickly evaporate and with it the glamor of trolley stock as a sound investment. A cash-poor company would then have little hope of shouldering its financial burden unaided and surviving with the all-but-universal nickel fare then prevailing. So, if the whole house of cards was not to collapse, even the most prudently run companies found themselves making glaringly obvious shortcuts, from construction to operation, in order to satisfy the insatiable craving of their owners for high yield and profit.

Caught in this bind, all too many companies refused to make allowances in their accounts for depreciation, maintenance and renewal, using money that should have been set aside for these purposes to pay dividends. In the early years, when everything was new, that was a chance one could take. But by the early 1900s age was catching up with even the newest installations and gradually slowly deteriorating service and increasingly surly officials became more common.

The electric trolley itself was a robust machine which regularly exceeded its predicted life span without distress, but the public perception of increasingly aged trolleys running on poorly maintained tracks was one all too true by 1910. Moreover, continued technological development within the trolley industry often made whole inventories of equipment obsolete before their time and eventually even the over-age trolley cars themselves began to wear out, along with the tracks and physical plant upon which they depended.

Thus when the greatest proportion of the continent's trolley fleets began to fall due for renewal after 1910, there was often no money to buy replacements. All money then came from the farebox, or from the issuing of new commercial paper. There were no federal or state subsidies. The manufacturing side of the industry was only just getting used to the realities of the situation. The trolley market became only a replacement market. In truth, the situation was worse than that, and those manufacturers who weren't already diversifying soon found themselves in difficulties when even replacement trolley orders did not materialize.

In theory, commercial loans for equipment renewal were always available, but many companies were already so saddled with debt that no bank would dare touch them. As a result, the gilt wore off trolley securities quite quickly, especially after the 1906-08 slump. Certainly, many big city companies and large traction groups continued to do well, but after 1910 the weaker companies were left to struggle on as best they could, hoping better times would return.

But better times did not return. In the next decade the automobile finally broke the electric trolley's monopoly on short-distance urban transit and, by 1920, the last of the major speculators had moved out of trolley securities and into oil or Florida land. Doubtless the widows and orphans holding such securities were advised to do likewise. A few flurries of renewed interest sparked the industry in the booming '20s, but came to nothing. The industry had not just stopped growing, it had begun to atrophy.

It was a painful process and the interurban railways were hurt the most. Almost always financially weaker than their city cousins, they could not survive the erosion of their revenues by the wash of trucks and autos flooding the land. Some undertakings were moribund as early as 1910 and a handful had torn up their tracks completely. But after 1925 it was clear the entire interurban industry was at risk. The Depression simply hastened its end. The building of state-subsidised concrete highways in the '20s, often by the side of an existing interurban right-of-way, encouraged the widespread adoption of autos for rural passenger and commercial use and most of the interurbans vanished as quickly as they had appeared. By 1930 the only hope of survival lay in offering high-speed commuter service to big cities, frequent medium-distance intercity passenger runs, steam railroad interchange, and good on-line freight services for local customers. The surviving inter-

By the second decade of the century, the sturdy single-truck closed city car of the 1890s was hopelessly obsolete, technologically and physically outclassed by newer and larger vehicles. Yet still they soldiered on, as witness this 1892 San Diego car (ABOVE), part of the original batch of single deckers with which the system began, battered but unbowed in 1912. Most passengers of the day would have been appalled to see this little car in rush-hour service, although had the car survived to have become a museum piece, today's visitors would have been enchanted. Essentially similar cars to this are, however, preserved in operational condition such as Rhode Island #61 at Branford, and its present stablemate, *Union Street Railway* (**New Bedford**) **#316,** cars dating from 1893 and 1895 respectively.

*Historical Collection,
Union Title Insurance Company/
Courtesy Edwin J. Klasky*

urbans offered such a mix of services and a few still survive today, having abandoned passenger and electric operation in favor of diesel traction and the haulage of freight. Almost all, of course, have been directly absorbed by steam roads, but those fortunate few amount to just 15% of the interurbans built, the rest having simply been abandoned and the money so lavishly poured into them irretrievably lost.

City trolley operators, too, were not exempt from automobile competition yet, most surprisingly, they made no serious attempts to deal with it, hoping the auto would go away of its own accord and quit bothering folk with real work to do! Some even saw the auto as a passing fad, rather as the bicycle had been in the 1890s. Few companies were in any position to make large-scale investments in plant and equipment needed to effectively counter the automobile in the 1920s. The gasoline bus was already an effective transit tool in the

hands of competing operators and many trolley owners took the hint.

Their experiments with gas buses were imaginative and the results were encouraging, for the bus was seen by potential passengers as a high-class and speedy alternative to the trolley, worth paying a premium fare to use. Others with a more thrifty eye looked to the electric trolley coach as a means of salvation, since apart from rails, the trolley coach made use of existing facilities yet was perceived as being both modern and economical. In both cases the new vehicles greatly lessened operating costs, while passengers flocked to the fast and comfortable new equipment.

Few investors were interested in new trolley securities. Company failures and reorganization became very common and the bulk of the continent's trolley service, once the marvel of the world for its comprehensiveness and efficiency, became considerably poorer.

Maintenance standards, too, continued to decline. In the most outrageous cases, virtually moribund plant and cars, dating from the turn of the century, were still in daily use, pitted against up-to-date buses or trolley coaches (often owned by the same company that ran the trolleys) and, increasingly, the private automobile. It really was no contest. While occasionally a quasi-public authority could gain control of a bankrupt trolley company, buy new cars, pull service standards up and win back passengers from competing transit modes, such bodies had their greatest success only in the very largest of cities, where all public transit modes could be integrated under their jurisdiction, and where large sums of public money could be made available. The efficient operation of electric trolleys thus quickly became confined to the largest cities. Elsewhere the decline became a tailspin, as the traveling public sought other ways to commute to and from the suburbs the trolley had helped create.

The alternative continued to be the automobile, now more comfortable and efficient than ever before. From the 1930s it was the automobile rather than the trolley (or the replacing bus) which became the transit mode around which cities and towns shaped themselves. While the trolley's decline was slowed by World War II, by 1960 the traditional trolley car had become all but extinct in North America.

Downtown Columbus, Ohio, in 1913, with the Ohio State Capitol Building at the right. Though the streets are paved and trolley service is well patronized, already private automobiles are in evidence. While they weren't all as luxuriously appointed as the little electric runabout on the left, without question they were well in front of the trolley in terms of passenger convenience in all but the foulest of weather. For ulti- mately, that's what a transit passenger seeks, comfortable, convenient transport. That is the reason the electric trolley swept aside all that came before it, and that is the reason it in turn was swept aside by the automobile that came after it. Though the trolley gave comfort, speed and convenience in 1913, so already could the private automobile.
Edwin J. Klasky Collection

(ABOVE) After World War One, the continent fell for the automobile as heavily as it had for the electric trolley thirty years earlier. The smaller trolley systems began to disappear, but for a while the larger systems continued to thrive. *San Diego Electric Railway #213 and #426 are seen at the Santa Fe railroad station loop in 1920, just around the corner from the present new Light Rail terminal point.* Historical Collection, Union Title Insurance Company/ Courtesy Edwin J. Klasky

Edwin J. Klasky Collection

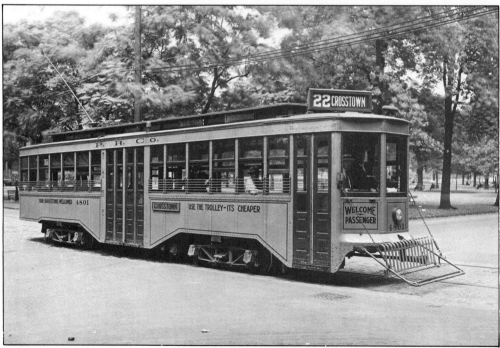

Owners of big city trolleys were not slow to see that the inflation-induced end of the universal nickel fare (and the losses that went with it) meant their monopoly on urban transit was in jeopardy. While new equipment could no longer be bought with the reckless profligacy of the old days, letting the passengers know you were just as glad to see them couldn't hurt. "Welcome passenger," says the slogan on the front dash of *Pittsburgh Railways'* low floor car #4801 in the early 1920s; and the company *meant* it. A similar car is preserved at the Arden Trolley Museum.

(ABOVE) The rural interurban was only just holding its own by the early 1920s, but the arrival of a car in a village was still one of the day's events. *Aroostook Valley* combine #70, now awaiting restoration at the Seashore Trolley Museum, pauses at Washburn, Maine, around 1922.
Willard B. Thomas Collection

(RIGHT) The interurban which ran from a large city, linking it with small and medium-sized towns with its own segregated right-of-way still had a fighting chance for survival and many of these lines, extensively and expensively modernized in the early and mid-1920s, survived a minimum of another fifteen years. Many survived into post-World War Two days, while the Chicago area lines ran until much later. Indeed, the *Chicago, South Shore and South Bend* survives still, thanks to an extensive modernization in 1926 and the delivery of a new generation of cars completed in 1983. The *Chicago, North Shore and Milwaukee* line, closed in 1963, gave a high-speed electric link between Chicago, its northern suburbs and Milwaukee, and is badly missed, though high-speed electric commuter service over a short surviving portion to Skokie is still provided. Equally as badly missed is the *Chicago, Aurora and Elgin,* a third-rail interurban which closed to passengers in 1957. Both these lines gave downtown access over the elevated tracks and into Chicago's Loop. Here is the *Chicago, Aurora and Elgin's* Wells Street terminal in the Loop, with many heavy interurban cars and throngs of homegoing commuters awaiting their trains, in 1925. Car #316 on the right is preserved in operating condition at the RELIC Museum in South Elgin.
Edwin J. Klasky Collection

(BELOW) By the time the Great Depression hit, most of the interurban industry was dying on its feet. Large-scale subsidies for concreting hitherto unpaved roads were universally available and often the roads paralleled interurban routes across the states served. The development of all-weather road traffic, both passenger and freight, robbed the interurban of the best of its remaining business frighteningly quickly. Even the largest modernized systems now began to succumb, though many fought a valiant rear-guard action which put off the day of reckoning for many years. The infusion of high-speed cars, parlor and express service, together with motor bus feeders helped the large midwest companies to survive beyond all odds from the late '20s to the early '40s, though increasingly their services shriveled to almost nothing in the process. Here a Reo bus of the *Interstate Public Service Corporation* is posed with one of the same company's massive 1920s steel cars, apparently holding down services on the line's crack *Dixie Flyer*, a five times a day express parlor-diner run connecting Indianapolis and Louisville.

William J. Clouser Collection

(RIGHT) Something better was needed to persuade people to come back to the city trolley in the 1930s. That there was now no chance of saving the small-town trolley or purely rural interurban was already generally agreed, but the largest city systems still had a chance to re-equip. It was the industry consensus that speed, silence, cleanliness and perceived modernity of style and components were the most successful elements of experimental cars produced in small quantities at the end of the 1920s. Here are the top brass of *Louisville Railways* swarming all over car #1050, a conservatively styled 1920s car, standing on its Timken worm-drive trucks. Testing of the trucks, a new design developed for silent city operation, revealed that worm drives were not suited for intensive city service. More "guinea-pig" cars would follow as the streetcar companies sought an alternative to abandonment.

Edwin J. Klasky Collection

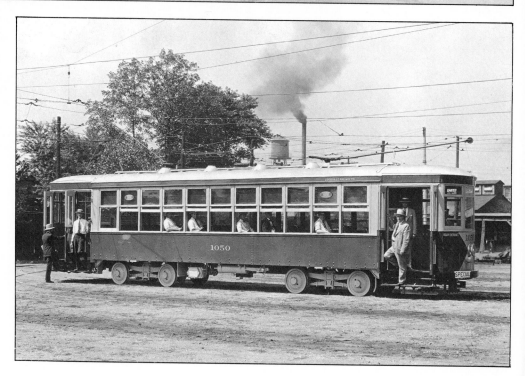

The expense of running the new heavy steel city cars with two-man crews in the smaller towns prompted the development of a small lightweight single-truck, steel-bodied car for more lightly loaded lines. Perfected just before World War One, these cars provided automatic safety devices, one-man fare collection and reduced power consumption, which allied with improved headways on a given line of route was supposed to bring customers flooding back to the ailing lines. More often than not it didn't work out that way, but for seven years the little cars were built in the thousands. Known as Birney Safety Cars after the master mechanic of the (still-existing) *Stone and Webster Corporation* which then had extensive holdings in small-town trolley companies, they could be seen practically everywhere, even in the largest cities. *Louisville Railways'* #419 is seen in 1926 in a congested area of the city. Note the tail of traffic behind it and the traffic lane on the right, blocked by parked automobiles.

Edwin J. Klasky Collection

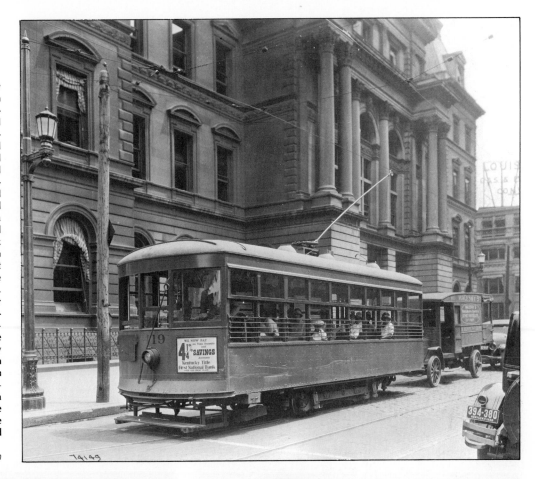

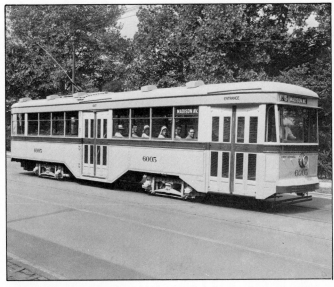

(ABOVE) Aesthetically, this style of car was the latest thing in 1930 and while marginally less noisy and heavy than turn-of-the-century cars, the overall smoothness of appearance was what really smartened up the city streets. This is Baltimore #6005, one of 150 similar cars delivered in 1930. It is termed a "Peter Witt" car, a name which referred to the dual door-way pay-as-you-pass system of fare collection in which passen-

gers paid a seated conductor as they passed his station. The name itself was that of a former Cleveland street railway commissioner under whose aegis the design was developed. Two of these Baltimore cars are preserved; one at the Seashore Museum and the other at its hometown of Baltimore at the Baltimore Streetcar Museum.

Baltimore Streetcar Museum/ Courtesy Andrew D. Young

(ABOVE) The curved side of this Cincinnati Car Company-built lightweight car was a style adopted by the builder in the 1920s in order to give additional strength in the side members. It had the incidental advantage also of producing a memorably styled and attractive vehicle and no less than 400 cars to this general design were produced between 1923 and 1932 when the company succumbed to the Depression. Only two cars of the type have survived whole, unfortunately, although

there were many good examples in operational service well into the trolley museum era. One is to be seen awaiting restoration at Shade Gap (Railways to Yesterday) while the other, a streamlined version for interurban use, is at the Arden Trolley Museum. Car #1218, sold to the *Dayton & Western* in 1932 by the newly defunct *Cleveland and Southwestern* system, stands here after a total refit outside the parent *Cincinnati and Lake Erie* shops.

Edwin J. Klasky Collection

Some operators, impatient at the delays in developing the research which could culminate in the new PCC car, decided to switch to motor or trolley buses instead. Two new Brill model TC-30 trolley buses for Philadelphia are dwarfed by the shipping on the Delaware River in this 1935 view.

Author's Collection

(FACING PAGE) One of the most strenuous efforts to make a still-strong interurban network pay in the 1930s was made by the *Cincinnati and Lake Erie,* a 1929 amalgamation of several independent lines, primarily in Ohio. This company possessed a 216-mile main line, almost all on private right-of-way, running from the outskirts of Cincinnati to Toledo, with a branch from Springfield to Columbus. Management firmly believed 1930s-built cars should be as technologically advanced as possible, providing high speed and superlative comfort. Twenty of these cars were ordered and delivered in 1930 to prove the point. With deep leather bucket seats in front and a beautifully appointed parlor lounge in back, a passenger could expect to ride at over 70 mph for scores of miles at a stretch; he usually did. A famous stunt was staged July 7, 1930, with car #126 and this specially chosen biplane on a carefully selected stretch of route near Dayton. The new car won, much to the delight of management and the newsreel audiences

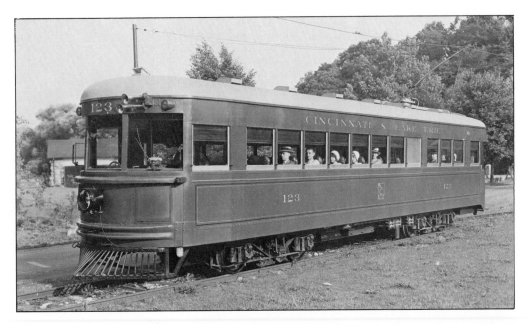

of the day. It made a top speed of 97 mph, but neither the speed of the cars nor their exceptional luxury could for long arrest the decline in passengers and freight brought on by the Depression.

The line was finally closed in the late 1930s, but the cars went to new homes and survived into the postwar years, albeit without the beautiful lounge furnishings. No less than four cars survived to be

preserved in operating condition and may be seen at Rio Vista, at Worthington, at Branford and at Seashore.

All: Edwin J. Klasky Collection

Chicago #7001, an experimental ultra-modern streamliner of 1934, is seen at the J.G. Brill plant in Philadelphia before shipment. The problem of developing a suitable modern city car had led to the formation of an industry-financed research project, known as the *Electric Railway Presidents' Conference Committee.* The ERPCC functioned from 1930 to 1934, when it was turned into a

commercial body known as the *Transit Research Corporation.* #7001 was one of two samples built for *Chicago Surface Lines* that year, and represented the first fruits of the ERPCC research. Light weight, strength, modernity, comfort, speed, silence, good lighting and good ventilation were mandatory, and mass production of the *PCC* car began in 1936, continuing to 1952, the near

nadir of the street railway on the North American continent. It is an ironic compliment to U.S. technological prowess that when manufacture for domestic use ceased that year, the West and East Europeans were just getting into their stride and mechanically identical cars, with restyled bodies, were produced for another 30 years over there, proliferating most thickly in Belgium and Holland, in

eastern Europe and in Russia. It is greatly to be regretted that this prototype car was not preserved, for though it never ran after 1947, the car survived almost complete until 1960. The body of its mate, an aluminum Pullman car numbered #4001 was, however, rescued and awaits restoration at the Illinois Railway Museum.

Author's Collection

The styling and performance of the PCC car were startling in a transit world not accustomed to streamlining and silence. The body was styled on automotive lines and in years to come many bus manufacturers matched the PCC car's lines. From 1936 to 1945, most PCC cars had this style of body, seen here on *San Diego Electric Railway* #528, running through Balboa Park in 1949, the final year of the trolley system. The car was then placed on display at the county fairgrounds and more recently was given to the Orange Empire Railway Museum. Though the very first PCC car to go into service, Pitts-

burgh #100 of June 1936 (a single sample car) was mistakenly allowed to go for scrap in 1962, *Brooklyn-Manhattan Transit* #1000, a unique Clark Equipment Company vehicle and Brooklyn-Manhattan Transit #1001, the first mass production car of the standard PCC type have both been preserved. #1000 is not currently on view, although it is being restored in the New York area, but #1001 is in operating condition at the Branford Museum. In addition, many other cars of this type can be seen at the museums, and in daily service in Pittsburgh, Boston and Philadelphia. *A.M. Payne*

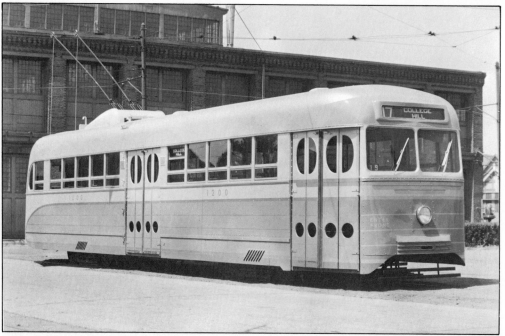

The J.G. Brill Company pulled out of the ERPCC in 1935 to develop its own designs. Between 1938 and 1940 it built a few dozen of these boxy, PCC-like, *Brilliner* cars. They were to be the last of a long line of rail transit vehicles built by the company which dated back to 1869. *Cincinnati Street Railway* #1200, seen at Brill in 1939 is fitted with double trolley poles for use within the Cincinnati city limits. Local ordinances, drafted in the wake of a ruling against the street railway company in the 1890s, prohibited the use of a ground return since it set up interference in the lines of the local telephone company which also used the ground for return. Though these cases were all universally decided the other way subsequently, Cincinnati stuck to its trolley-bus-like overhead system to the end—within the city. *Philadelphia Transportation Company's* **Brilliner** #2021 and a Mack bus are pictured being outfitted for an American Red Cross membership drive in late 1940. No true Brilliner city cars are preserved, although all survived well into postwar years. However, a pair of Brilliner trucks are preserved as part of the equipment on *San Francisco Municipal Railway's* "Magic Carpet" car #1003 at the Rio Vista Museum. One further order, considered by some to be Brilliners, were double-ended cars for the *Philadelphia Suburban Transportation Co.* (**Red Arrow** lines). These were the last electric railcars to leave the Brill plant and almost all survived until the end of 1982 in daily service on the Red Arrow lines. The majority have now been sold for preservation. *Top: Author's Collection Bottom: Edwin J. Klasky Collection*

An extraordinary addition to any interurban's roster, particularly at so late a date in that transit mode's history, were a pair of air-conditioned four-car articulated trains delivered in 1941 to the *Chicago, North Shore & Milwaukee.* **One unit is seen here in early years at Madison and Wells on the Chicago el. Both units went to Red Arrow's Norristown high-speed line after closure of the North Shore in 1963, operating until 1980. They have both since been preserved in operating condition, one set at the Illinois Railway Museum and the other at Shade Gap, Railways to Yesterday.**
Edwin J. Klasky Collection

The second basic style of PCC carbody was evolved during World War Two and had great styling affinity to the contemporary General Motors city bus. A little wider and with other small refinements in appearance and passenger comfort, by far the majority of preserved PCC cars are of this pattern. *Johnstown Traction Co.* #413 was one of 17, the smallest lot of PCC cars purchased new by a U.S. operator and is seen in 1947 when new. When the system closed down in 1960, the trucks, motors and electrical equipment of these cars were sold to Brussels, Belgium, where they were fitted with new bodies and run to this day, along with 80 of their brethren from Kansas City, similarly treated. Preserved cars of this type can be seen at the Orange Empire Museum, Rio Vista, Midwest Electric Railway, Illinois Railway Museum, and Halton County Radial Railway, while many hundreds were still holding down daily service for passengers during 1982 in Philadelphia, Boston, Newark, Toronto, Pittsburgh, Cleveland (Shaker Heights) and San Francisco.
Author's Collection

The trolley line to the lake or amusement park was not quite a thing of the past in the 1940s, but the tone of the parks had gone down considerably as the middle-class found other amusements. Many of the parks were by now rather tawdry and not a little tacky, but perhaps that's why they continued to delight so many! San Francisco's *Market Street Railway* cars loop at Playland-at-the-Beach, a seaside attraction inside city boundaries, in 1941.

Edwin J. Klasky Collection

Only lines with embryonic Light Rail characteristics: large stretches of dedicated right-of-way, passenger demand upwards of 4,000 an hour at rush hours, and modern cars that could be run in two, three and four-car trains, had any hope of surviving after World War Two, and then only as a subsidized social amenity, necessary to keep the quality of urban life high, undamaged by the intrusion of the private automobile. Although many lines with this potential still failed to survive the onslaught, single and multiple-unit PCC cars have helped the rest survive into today's Light Rail era.

SEPTA's **Red Arrow** lines in Philadelphia are an example. This is car #18 at 69th Street in June 1949, leading a multiple-unit train on one of the lines that did not survive, the West Chester route. But in every way these cars were Light Rail vehicles and their retirement in 1982 in favor of new Japanese-built LRVs, running on refurbished, but not otherwise modernized lines, only shows how viable Light Rail is in today's conditions. Car #18 is now at the Branford Museum. *Author's Collection*

1952 saw the end of trolley service in the Pennsylvania coke region. *West Penn Railways #725* was one of a series that maintained service on the lines for decades. Curiously it was neither the automobile nor old age which killed this operation, but television, robbing the line of off-peak and evening riders. Rather than head out to the movies, or to shop, former patrons now stayed home, glued to the "tube." #722 of this series is being restored at the Arden Trolley Museum.

Edwin J. Klasky Collection

Not even modernity of equipment could save a big trolley system when economical public transit alternatives existed. *Chicago Surface Lines* ordered over 600 PCC cars long before it was taken over by the new *Chicago Transit Authority* in 1947 but deliveries were slow, not being completed until well after the takeover. Since the new CTA also took over the subway and elevated lines, it theoretically could better integrate transit by concentrating future rail development on high-speed operation, with segregated rights-of-way — conditions found already on the el and almost-new subway. These were to be extended in a system modernization and expansion which began in the 1950s and continues to this day with the new line out to O'Hare airport. For the surface, however, the CTA preferred cheaper transit modes, feeding the railed el and subway stations as far as possible. They chose to concentrate on the motor and trolley bus. All the surface car lines were phased out by 1958 and these fine PCC cars, among the longest ever built, were recycled into PCC rapid transit cars. New bodies had to be constructed, but nearly all the rest of the equipment was refitted and the last of the PCC rapid transit fleet can still be seen in Chicago service today. A very few PCC cars escaped the recycling, either because they were early losses in accidents, or because they were set aside for preservation. One car is kept as part of the CTA's private museum collection of historic Chicago cars, unhappily not on public view, while another is in operating condition at the Illinois Railway Museum. The unique door arrangement of #4130 in this photograph was installed because of a two-man operation mandate in a union contract. Undoubtedly that was a major reason that the CTA found one-man operated buses an attractive alternative.

Edwin J. Klasky Collection

Trolley junking; the ultimate fate for any fleet and the inspiration for the museum movement. The long lines of cars were first stripped of anything salvageable and then turned over and burned to eliminate non-metallic content. The metals were then sold for reuse. This is illustrated here by a 1947 scene at Quebec City, Canada.

Edwin J. Klasky Collection

(RIGHT) This may be the first photograph of a car at the Seashore Trolley Museum, *Biddeford & Saco* #31, the "mother" car of the whole museum movement. It is the summer of 1940, and the site has just enough track to hold the open car. *Charles Duncan* (BELOW) Here it is again, the first car to be preserved as part of an operating museum scheme, #1, as restored and in service at the Seashore Museum in the 1980s. Instead of an empty field, the new visitors' center is in the background left, while the signal tower which formerly graced Boston's elevated line is on the right.

C. Woolnough

Chapter 2
Aficionados to the Rescue

WHEN SO FAMILIAR a part of everyday life disappears, it would be odd if there wasn't someone to mourn its passing. That certainly has been true of the trolley, and today millions recall it with nostalgia and affection. Such wasn't always the case. When trolleys were still fairly thick on the ground, it took courage to admit affection for so old-fashioned and noisy a contraption. But, with the formation of the still-active Electric Railroaders' Association in 1934, embarrassment gave way to organized enthusiasm, and the precedent set by that group was quickly followed by others. These groups were primarily devoted to riding and observing the old trolleys, while boosting the concept of the modern trolley, using grade separated private right-of-way, as an integral part of up-to-date city transit. In truth, these groups envisaged today's hot new Light Rail transit concept over 40 years ago!

Those with a nostalgia for the old cars and the way of life they had been built to serve found such groups had less to offer them. But, because trolley fan clubs for the first time gave such people a forum to come together and share interests without ridicule from family and friends, it wasn't long before the more historically minded found each other. Shortly thereafter, one group began to do something more constructive than merely talking.

An April 1939 fan trip in New England led directly to the formation of the New England Electric Railway Historical Society. The 12 charter members set themselves the immediate task of acquiring a New England open car and with it to preserve something of the New England trolley era by actually operating it as part of a living museum devoted to the electric trolley and its times. What could be more constructive than that? And yet what could be more difficult to do? Individuals had for some years been "preserving" single trolley cars in fields or backyards with limited success, but had never considered operation. Regular museums, too, were by then familiar with trolley cars as potential exhibit material, but were unable to do much with them except mount them on a plinth and encase them with glass. If the professional museums were so ill-equipped to deal with the preserved trolley's unique problems, how was a group of untrained amateurs going to do any better? Why go to all that trouble?

The answer was glaringly obvious and admirably logical. It had never been done before and someone had to be first. If the amateurs didn't do it, then likely as not no one would. The only possible way to preserve a trolley car was to build a special museum around it in which it could be operated. The trolley was a machine whose function was to move people. If its full impact

The summer of 1940 saw things begin to move at the new Seashore Museum project as cars began to come to the site. Here is Manchester #38 being trucked in from the Kennebunk RR station to the museum in July 1940.
Charles Duncan

Seashore Museum, summer of 1941. Track and switchwork is coming along, but America's entry into World War II is less than six months away. *Biddeford & Saco #31 and Manchester #38 are seen.*
Charles Duncan

A wartime work party at Seashore, seen here in the summer of 1945 working on *Biddeford & Saco #31.* A few more cars are on site.
Charles Duncan

was to be recreated in a museum setting, if its history was to be brought to life for future generations, it had to run. There was no other way.

An idea so radical, expressed by a group so inexperienced, was slow in making an immediate impression. After all, this fledgling group was wholly amateur, practically penniless and totally ignorant of professional museum display and restoration techniques. Even worse, there was no one to turn to for guidance on such matters. Nostalgia for artifacts of the recent past was not then a national pastime and items which would be greatly prized now had almost no value or interest then. The new group was beginning a venture with absolutely nothing going for it—not the best indication of a successful outcome!

Yet, in spite of the European war, they persevered, encouraged by the formation of another small group sharing their aims within the year. America's entry into the war made it difficult for much active work to be continued, but the degree of progress made by the groups in the early '40s was heartening. Cars and property were obtained. There seemed to be just enough labor and know-how to keep the projects alive on a care-and-maintenance basis, and occasionally a member or friend could make money available to help complete another purchase.

The groups thus proved conclusively that preserving trolley cars in the way they felt to be necessary was not an impossible task, even in wartime. Moreover, the experience they had after five years of effort could not be bought at any price. So, when peace came in 1945, their continued survival provoked an explosion of interest in operating trolley museum projects and a great number of the museums examined later in this book can trace their origins to this time.

Originally it had been assumed that car and land purchase, together with the building of shelter, were a group's first priorities, only then to be followed by operation. But the group which established the Branford Museum surprised many by reversing that procedure. They were able to buy a completely equipped section of line after its abandonment, and immediately operate revenue-raising trips on their museum trolleys. This, they felt, would enable them to build their museum around the small but hopefully steady income derived from car operation, and plan systematic and orderly growth. The advantages of this new approach were many, not the least of which was the ability to get cars moving within a very short time; a big psychological boost to the membership.

Branford was thus the first of the operating trolley museums to actually operate trolleys on its own property, becoming a major stimulus and encouragement to the rest of the new movement. As a bonus, the Connecticut Company, from whom the right-of-way had been purchased, obligingly left in the track and electrical connections to the remainder of its system for more than a year after transfer to the group, thus simplifying the task of transporting Branford's Connecticut Company exhibits to museum premises.

Regular car operation did not guarantee an adequate supply of revenue, nor was it the end of the development possibilities inherent in the growing movement. But it was the final proof that amateurs could create the operating museum they insisted was the only correct environment for the preserved trolley. As a result, by 1955 (only eight years after Branford ran its first trolley in museum service), there were no less than 16 groups attempting to create operating trolley museums in North America.

Their originally "radical" philosophy became the new orthodoxy in industrial museum projects generally, while their influence on steam railroad preservation groups was such that the 1950s saw many other successful museum schemes established centered on steam railroad locomotives and other bulky old machines. Moreover, the professional museums, too, were beginning to see possibilities.

Of the amateur trolley museum groups existing in 1955, Seashore (the location of our old friend the New England Electric Railway Historical Society's museum), Branford, Worthington and Warehouse Point had already begun electric operation, while the Iowa Railway Historical Society, an offshoot of which today runs the Old Threshers' line in Mt. Pleasant, Iowa, had the occasional use of a still-operating Iowa interurban line on which to exercise its elderly cars. The remaining groups intended to run their cars as soon as they were able.

Unfortunately by the mid-1950s operation, and the revenue derived therefrom, had ceased to be the main priority. The decline of city trolley services had resumed at war's end and, by 1960, was practically complete. The few city lines to survive this wholesale closure generally had extensive stretches of private track, subways or tunnels which could offer suburban commuters appreciable time savings as against their automobile in making trips to the city. It should be pointed out that many of the lines still operating in 1960 operate today, and that the special features to which they owed their survival were those of today's Light Rail. Most of the surviving lines either have already been or are shortly to be reequipped and modernized to Light Rail standards, while other towns who scrapped their trolleys after the war are bringing them back in the guise of Light Rail lines.

Until the mid-1950s, these embryonic Light Rail systems had been replacing their old trolleys too, but rather than buy buses or trolley coaches as did the majority, they instead bought new or nearly new lightweight, streamlined trolley cars. These cars' comfort and performance closely matched the private auto with which they had been designed to compete back in the 1930s, when their radical design was first mooted. So far as the trolley museums were concerned, the end

The early days at the Branford museum. A *Connecticut Company* closed car and work motors are viewed in the carbarn area in 1950. *William E. Wood*

Connecticut Company open-bench car #923 is waiting at the siding in September 1953. This design has been the mainstay of the New England museums on summer days. *William E. Wood*

result of both scrapping and modernization was the same: the speedy junking of old trolley cars by the thousands, some dating as far back as the early 1890s. Cars had to be acquired, and quickly.

Thus from the end of the 1940s, but especially in the 1950s and early 1960s, car acquisition became the dominant thrust of the trolley museum movement. Very few new electrifications were completed between 1955 and 1965 while, instead, the groups concentrated their main efforts into locating, purchasing and shipping cars across the length and breadth of the continent. The new acquisitions were not always in the best of shape but continued to descend on the museum sites in ever-increasing numbers.

Once safely arrived they would sit outside (in full view of the visiting public) for lack of funds to provide shelter, until they could be restored to their former glory. Ironically, the cars in the worst condition were invariably those which presented the greatest difficulty in restoration. They tended for years to remain in derelict condition, while attention was given to readying cars in better shape for revenue service. Many museums thus unwittingly converted themselves into what a lay visitor could only have regarded as a junkyard.

Yet the situation was desperate. The museum groups rightly felt they had no choice but to saddle themselves with what the visitors only saw as wrecks. If cars were not bought when the opportunity arose, they would be lost forever. When exhibit collection has to be done on this basis, there is left little room for discrimination in purchase, or time to work out the niceties of an elegant

Looking toward Quarry Hill from the Short Beach end of the Branford museum's line in December 1952. The *Connecticut Company's* double-track line was made single-track by the museum for financial reasons and operation did not resume to this point for many years due to a washed-out trestle. *William E. Wood*

display, while the best-planned acquisition program becomes meaningless. Thus the determination of the groups to get needed vehicles at any price (and in any condition) was in the final analysis praiseworthy.

At the same time, it was becoming increasingly clear that simply preserving and operating the machines was not enough in terms of the overall museum experience. But it was not generally appreciated in the movement that if a museum was to succeed in its aim of both informing and entertaining the visitor by bringing the trolley era back to life, it was vital that each exhibit have some recognizable relationship to the others in the collection. A balanced and integrated collection of vehicles and their accessories, which could together demonstrate a particular aspect of the trolley's evolution, interpret the trolley's function in the development of the American city, or simply tell the story of the trolley in a particular region, could spell the difference between visiting a well-organized and informative museum, or watching a bunch of grown men playing with a full-size electric trolley set.

At that time of intense activity in car purchase, almost every group insisted that its collection goal was to build nothing less than a full-scale museum. The idea of doing something less or something different was rarely considered. Insisting therefore that car buying was their last chance to build a balanced and representative collection which would tell the complete story of the trolley's evolution either nationally or in their region, many groups at this time ignored other equally fruitful display techniques which might have influenced their purchase decisions.

Moreover, because all of them were locked into this image of themselves as full museum operations, they began to compete with each other in their need to get examples of cars which could plug gaps in their story

of the trolley's development. Consequently many car types were duplicated in museums across the continent, often after intense competition to buy them had pushed the purchase prices to unrealistically high levels.

A classic example of this state of affairs was to be seen at the closure of the Chicago, North Shore & Milwaukee interurban in 1963; an operation widely felt to be the last of its kind. Literally dozens of identical or near-identical cars from this line were bought by the museums and as the years have gone by only a very few have actually been restored to first-class operational condition, simply because they are too big and powerful to operate in any but those museums that had planned interurban displays. At the same time, other important car types of more local or regional significance were frequently passed over, the more so if no detailed long-range museum display policy had been worked out by the group concerned.

In fairness it must be said that the amateur trolley museum then consisted of individualistic and outspoken young people, for whom it took an enormous effort of collective will to subdue individual preferences in favor of their museum by means of a properly thought-out collection philosophy. It took even more effort to stick closely to an acquisition program in the now-or-never conditions that prevailed in the '50s and '60s. No rational policy of any kind could long survive unchallenged when crucial purchase decisions had to be made at 24 hours' notice. Much had already ceased to exist and if even one more car of potential museum quality was allowed to go for scrap for want of effort on their part, then they weren't doing their job. Not surprisingly, then, planning was a luxury few groups felt they could afford.

Planning also called for a degree of structural for-

Just after World War II, all of the Connecticut Electric Railway can be seen in this shot, looking east from the location of today's gift shop and driveway. The original station was being built and the first track after the war was being worked on by the volunteers. Cars #10 *(Springfield Terminal)* and #65 *(Connecticut Co.)*, in the background, sat at the museum all during the war years.   *Roger Borrup*

malization that many groups did not want and did not intend to create. Lack of a hierarchy had the major advantage of encouraging camaraderie, enthusiasm and equality, the only real and sustaining strengths groups possessed in the early days. The new trolley museum groups were little more than clubs, with all the strengths and weaknesses such organization implied. But, since their clublike structure helped conserve their most valuable human resource, such an asset could not lightly be squandered.

Early formalization of the museum administrative structure was too risky if the long-term survival of the group was to be assured; but once the cars were running for the public it had to be done. However, once the cars were running, most groups were no longer battling quite so hard either for cars or for continued existence and on the operational side at least a recognizable administrative hierarchy has appeared in most museums.

Formalization of structure is an essential prerequisite to safe operation, future growth and long-term stability. Professional museums have long recognized that they exist to provide their exhibits a safe home for all time and a great deal of time and effort is spent to secure that goal. Amateur-run or private museums have many

more hurdles to cross than the professional museum in order to reach that same goal.

Many of the existing trolley museums have yet to become independent of the whims of the individual member and that can be done only by the election of a board to set policy and an administration strong enough to carry it out. It makes no difference if these bodies come from within the amateur museum's membership or elsewhere, for they are charged with the same grave responsibilities. They are trustees, not just for today's members and the public they serve, but for generations to come. Establishment of a rudimentary museum hierarchy other than merely on the operational side, responsible to a board of governors or trustees is therefore the hallmark of an amateur-founded trolley museum that intends to survive and function as the charter members intended.

This formalization of structure has not occurred overnight. Even the oldest trolley museums are still struggling with this painful yet vital process and the pages of their members' newsletters are regularly filled with anguished debate.

The core of the problem, which is still very troubling today, lies in the age-old psychological split between the "hands-on" worker and the "paper-pusher." This may be a valid response to working conditions in the outside world, but it seems a needless luxury in a museum framework where everybody is a member and supposedly pulling in the same direction to achieve the same ends. Yet since the bulk of early-day museum

It is the winter of 1948-49 at Warehouse Point, and #840 has arrived from the *Connecticut Company* after closure of its New Haven routes that year. *William E. Wood*

The Connecticut Electric Railway line had just reached Borrup Road in March 1959 and Springfield #10, freshly repainted, was out for a spring trip; #840 is behind. *William E. Wood*

Kelley Barn is underway at the Connecticut Electric Railway in 1961. It is the center barn of today. *William E. Wood*

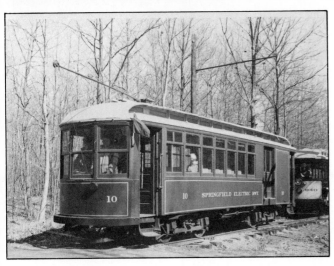

work was "hands-on" there has grown up an unspoken contempt for administrative work, expressed in the unwillingness of all but a few to put their minds to it.

In a sense some museums are run as 12"-to-the-foot model trolley clubs as a result of these attitudes and there is no core of experienced individuals able to handle the paperwork that a large and attractive museum of necessity must generate. This leads to haphazard and arbitrary rule, subject to the passing fads of individuals which may or may not survive the season.

This same psychological split is at the root of the continued reluctance of many groups to set out their goals and objectives in formal fashion. On the face of it, many of the most active members seem to have no interest in doing so, as one newsletter put it recently, they prefer to "just keep on struggling from day to day, year to year." Yet if one probes deeper, one finds less to condemn the individual member for than the above quote might imply, since without leadership there is

little else they can do. Leadership does not arise spontaneously, but it can evolve with encouragement.

The museums recognize that the problem exists and are quite blunt about what the future holds if nothing is done. Here is the *Branford Electric Railroad Journal*, house magazine of the large, well-run Branford Museum laying it on the line to its members in the summer of 1982:

Long-term goals must be decided upon, short-term objectives must be established . . . and adhered to until the desired results have been achieved. The [museum] cannot continue to shift . . . attention to whatever project strikes our fancy at a given moment. The enthusiasm generated by new projects, we have learned, wanes very quickly. The short-term objective which should be given priority is the establishment of an effective, efficient administrative system . . . under the jurisdiction of a full-time Museum Director. If this

Early days at Rio Vista Junction, Calif. One of the two ex-New York elevated cars has arrived by rail in 1963 and a crew labors to complete an unloading ramp. The Bay Area Electric Railroad Association's site is one of the few that provides direct rail access.
Addison H. Laflin, Jr.

Temporary refuge for the fast-growing collection of the Illinois Railway Museum before it located at Union was on the grounds of the Chicago Hardware Foundry. Illinois Terminal #101 and Milwaukee Electric #972 are seen in the cramped conditions the yard offered. *William E. Wood*

"club" cannot ensure that its affairs are properly managed, it is unlikely that it will ever develop into the public institution we . . . think . . . we are.

That strong comment comes from a museum which is one of the oldest and largest in the country. It was one of the first to understand the critical need to establish an administrative hierarchy on the operational side since it was the first of all the museums to operate its cars for the public. As a result, codes of conduct, operational and safety rules, disciplinary procedures, staff schedules and command chains all had to be evolved as the years went by for the museum to take life. The museum has taken life, of course, and without this operational administrative framework neither Branford

nor any of the other operating museums would be providing a safe home for its exhibits, nor be able to operate these elderly high-voltage machines without hazard to life and limb.

Formalization of the rest of its structure now is the logical next step and with it will come the proper institutional leadership that is needed. At that point the museum will be able to channel the individual member's immediate personal gratification from working with old trolleys into something of benefit to the institution as a whole. A less ad-hoc approach to decision-making at all levels will be one advantage which will be of immediate benefit to the museum's members and its public. Most of the museum groups are already bracing themselves to deal with this problem and will

The first cars at the Orange Empire Railway Museum are seen just after their arrival at Perris, Calif., in February 1958. *San Diego Electric Railway #508 is in the foreground; a Los Angeles Railway flat car sits behind.* Ray Ballash

soon have settled down to a sound hierarchically planned approach to their existence.

Not the least advantage of a formalized structure is the opportunity it provides to exchange information and techniques with others on a more formal and scientific basis. An attempt was made in the 1950s to create a professional association for the museums and though this effort failed a later attempt led to the establishment in 1961 of today's Association of Railway Museums. The work done by that body in helping its member groups on the one hand and representing them to the outside world on the other has been monumental. Negotiation of bulk purchase agreements, recognition of museum operation as an insurable activity, public relations, the compilation and distribution of handbooks on preservation and restoration techniques are all jobs the ARM has successfully undertaken for the benefit of its members.

The real problem facing the museums in the immediate future is the need to try and reconcile a more formalized structure, which they need to survive, with the essentially democratic and amateur nature of their working membership. That is a hallmark of the early days of the movement which still sets the tone of the museums and which they are reluctant to lose completely. The enthusiasm and camaraderie of young volunteers working within the established framework of a museum continues to be one of the movement's greatest assets, especially in these times of reduced public funding.

Since most trolley museums have never been able to afford full-time salaried professional staff (though some are inevitably moving in this direction) permanence and continuity of operations in vital areas remain largely in the hands of dedicated unpaid volunteers. Though the largest museums now have a paid skeleton staff in the busiest seasons (usually drawn from their members) payroll costs are not normally part of a trolley museum's budget. If you should visit a trolley museum that appears polished to the nth degree of professionalism and then see their many appeals for cash donations, please don't be surprised or upset. Even without a payroll, there are other bills to be paid!

The largest of the museums are in many ways major enterprises and have to be built on a large scale. Here is one of the Illinois Railway Museum's huge modern barns, seen here with Cornwall (Ontario) Street Railway #14, a 1929 Baldwin electric locomotive. (BELOW) Not only must carbarns be erected to house the collections, but facilities must be created to provide workshops to keep them in operating condition as well as structurally sound. This building at the Orange Empire Museum houses a machine shop, welding and blacksmith areas, an airbrake and electrical components testing room, plus parts bins and tool storage. In the future it will be connected to a large bay (along the wall at right) in which cars and locomotives will be placed during work. *BOTH: Jim Walker*

Chapter 3

Preservation: A Formidable Enterprise

WHEN WRITTEN down on paper, the word *survival* has a dry and academic ring to it, which completely misses that elemental overtone of titanic struggle and of grinding physical toil against the odds that was the lot of all the museum groups in their early days. Let there be no doubt about it, the creation of a trolley museum and the navigation necessary to put it on a secure and steady course is frighteningly hard, even for the most generously funded public institutions. If you are a group of amateurs with no backing except for a few dollars and your own enthusiasm, the constraints on you are horrifying.

Land and cars have to be located and bought when money is at its scarcest. Naturally nothing can be spared to hire professional labor and the volunteer help is always far less than needed even on weekends or holidays, family circumstances permitting. Virtually none of the labor is skilled and once the museum is over its birth pangs, the remaining tasks are just as horrendous. Exhibits bought and owned are not necessarily at the site. They have to be brought there. That is a story in itself in which low loaders, low bridges, narrow roads, treacherous weather and mountain passes all have a part to play along with the tractors of GMC, Ford, Kenworth, Peterbilt, and the rest.

Once arrived at the site, unloading is long and hazardous without cranes, while damage sustained during shipment must be made good so as to keep out the weather. Since shelter for the exhibits usually has yet to be erected, and the cars themselves are in less than wonderful condition, the site quickly begins to look like a scrap dealer's yard and then hostile neighbors and local authorities have to be placated. Shelters have to be erected (apparently an optional step, looking at some museum histories) and the tracks and electrical system installed.

The trolley, together with the spares, tools and machinery needed to sustain it and the track and electrical work which nourished it, came and went decades before OSHA became a power in the land. Thus, reconciling the trolley's work standards (often seemingly set in 1903) with those of 1983 is no easy task. All this has to be done at a time when no protection from the elements can be offered the crews. Toilets, showers, locker rooms, and recreation areas are just a dream.

Once in place at the museum site, the exhibits cannot conveniently be moved without electrical power or at the very least the help of a diesel tractor. Most groups in the early days had neither convenience. Then the only power available to move cars around was the sheer brute force exerted by strong young backs and shoulders.

It is this undeniably physical element that continues to be present in all that a trolley museum does. In the early days, a group's uninhibited enthusiasm and physical strength were vital to keep a project going. Even today both these elements are needed badly. There are no cheap labor-saving shortcuts to many of the jobs which must be done, at least if there is no money available to use mechanical aids.

Take trackwork, for an example. Without machinery, trackwork is the most brutally demanding of all jobs. If a group can't find money to hire contractors and their machines to grade and lay track (and most museums in this book could not), then they've got to do the job by hand, like the "gandy dancers" of the last century. It is heavy and grueling work, and it is work that requires young people in good physical shape, willing to work all hours for no pay. The only immediate reward is the satisfaction of a job well done and the knowledge they are one step closer to their goal. Considering how heavy the work is, it is ironic these folk undertake such labor in what the outside world would call their *leisure* time!

Planting poles, stringing overhead, moving cars, building barns—these are all jobs which entail back-breaking effort. And they all have to be done on a self-help basis. Recent museum eligibility for local, state or federal monies, while of enormous help to ongoing projects, has a doubtful future, and in any event came too late for most museums.

It's hardly surprising, then, that every attempt would be made to secure an existing right-of-way for a museum site, preferably with track and overhead still in place. Most museums and tourist lines are therefore located on some form of abandoned trolley, interurban or railroad right-of-way, so avoiding much of the hardest of the initial trackwork. But trackwork cannot be avoided altogether. The best-laid tracks need constant care, while periodically they have to be completely replaced. Moreover, simply getting them into first-rate condition can be a task that consumes years.

If there is no real shortcut to establishing an amateur-sponsored trolley museum, neither is there a shortcut to restoring the exhibits. Thousands of hours of work, taking many years, may be necessary to bring just one trolley car back to presentable condition. It is work that requires the revival of many long-dead skills. Trolley manufacturers are long out of business, and plant staff who actually built the car may have been dead the better part of a century. Those who practised the ancient trade and who are still with us, suffer as we all do from dimmed memories. The paper records relating to the car have largely been lost, of course.

So, in the absence of any formalized guide, how does one set about restoring a trolley car? Finding the answer to that question has attracted many men and women to car restoration, not merely as a hobby, but as their life's creative work. Trolley car restoration by these people on museum premises has rightly been praised as one of the greatest achievements of the

So many of the facilities from prototype railways have had to be duplicated at museums, including this service pit under construction at Orange Empire. Volunteers have developed skills at the museums to undertake these jobs.
Jim Walker

A track gang at the Arden Trolley Museum spikes in heavy rails for a public street crossing. The museum's #2, formerly SEPTA #C-125, serves as a line car for later installation of trolley wire.
Arden Trolley Museum

The creation of the physical plant has only been possible at most museums through use of volunteer labor. Member Danny Giles pounds nails on a carbarn at Orange Empire. *Jim Walker*

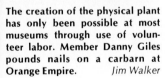

The route of the Branford Trolley Museum crosses a river at two points, and rehabilitation and maintenance of trestles is a major undertaking. This bridge over the Farm River was once double-track, of which one track space is now a foot passage. The Sprague Building lies across the trestle at the foot of River St. *Mark G. Effle*

amateur trolley museum movement. Working from memory, a faded photograph or two, perhaps if they are lucky a series of shop drawings, or if not, then from measurements they've had to laboriously take themselves from the hulk they're working on, these people work miracles.

Their task requires immense patience, great ingenuity and well-honed detective skills. No two individuals have quite the same approach, and their work tech-niques can further be varied by the geographic diversity of museum location. The facilities and techniques needed to restore and maintain cars at Orange Empire in arid Perris, California, are in many respects different from those of a midwest museum such as Union, sited squarely in flood-prone and tornado-threatened corn-fields, a mountain museum such as Shade Gap in the high Alleghenies or Seashore, on Maine's bleak Atlantic coast.

Even within a particular museum, the guidelines have a certain degree of flexibility built in, and to the outside observer it may seem as if there are no hard and fast rules at all. Perhaps they are right, for when brought down to basics all the museum wants from a car restorer is a car accurate for the period chosen, and representing precisely what the museum needs for its collection. Needless to say, despite the best efforts of the restorer, the degree of accuracy can vary.

Not surprisingly then, it is in this area that the greatest amount of in-house controversy seems to be generated, and where the lack of a comprehensive acquisition policy may make itself most greatly felt. Without a master plan for the collection, it is difficult to answer the basic visitor question of *why* a vehicle is there and therefore what kind of a restoration is called for. Basic questions that many times seem to be unanswered are those which would best define what the museum is trying to do and how each vehicle in the collection is helping them do it. With those questions answered and collection policy set, one then has a better idea of why, how and to what condition one should restore a given car.

Once those questions are settled, a whole new crop emerges. What about the restoration techniques to be used, for example? Can one possibly restore every piece of a car's original equipment, no matter how bad its condition? Can one indeed define the term "original condition" since by the time a vehicle gets to a museum it must have had many original parts repaired or replaced over the years? When wooden framing is completely rotted away, does the new wood one must use in its place to reconstruct the car thereby detract from the car's authenticity? And what if the appearance or specification of the car has changed from the original in the course of its life? How then should one restore the vehicle to preserve its authenticity?

There are two schools of thought on these problems. One takes the strict view that whatever happened to the vehicle during its life, its authenticity is fixed at the time it is handed over to the museum. From that point on, nothing should be done to compromise that authenticity; no restoration, no repair, no painting and certainly no operation. It is a view which seems to be grounded in traditional museum practices of 70 years ago, practices which evolved from work with single artifacts of a decorative, fragile or esthetic character. It is a view which does not encompass the realities faced by any museum of industrial technology. That reality is machinery, composed of many component parts, whose total function is movement.

Which brings us to the second, and fortunately, dominant school of thought in the trolley museums, that of the preservation of both the artifact and its function. It is a *sine qua non* of the trolley museum movement that exhibits must operate if they are to recreate the whole dimension of the trolley experience. But one is not necessarily compelled to go back to original specifications if the need is for an operating vehicle that represents a later period. The nub of the matter is the preservation of the vehicle in a state compatible both with authenticity and safe operation.

Obviously in a machine with many component parts, all needing restoration, it is next to impossible to maintain the standard of authenticity laid down by the strict school. But, with the flexibility of the majority view, all sorts of things can be done to the vehicle and its individual parts without detracting from its overall value as an authentic museum piece. And if the basic questions concerning the museum's purpose and acquisition policy are already settled, it is a lot easier to determine to what particular condition, representative of a specific time, one can restore a car and have it retain reasonable historical accuracy.

But then a further set of questions arises. What sort of materials should be used in the restoration? Should one laboriously beat out dents, weld tears and chemically de-rust metal panels, the way they did years ago? Or is it ethical to bypass those jobs completely by using the newer epoxy fillers which do a better job and are undetectable once the job is done? Today's technology can coat wood and metal with materials that can prevent wipeout by rot and rust. Though these materials were not around when the trolley rolled through our streets, is that a sufficient reason for not using them now on an exhibit intended to serve generations to come?

There are no absolutes yet in trolley restoration but consensus answers do seem to be forthcoming. Yes, one can use epoxy fillers, for they do a better job. No, one can't use modern paints in place of the old lead-based formulae, for the pigment of a lead-based formula lasts and the modern ones don't. Yes, one can substitute trucks and motors from other cars to replace missing originals, since not only would the car otherwise be inoperable, it is almost a certainty that that was done as part of normal maintenance during its operational lifetime.

Those are just a few of the questions and answers which arise, and areas where some compromises must be made if any meaningful restoration work is to be done at all. What a museum needs from a restorer is not just a revival of old skills which will reproduce the vehicle in the historic form wanted. No one sees much virtue in sticking to 1893's safety standards on an 1893 trolley car if that vehicle is to run in 1983 and 1983's standards are substantially different. If it is historically important for the museum to demonstrate such historical standards, that can be done in other ways besides on an operating car.

The museum car department needs vehicles that can be operated safely by today's standards and which are compatible in their operation with other cars on the line. They also need cars which satisfy the heavy demand for rides. In this way, then, there is a balance of forces between the various departments of a museum when it comes to deciding which car shall be restored and what form that restoration shall take.

That last remark should be qualified, however, by reminding the reader of the continuing problem of the amateur membership. Often a restorer has a particular personal reason for wanting to select one car over another when a restoration project is mooted. Perhaps he might insist on doing that car, or no car. There are not yet so many skilled restorers that a museum can afford to be inflexible when it comes to balancing its priorities against the members' own needs and creative urges. Consequently, there are many occasions when even if there is a priority schedule, it is waived to accommodate the particular individual concerned. When your staff is all volunteer it is only sensible to accommodate them.

All these constraints have of necessity led to a pragmatic rather than a dogmatic approach to restoration, flexible enough to correct mistakes if need be. Let's return to paint as an example. Since the old lead-based formulae are ecologically suspect, and for some of the cars probably forgotten, it made sense to try to use some of the more modern non-lead formulae on the cars. Though the results were fine for a while, in the long run they brought nothing but trouble. Bright reds quickly weathered to dirty pink in an operating season and the trouble was traced to poor pigmentation. It seems that only lead-based paints can give the richness and durability of color needed and so, once again, lead-based paints are being used for exterior car work.

All the same, one isn't always compelled to abandon modern methods in favor of the traditional ways and sometimes not even old methods will do the trick. Then only ingenuity and improvisation can save the day. A famous story is told of a restoration group back in the '60s, faced with the problem of stretching canvas on a car roof prior to painting. This was a routine maintenance task in the trolley's heyday since painted canvas provided a watertight cover for the lightweight wood roof normally fitted to a trolley car. But one group found it impossible to do the job with the tools on hand. The solution? Jack up someone's VW Beetle alongside the trolley, attach the edge of the canvas to the VW's fender and slowly let the VW down. The auto's weight stretches the canvas and as it stretches the crew is able to tack it down.

There's a moral to these stories, of course, and it is this: As long as the end result is what you and the museum are seeking, it isn't always vital to use the old techniques to get you there. Indeed, in the 20 years since the canvas incident occurred, new water-based latex paints have eliminated the need to stretch canvas, since they cause the canvas to shrink as they dry. Traditional techniques on one part of the car, modern techniques on another, yet who is to know from the outward appearance of the finished product?

To keep cars in the collections in operating condition, most of the museums have created shop facilities to some extent. At the California Railway Museum, rehabilitation and maintenance take place in this steel building. Its facilities include a pit, machinery bays and areas for stores. *Harre W. Demoro*

One of the earliest shop facilities, and now one of the best-equipped for restoration, is the Town House shop complex at the Seashore Trolley Museum. Manufacture of doors and windows, resheeting of both wood and metal coverings and fabrication of structural members are some of the tasks which are carried out in its confines. *Mark Effle*

Strict authenticity in restoration is thus nearly impossible to define satisfactorily, much less achieve, but no establishment examined in this book has been unwise enough to suggest that restoration should not be undertaken. They recognize that however close to the original the restoration may be, it can only approximate the original. But, provided the museum has some overall concept of where it is going and what part of its story the car in question represents, one can't reasonably ask for more. Then any further restoration questions can be reduced, at least on the non-mechanical side, to problems of cosmetics, of which the geometric shape, color and texture are the most critical.

If these elements together give an overall visual impression of authenticity when checked with photographs, drawings, measurements and other car records relating to the condition the group is attempting to recreate, the battle is almost won. It is true that more than just a general impression of authenticity is desirable, but *how* much more is debatable. The fact has to

An extremely high water table, a unique local problem due to the close proximity of the Branford Electric Railway to a tidal marsh, caused construction of pit facilities to be above ground on a trestle. *Mark Effle*

be faced that vehicles can almost never be restored to original condition, or to specific condition at a given date, if by that one refers not just to appearance, but to every single component with which the car was equipped. Why? Because most trolley cars have had the same kind of treatment as the lumberman's fabled "original axe" which though it had had three new heads and two new handles in its long life, was still the original axe!

Fortunately, no one seems to have been deterred by these problems and the debate seems to pale into insignificance when one sees some of the remarkable re-animations a dedicated restoration group can come up with. From a collection of rusted metal and rotted timbers, these people can re-create the most sumptuous of vehicles. If there is any lingering doubt on the matter, go to the Seashore Museum and take a look at the private car, *City of Manchester.* You might care to recall it took nearly 20 years to restore this vehicle from the decayed chicken coop it had become. You might also bear in mind that this car is but one of scores that have been similarly rejuvenated all over North America.

Even if a car is structurally sound and operable when it gets to a museum, the work still to be done can be intimidating. The exterior, grim as it may seem, is at least visible to all, but the interior is not, and after long periods of storage has probably become a disaster area unbeknown to anyone. Typically, one might find it to be dank, evil-smelling and bug-infested. Frequently, the interior fittings are missing, and only with luck might you find the missing seats stacked in one end of the car.

Flaking paint, dangling fixtures, leaky roofs, rust in vital structural components, damaged electrical circuits, missing controllers, holes in the floor, broken windows and corroded brass can all be found in abundance. Yet paradoxically it is easier to restore a carbody in this kind of shape than it is to repair or replace its missing mechanical components such as trucks or motors. Not a few restorations are hung up for lack of traction hardware and it really seems as if there are too many carbodies chasing too few trucks nowadays.

Car trucks can still be found, of course, if one is prepared to buy them in Europe, India or Japan, and assuming their current owner wants to sell them. Otherwise, the museum is compelled to make its own, and since no museum has a heavy forge, or triphammers, or (in most cases) any facilities larger than a small metal-working shop, not one museum has been able to attempt such a feat. Electric motors and air-brake equipment present less of a problem though armature winding and heavy motor repairs are also beyond a museum's present ability to cope.

The greatest collection of fully restored cars, and the facilities to maintain them that way, are to be seen at the oldest of the museums such as Seashore or Branford, but many superb examples can be seen elsewhere. Not all restored cars are in regular museum service, but most operations try to run them all several times in a season, while many go further than that. Parades of restored cars are frequently organized by the larger museums, and they are conducted on such a scale as to be events of regional importance.

Operating museums rely heavily on local or regional visitors and the usual operating season other than on the Pacific coast is generally confined to summer weekends and holidays, times when the visitors are in a relaxed mood. But during the 1960s a most unhappy fact became apparent. Weekend and summer visitors in a holiday mood were less inclined to examine displays than they were to ride cars, open cars for preference. No matter how painstaking a restoration, no matter how intricate the display, no matter how effective the presentation, 20 minutes were about all the average visitor seemed to want to give. After that, riding was the main attraction and open cars the target. And there simply were not enough operable open cars in the museums to satisfy this riding preference.

But so marked was the demand for summer open

car rides that the lack threatened museum revenues. A visitor might pay his fare once to ride a closed car, but would pay many times over for the pleasure of repeated rides on an open car. Something had to be done to cater to this summer visitor preference. If open cars could not be provided, perhaps a change of display emphasis might work.

Visitor preference for open cars was first noticed at Glenwood, some 40 miles west of Portland in Oregon's mild summer climate. While this small operation intensified its efforts to find open cars by shipping in vehicles from Australia and Britain, it was one of the first to make a break with the "total museum" concept, in order to attract the desperately needed visitors. In the early 1960s, the trustees decided gradually to develop the beautifully located museum site as a trolley park. It was to have woods, camp and picnic grounds, nature trails, fishing and swimming holes and, of course, trolley rides. In short, it was to become the ideal place for a city family to spend a day or weekend out in the country.

Glenwood thus became a prototype of the "second generation" trolley museum, those in which the restoration and operation of the trolleys is but one part of the total package offered by the institution rather than the main focus.

It is not possible to formulate an exact definition of the term "second generation" trolley museum, but broadly speaking the term does not refer to the date of the museum's establishment. Rather it is a question of its initial attitude towards function. The "first generation" museums concentrated on building collections of historic trolley cars, selected for their place in the museum's animated display of the trolley's story.

By contrast, "second generation" operations have a more relaxed and flexible approach to their intended function of preserving and operating elderly trolleys. They have utilized an impressive repertory of display techniques in order to preserve visitor appeal. Several run as adjuncts to preserved live steam railroads, operating Toonerville fashion as "trolleys that meet all the trains." There are tourist trolley lines, trolley parks and lines which take the visitor on a journey to visit much larger collections of mechanical antiquity, such as those assembled at Chattanooga, or at the extraordinary Old Threshers meet in Iowa.

Many of these ideas have been taken up by what were once thought of as "first generation" museums, such as those at Arden, Seashore, Worthington, Orange Empire and Rio Vista. As a part of the process these places are slowly enlarging their horizons and becoming museums of transportation, rather than just trolley museums, specializing in collecting transport artifacts of their own region. The operating trolley, of course, remains a vitally important element, the point of focus which draws the other more disparate collections in the museum together. So widespread is this tendency now

The horrors of restoration don't manifest themselves at first glance. You've got to look long and hard to really take in all the damage that years of neglect can do. For example, many wood-built cars were modernized in later years and masqueraded behind panels of sheet steel. The steel panels reassured the passengers that the car was sturdy enough to withstand major collisions (it wasn't, but luckily for their peace of mind, they didn't know that) and at the same time gave the operator a cosmetically modern-ized car for a fraction of the cost of a genuine new vehicle. This rotted end sill was hidden beneath steel for many decades of use on the Los Angeles streetcar system, and came to the attention of owner Orange Empire Railway Museum when the piece would no longer hold up hardware attached to it. Since Southern California is probably the least damaging of climes for the cars, it takes little imagination to conjure up an image of the damage not yet found to cars from less benign climates.   *Jim Walker*

More than a few of the museums now contain marvelous examples of "miracles," such as Seashore's "City of Manchester." In the small photo it has arrived at the museum and has been placed on a temporary truck, and after years of patient work, it has returned to life (large photo). In the parlance of the fraternity, it began as a "chicken coop," simply the leftover body of a car used for that purpose, as a summer house, or tool shed in someone's back acres after being stripped of its mechanical gear. Often examples of long-vanished types, "chicken coops" provide a challenge in that trucks, motors and control equipment must be located, often long distances or in other nations.

Small Photo/Charles Duncan
Large Photo/Seashore Trolley Museum

that in all but a few cases it is impossible to label a museum first or second generation. The terms are meaningless, except as a way of understanding how a given museum came to cope with visitor preferences by changing its attitude to function. In short, the terms indicate only the path the museum took to survive.

Of late, the success of the operating museums and the nostalgia for the trolley which they have unleashed, has spilled over into more widespread areas. In particular, cities which still have trolleys have been most interested in the idea. Philadelphia and Boston have seen a number of privately preserved cars grace their streets in recent times, and small fleets of old trolleys from various museum sources are now on loan to both towns and operated on suitable occasions, to the delight of the public. Toronto has for some years been maintaining an "obsolete fleet" of 1920s' cars of its own "Peter Witt" pattern. They are owned by both Toronto and the Rockwood Museum and have for some years been operating regularly scheduled tourist sightseeing services around downtown Toronto.

The Cleveland RTA, as successor to the City of Shaker

Heights, has continued that operator's tradition of maintaining and occasionally operating a nicely restored Cleveland city car that is now more than 70 years old. The same operator, during a period of critical car shortages, pressed two other cars back into service in the mid-'70s, loaned from the Worthington and Warehouse Point museums. The cars stayed in service some years before return to their owners, and the public was impressed with these nicely restored cars. San Francisco, of course, has its own operating trolley museum in the surviving cable car network, now undergoing lavish restoration. As the symbol of a city known the world over, the system is lovingly cherished. The city's electric trolley network, recently upgraded to 1980's Light Rail standards in superb fashion, is less well known.

San Francisco's Municipal Railway yearned for decades to get the electric trolleys off the surface of Market Street and into the oft-projected and finally built subway. But a scant few months before all services were due to be transferred underground, the city changed its mind about clearing Market Street of trolleys altogether. Why? Because though there was a perceived need to retain some local trolley transit along downtown Market Street, there seemed to be as great a desire to save something of San Francisco's last downtown trolley line *in toto* as an historic exhibit.

Trolleys are to Market Street, San Francisco, as the Loop is to Chicago. A traffic-free mall has been considered, with only trolley transit, and other schemes too have been discussed. The city borrowed back one of its old cars, now owned by the Rio Vista Museum, during portions of 1981 and 1982, while it still possesses two other similar cars which have occasionally had an airing in recent years. No firm decision has yet been made since total elimination of regular trolley service on Market Street was so long postponed and what will ultimately happen is in the lap of the gods.

But one is forced to conclude that the role of the trolley museum in sensitizing people to the trolley's significant place in this continent's history, has had a lot to do with San Francisco's thinking. In the same vein, there are towns who are prepared to bring old trolleys back again after decades without tracks on the streets, sometimes as part of a brand-new Light Rail installation but more usually as focal point of an historical district restoration project. The next few years will see many such projects, now in the planning stages, finally completed, but already Detroit and Seattle are running while tiny Fort Collins in Colorado will not be too far behind.

The supply of suitable cars for museum collections, while now very limited, has not entirely dried up. Car acquisition is still an important museum function and cooperation rather than competition between the groups in making purchases can yield spectacular dividends. When the shortage of open cars became acute in the 1960s the ARM made an offer for some of the ex-U.S. open cars still running in South America. After trips to Brazil, Argentina and Peru to negotiate terms, no less than 14 open cars plus spares were shipped back to the U.S.A. from Rio de Janeiro for distribution among the ARM's constituent museums. Those that have so far been restored are, as one might expect, among the star attractions in their new homes. One hopes the ARM can accomplish the same feat with the ex-U.S. cars recently made redundant in Vera Cruz, Mexico.

The import of purely foreign cars has been another successful technique employed to fill out collections, since these cars point up the marked contrast between North American and European practise in vehicle design, function and technology. After the initial American influx in the 1890s, European trolley technology went its own way, producing some very distinctive vehicles to work in conditions very different from those found here. Ironically, it is European trolley technology which is now the world leader and which the North American Light Rail operators have had to import in order to restart or reequip their systems.

The Seashore Museum was the pioneer in importing museum cars of European origin and, in the late 1950s, the face of their representative became a familiar one in Britain, seeking out cars and spares whenever a trolley system there was about to close. Since then other museums have followed Seashore's lead, sometimes on their own, sometimes using the good offices of the ARM.

As a professional association, the ARM has become of great value to its members in recent years. It has for some time issued regular bulletins. Its annual conventions are held at the different museums. ARM serves as a forum for exchange of news and information and can act to put museums together with suppliers with obsolete material for sale, or who are willing to fabricate unobtainable parts for purchase by the museums on a cooperative basis. And, of course, the ARM remains a principal channel for the average museum member to socialize with like-minded people from other museums widely scattered over the continent. This is an important function for which there seems all too little time during an average museum season.

Chapter 4

Interpreting and Documenting the Collections

THERE ARE CERTAIN intellectual functions *all* museums must perform. Chief among those are the obligations to preserve, to restore and most important of all, to interpret. It has unhappily been true of the trolley museums that their continued amateur character, in so many ways their greatest asset, has here become their greatest liability. The concentrated effort of *will*, the single-mindedness of purpose a group must maintain when building their museum, has blinkered too many into the neglect of some or all of these fundamental museum functions.

A typical omission is the neglect of informative or interpretive descriptive display. Viewing and riding the trolleys is a basic part of the visitor experience at a trolley museum, let there be no doubt about that. Moreover, if the visitor pays attention, he or she might pick up something about the museum, or the car being ridden, from the little speech given by the driver or conductor at the end of the line. Or, if eyes are sharp, the visitor might be able to spot the informative car card, typed in excruciatingly small letters on paper brown with age and weather stains, often posted in some inaccessible dark corner of the car. But that's not the most imaginative way to impart information, and it doesn't do justice to those who compiled it.

At the very least a visitor should be able to inform himself as to why this vehicle, as opposed to any other, has earned a place in the museum's collection. Obviously in a museum which itself has yet to acquire a cohesive acquisition policy it is asking a little much to expect the members to be able to explain exhibits to a visitor. But what kind of a museum then is it supposed to be? If it is so confused about why it exists, or why its vehicles are there, how is it going to inform the visitor? Those with a properly formulated collection policy aren't always much better equipped to inform a visitor. Without adequate descriptive information, without some understanding of the way in which one exhibit dovetails with another in telling the story the museum wants, and without some overall interpretation of the exhibits, the display can't make sense to a casual visitor. All he or she can do is wander aimlessly around the site, drawn only to the patently odd or unusual. In their eyes you can see the unanswered questions. "Why is this wreck here? Why did these guys think it was worth saving? What was it for?" Too many institutions do not provide such basic information as part of their displays. It is no solution and it is bad public relations to tell a visitor that if answers are wanted the visitor must buy and study the museum's guidebook; always assuming there is a guidebook and that it addresses itself to such topics. Not all do.

Another fundamental problem with far graver, long-term implications has been the almost total neglect of raw historical data in museum collections. Collecting and preserving the papers that went with the trolleys is a crucial museum function. It is the foundation which is needed to create sound and reliable research collections devoted to the history of urban transit. Such collections are badly needed and do not exist in easily available form today. For lack of them, transportation history is not recognised as a legitimate field of scholarly endeavor, save as a derivative of some other historical discipline such as economic or urban history, and fettered by that discipline's historical outlook and methodology.

Presently, only a handful of museums systematically collect paper materials on the trolley and its era and all praise is due them. Other data that survives is widely scattered and largely denied the scholar or researcher. Far too much is in private hands. That is a major hazard to the researcher, since private collectors are notorious for their single-minded determination to sit on their acquisitions in total silence. They seem unable to muster either the energy or the intellect required to do meaningful work on the papers themselves, while allowing no one else near.

When they die (and many have died over the years!) the situation becomes far worse. Since they have never been seen to do much with their collection, probably keeping it in a damp basement along with the other household junk, their widows and executors, perhaps bowed down with grief and certainly determined to respect the deceased's memory by clearing up the estate quickly, assume the papers had no intrinsic value except to the dear departed, and destroy them.

Ironically, even if the grieving widow does appreciate the value of the papers, there are almost no channels open to her which can assure the papers' safe long-term preservation. Consequently another private collector, alert and fully cognizant of the situation, will likely as not be waiting in the wings, anxious to take possession. The grieving widow is hardly in a position to make a sound judgment on the merits of the collector's claim, nor his financial offer (if made). The usual result is that, if not destroyed, the papers are given or sold to the first who asks for them and the whole cycle begins again.

The logical places one might consider lodging the papers, such as a local historical society or a university manuscript collection, are hardly the most ideal repositories, either. Generally these institutions tend to be overwhelmed by the size and scope of these kinds of collections, and by the special storage and access needs of transportation documents. Moreover, they have little experience of the specialised techniques required to accession, rehabilitate and index this type

of collection so that it can be of use to a scholar or researcher, let alone an ordinary person with a passing interest. Many times the staff is without anyone who can correctly assess the worth of these materials, which on their face may appear to have no scholarly or historic value, the usual criteria employed when making an acquisition decision in an historical society or university collection. Here, then, is a place for the trolley museum movement to expand its genuine museum function, one literally crying out for attention.

One can make the same criticism concerning the neglect of secondary material collections, that is to say collections of books, pamphlets and other published documents relating to urban transit. There are no reference libraries open to the public at any of the museums, though some are planned way into the future. But, in the 45 years since the movement started, so much has been published on transit topics that a complete (or nearly so) collection would in itself be an extraordinarily valuable research tool. What makes the lack of secondary material collections utterly inexcusable is that for years the museums have been selling a goodly proportion of such stuff in their gift shops as a way of raising funds, without ever having set aside one copy of everything stocked for their own use! If a lay visitor wants printed information on transport history in general, or needs to research something in particular, the bookstore is usually the only place at a museum which can help, and that only at a price, and subject to what may be in print at the time. The serious student of transport history will find little to help him at *any* price.

This is a national tragedy. So much needs to be studied. As we have seen, public transport in the form of the trolley was for decades the prime tool of city growth at precisely the time the continent felt a civilized future was possible only within the city. A similar kind of reasoning, incidentally, can be found in the new Light Rail installations of the 1980s, namely that commitment to a permanent line of route creates an artery around which new city growth will cluster. Early indications are that the reasoning is absolutely correct.

But the dimensions of the process in the trolley's heyday are as yet undetermined, while the simple factual record is terribly incomplete. The trolley museums ought to be at the cutting edge in this kind of work, functioning as regional research and learning centers, yet not one has seen its functions as encompassing such a task. It is a problem which has been engaging the ARM of late, and time might see attempts made to tackle it. One would hope so. The museum which first assembles and opens to the public an archive or library devoted to the trolley or urban transit in general will advance the status and reputation of the amateur trolley museum movement just as surely as did that band of pioneers who first suggested preserved trolley cars should be operated.

Another kind of problem which is arising is more

closely connected with display techniques. It has to do with presenting the preserved trolley car in an authentic setting. With the exceptions of the East Troy interurban museum, Branford (with a genuine country trolley right-of-way sliding imperceptibly into a surviving streetcar suburb), and the Minneapolis and Baltimore museums in their genuine midtown settings, only a handful of museums have begun to grapple with the problem of reconciling a country location with the essentially urban character of their artifacts.

In a way, the tourist trolley lines at Detroit, Seattle, Philadelphia, San Antonio and Yakima have this problem licked. Their trolleys run on ordinary city streets, just as they did in the old days; so will those at Fort Collins. In a sense their very location has enabled them to possess at one stroke what the more traditional trolley museums have labored years to achieve: a genuine urban environment for their trolleys. It isn't just a question of building stage sets, though all the museums could benefit from a touch of the theatrical in their presentation. No, it is more a question of re-creating the environment out of which the trolley sprang and helped shape.

Trolleys were preeminently creatures of the street. That was their true context. They are out of place in any other setting. By contrast, interurban cars were designed for fast running in the country. The average trolley museum's environment is much closer to that of a typical interurban line so, while the experience of riding a Chicago city trolley through an uninhabited Illinois cornfield might be an attraction for the trolley fan, and certainly wasn't unprecedented on the sprawling Chicago Surface Lines of the 1940s, the average visitor can't be expected to know that. To him it is an anomaly. The car is out of context. It belongs on prosperous, well-lit, downtown shopping streets, in the gloom and grime of industrial areas, or among the green trees, red brick, white clapboards and summer lawns of an early 20th-century suburb.

Most visitors can't recall the trolley in any other setting, except perhaps for the very special open trolley which in the summer served a lake or a park. As a result, none of the city trolleys look right among the fields and trees of the museums.

Yet only a few museums propose adding appropriate urban settings. That is a pity, for the creation of a city street or two, set in a time period appropriate to the majority of the collection, would unquestionably help further a museum's aim to make the past live. Let there be no doubt that it can be done; the creation of an urban setting in a museum is entirely within the realm of possibility. The National Tramway Museum of England, a wholly amateur group, has started to do exactly that, using as its model other British folk and industrial museums which seemingly without effort have re-created whole streets from other ages with a style and grace that takes one's breath away.

Moreover, it has been done in North America, too. Some very professional Canadian groups, in partnership with amateur-sponsored historical societies, have been creating some marvelous parks which give the visitor the impression that the clock has literally been turned back. Heritage Park in Calgary, for example, re-creates many eras of Calgary's past simply by re-erecting old buildings on the site in appropriate groups. Naturally, the trolley fits into the overall scheme of things as a people mover, but also as something typical of all Calgary's past. In the Fort Edmonton project the trolley museum is to be a part of the 1920s section, in which, again, an entire set of buildings of that vintage will be brought together, with the trolley serving them.

The spinoffs in space, facilities and commercial enterprises are infinite. One can easily envision space for offices, a library, an archive, a workshop, stores typical of the period selling merchandise of the period, perhaps even whole buildings given over to other kinds of museum collections, but all focused on the operating museum trolley line. The scope for parades, vintage car meets, old movie conventions, and the like would be unlimited, and they would all be based around the successful marrying of the city museum trolley with its appropriate surroundings. For myself, I see this as the only way the trolley museum movement can go in the future if it is to survive. And for the museums, survival is the name of the game.

In this day and age, survival means money, and money means visitors dropping fares in the farebox. They will only drop fares in the farebox if they can be both informed and entertained. In short, the amateur museums are at a takeoff point. They can, if they so wish, join the leisure industry and be successful at it. They have something unique to offer. But, in order to do so, they must begin to plan their activities around proper development of their institution and its site.

It is the professional touch that is wanted in everything that comes before the public's eye. To acquire that, one need look no further than a well-run amusement theme park. Look at the joy Disneyland's replica horse cars and motor buses bring its visitors as they roll down Main Street Yesteryear. Disney himself conceived the idea of re-creating a main street of a typical Missouri town of his boyhood, complete with horse cars, as part of his theme parks and he coupled that with the knowledge that the public responds best to a clean and well-run operation.

Trolley museums aren't Disneyland, but they are in the business of entertaining as well as informing their visitors. To that extent, then, landscaping, cleanliness and overall tidiness have to have higher priorities than they do now. It is amazing the effect that adopting so simple a device as a standard and legible house style for all display signing can have, for example. Doubtless the reader will have as many ideas as the experts as to what else can be done to please the public.

But somehow it must be done, for if the museums do not act imaginatively, their long-term survival is at best questionable. There is a very real argument for the proposition that the amateur trolley museum has gone about as far as it can go on its present course. As the Branford house journal pointed out, too many of even the biggest museums are still no more than glorified fan clubs, steered by the whims of the membership. One hopes the movement has the flexibility to be able to chart a new course for itself in the years to come.

But let us not get so carried away with the problems and the omissions of the present that we lose sight of the trolley museum movement's very real and solid achievements to date. No visitor leaving an operating trolley museum, whatever its size, can fail to be convinced that restoration and operation of the cars is a vital component of the institution's museum function. To speak plainly, a museum that can't (or won't) operate its cars denies the visitor the complete experience of the very thing it is supposedly preserving. The trolley, moreover, is an object not merely of historical curiosity, but of nostalgia, recalled with affection and even love. Undoubtedly the museums which cater best to these basic emotions are those which run their cars. Thus even the smallest tourist trolley line can give to its visitors an experience of far greater depth and historic significance than can any purely static display, no matter how comprehensive or sophisticated.

Words do not adequately convey the immediate and overwhelming impact that the living trolley has on its visitors. It weaves a spell of hypnotic proportions over all the generations. The older visitor greets them as the long-lost friends they undoubtedly are (like stepping back 40 years, many of them will delightedly tell you), while the youngsters, who never saw the trolley at work on their city streets, are at first awe-struck and then captivated by these unfamiliar yet friendly machines. So powerful is the dramatic effect of the living trolley upon the young that all over North America hundreds of youngsters who probably never saw a working trolley in their lives have joined museums as members and volunteers. They are the young blood such voluntary organizations must have to keep alive and vital. It says much for what the museums have done already that the living trolley has this power.

The amateur trolley museum movement of North America has single-handedly kept the trolley-car era alive. By adding the missing element of movement to their displays, they have created a new and priceless national treasure: the operating trolley museum. Their millions of visitors owe them an immense debt of gratitude. Against all odds, against all advice, the men and women who built these museums have created an enduring memorial to a vanished way of life.

PART 2

PART 2: The Museums

ORANGE EMPIRE RAILWAY MUSEUM. Humming south along the main line, *Pacific Electric* "Blimp" combo #498 travels through a rural valley. It ran for many years in the San Francisco area.   *Craig Rasmussen*

ORANGE EMPIRE RAILWAY MUSEUM. The dual-gauge (3'6"–4'8½") operation at this museum is unique among the U.S. displays. This portion of the "Loop" line is reminiscent of street trackage. **Behind** *Los Angeles Railway* #1201 is the 60x200' carbarn that houses the narrow-gauge fleet.
Norman K. Johnson

California • Perris

Orange Empire Railway Museum. South A Street, Perris, one mile south of town, 18 miles SE of Riverside. Use Perris exit (Ca. 74) on I-15E temporary. Museum owned and operated by the Orange Empire Railway Museum, P.O. Box 548, Perris, CA 92370. Standard gauge and 3'6" gauge tracks.

IN 1956, 14 young men, concerned that the trolley museum movement include Southern California's highly individualistic trolleys, banded together to consolidate early preservation efforts. They soon found that while car buying was only a question of money (and not very much money at that), housing the cars was a very different matter. It took two years and much heartache before a suitable home was found at the present site, already in the hands of a railroad preservation group. Negotiations led to the lease from this group of a portion of the site and its trackage, and the trolley museum was underway. Soon an adjoining eight acres was purchased, and the first 1,000' of electrified track was opened in 1960.

At that time the site was virtually desert, and in the intervening years landscaping has been given a high priority, softening the bleak harsh and dusty scene. Priority, too, was given to vehicle acquisition and, since the beginning, more than 140 vehicles have come to the museum. The host California Southern Railroad Museum has now merged with the Orange Empire group, bringing with it a fine collection of railroad locomotives and cars, and transforming the trolley

ORANGE EMPIRE RAILWAY MUSEUM. *Pacific Electric Ry. #717, a "Hollywood" class car (shown on roster as #5167) loads on the museum's main line. The track at right leads to the yards and carbarns.* *Jim Walker*

ORANGE EMPIRE RAILWAY MUSEUM. The beautiful station, completed in the late 1960s, is at the right of Los Angeles PCC car #3165, the last car bought new for the city when it arrived in October 1948. Most of Los Angeles' 165 PCC cars still soldier on in Cairo, Egypt (three are at this museum). Noticeable here is the width of the car, the same as on other systems despite the use of narrow-gauge trucks. *A.D. Young*

ORANGE EMPIRE RAILWAY MUSEUM. Part of the "flavor" of the interurban was trolley freight operation, *Pacific Electric #1624* switching a cut of wood-side box cars, also from that very large system.

Orange Empire Railway Museum

museum into an all-around museum of rail transit.

Though the ambitious multi-gauge track layout was envisaged by the trolley museum from the beginning, the present extensive covered carbarns were not, for it almost never rains in this part of the world. The sun is hot and shines on almost every day of the year, while most of the cars from the region now in the collection spent all their working lives in the open. So, for about 12 years, it was felt carbarns were not an urgent need. By 1968 shrinkage of wood and other evidence of vehicle deterioration could be ignored no longer and a start was made on the first of the carbarns.

The museum's main line was once a part of the Santa Fe's old San Bernardino–San Diego route, and is of standard gauge, with a long stretch of double track outside the main entrance to the museum. It is about one and a half miles long and of decided interurban character; very appropriate for predominantly Pacific Electric cars which regularly operate over it. There is a loop line of dual 3"6" and 4"8½' gauge which runs from an immaculate trolley station at the museum entrance, encircling the landscaped area, picnic grounds and storage yards.

A third narrow-gauge line traverses the proposed main street ("Broadway") of the museum, with shuttle service provided by a typical U.S. "dinky" car, except that in this case the normal vehicle provided is an export model which spent all its working life in Kyoto, Japan. There is an impressive amount of mixed gauge trackage in the museum and in busy times or during special events, this museum can provide five separate rides in five different cars over five different routes, on

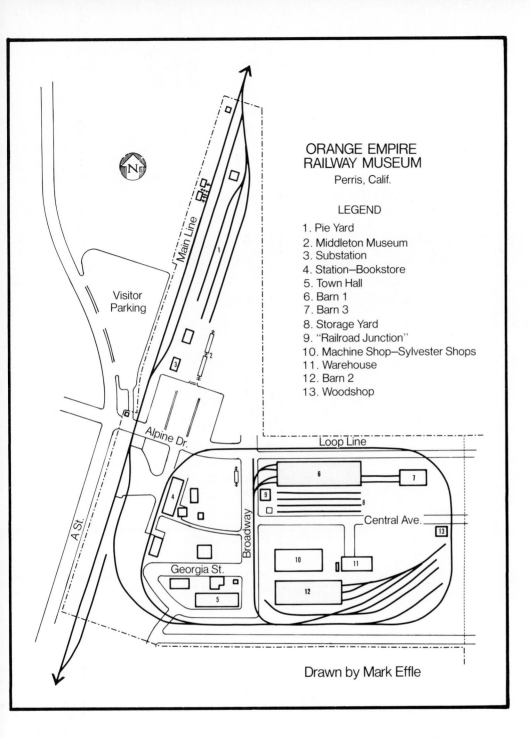

MAP 1

ORANGE EMPIRE
RAILWAY MUSEUM
Perris, Calif.

LEGEND
1. Pie Yard
2. Middleton Museum
3. Substation
4. Station—Bookstore
5. Town Hall
6. Barn 1
7. Barn 3
8. Storage Yard
9. "Railroad Junction"
10. Machine Shop—Sylvester Shops
11. Warehouse
12. Barn 2
13. Woodshop

Drawn by Mark Effle

two separate gauges; a remarkable achievement.

Normally the narrow-gauge loop is traversed by Los Angeles cars, stopping at various points of interest en route while the operator tells the passengers something about the museum and the reason for its existence. Almost every type of car run by Los Angeles Railway between 1900 and 1948 is represented at this museum, though by no means are all yet fully restored. A similar broad range of vehicles comes from the standard-gauge Pacific Electric system. For breadth and for contrast there are a few choice examples of cars from other areas in California such as the Municipal Railway of San Francisco, the Key System, plus more distant systems in New Orleans, British Columbia, and (surprisingly) Ireland.

This intelligent acquisition program has been complemented by an equally well-thought-out display policy. Orange Empire is one of the few museums sufficiently developed to go beyond simply providing rides on restored cars. An early supporter of the ARM and one of its principal activists to this day, Orange Empire's museum manuals are among the most important documents so far produced by the movement as a whole.

Moreover, it is the museum's intention to create on at least a portion of the site a period "trolley street," to be set in the 1930s. Work began on this project during 1969, and a collection of other transit modes is being assembled as part of that display, together with appropriate street furniture, shop fittings, and carbarns.

Re-creation of the trolley's environment is a big feature of this museum's future plans, since current proposals call for constructing additional storefronts, streets, picnic groves, bandstands, soda stands and hot dog counters, to be located in the center of an expanded main property. May that day soon be here! In the meantime, this is one of the most satisfying of all trolley museums to visit. There is plenty of space to sit down, freshen up, snack, picnic or make purchases from the gift shop in clean, lushly vegetated surroundings typical of California's southland. The flowers, shrubs and lawns are abundant, providing a powerful contrast to the semi-desert beyond and is a peaceful setting from which to watch the trolleys go by, just as they did in the old days. And that's really what trolley museums are all about.

ORANGE EMPIRE RAILWAY MUSEUM. The "Huntington Standard" streetcar is the symbol of the *Los Angeles Railway,* and has become famed all over the world thanks to the use of the Los Angeles Railway in Laurel & Hardy and other early two-reel film comedies. #665 pauses during evening operations at the loading area.
Mark G. Effle

Fleet No.	Principal Owner	Builder, Year	Remarks
City and Suburban Cars			
2	Hill of Howth (Dublin, Ireland)	Brush, 1901	Open Top Double Deck
4	Bakersfield & Kern Electric Ry.	Holman, 1900	California
7	Los Angeles Railway	St. Louis, 1895	California—Type A
19	Kyoto, Japan	Brill, 1898	
51	Fresno Traction Co.	Brill, 1913	Hedley Doyle Stepless
83	Fresno Traction Co.	St. Louis, 1925	Birney Safety
152	Los Angeles Railway	St. Louis, 1898	California—Type B
162	Municipal Ry. San Francisco	Jewett, 1914	Type B
171	Municipal Ry. San Francisco	Bethlehem, 1923	Type K
179	Pacific Electric	Pullman, 1912	Center Entrance
331	Pacific Electric	American, 1918	Birney Safety
332	Pacific Electric	American, 1918	Birney Safety
508	San Diego Electric Ry.	St. Louis, 1937	PCC
511	Pacific Electric	St. Louis, 1901	Suburban
525	Los Angeles Railway	St. Louis, 1906	California—Type BG
528	San Diego Electric Ry.	St. Louis, 1937	PCC
538	Pacific Electric	St. Louis, 1909	Suburban
665	Los Angeles Railway	St. Louis, 1911	California—Type B
913	New Orleans Public Service	Perley Thomas, 1923	
936	Los Angeles Railway	St. Louis, 1913	"Sowbelly"—Type C

Fleet No.	Principal Owner	Builder, Year	Remarks
1003	San Diego Electric Ry./Salt Lake City	St. Louis, 1913	
1039	Municipal Ry. of San Francisco	St. Louis, 1952	PCC
1069	Los Angeles Railway	American, 1921	Birney Safety—Type G
1160	Los Angeles Railway	Los Angeles Ry. Shops, 1923	California—Type F
1201	Los Angeles Railway	St. Louis, 1921	California—Type H4
1423	Los Angeles Railway	St. Louis, 1923	Type H3
1450	Los Angeles Railway	St. Louis, 1923	Type H3
1559	Los Angeles Railway	Los Angeles Ry. Shops, 1925	California—Type K
2501	Los Angeles Railway	St. Louis, 1925	Type L
2601	Los Angeles Railway	St. Louis, 1930	Peter Witt, Type M
3001	Los Angeles Railway	St. Louis, 1937	PCC Type P
3100	Los Angeles Railway	St. Louis, 1943	PCC, Type P-2
3165	Los Angeles Transit Lines	St. Louis, 1948	PCC, Type P-3
5112	Pacific Electric	St. Louis, 1922	"Hollywood" Suburban
5123	Pacific Electric	St. Louis, 1922	"Hollywood" Suburban
5166	Pacific Electric	Brill, 1925	"Hollywood" Suburban
5167	Pacific Electric	Brill, 1925	"Hollywood" Suburban
Descanso	Los Angeles Railway	Los Angeles Ry. Shops, 1909	Funeral Car

Interurban Cars

127	Bamberger (Utah), Fonda, Johns & Glover	Brill, 1932	"Bullet"
167	Key System	Bethlehem, 1937	Articulated
301	Visalia Electric	American, 1918	Trailer
302	Visalia Electric	American, 1918	Trailer
314	Pacific Electric	St. Louis, 1930	
418	Pacific Electric	Pullman, 1913	
498	Pacific Electric	Pullman, 1913	Combine
1000	Pacific Electric	Jewett, 1913	Business Car "Commodore"
1001	Pacific Electric	Jewett, 1913	
1225	British Columbia Electric Ry.	St. Louis, 1912	
1440	Pacific Electric	Pacific Electric, 1910	Box Motor

Electric Locomotives

1	Hutchinson & Northern	General Electric, 1921	Steeple Cab
1	American Smelting & Refining (Arizona)	Westinghouse, 1912	Mining (250-volt)
653	Sacramento Northern	General Electric, 1928	Steeple Cab
1624	Pacific Electric	Pacific Electric, 1925	Steeple Cab

Maintenance of Way Cars

9209	Los Angeles Railway	Los Angeles Railway, 1913	Power Car
9225	Los Angeles Railway	Los Angeles Railway, 1912	5-ton Derrick
9310	Los Angeles Railway	Los Angeles Railway, 1925	Rail Grinder
9350	Los Angeles Railway	Los Angeles Railway, 1907	Tower Car
9351	Los Angeles Railway	Los Angeles Railway, 1907	Line Const. Car
9550	Los Angeles Railway	Los Angeles Railway, 1904	Shop Switcher
9614	Los Angeles Railway	Los Angeles Railway, 1907	Flat Car
9615	Los Angeles Railway	Los Angeles Railway, 1908	Flat Car
0036	Pacific Electric Railway	L.A. & Redondo, 1896	Caboose/Box Car
00150	Pacific Electric	L.A. Pacific, 1899	Trolley Greaser
00157	Pacific Electric	Pacific Electric, 1915	Tower Car

Steam Locomotives

2	Mojave Northern	Davenport, 1917	0-6-OT Saddle Tank
2	Ventura County Railway	Baldwin, 1922	2-6-2

Steam Railroad Passenger and Baggage Cars

20	Virginia & Truckee	Hicks, 1908	Combination
54	Soo Line	Barney & Smith, 1914	Business Car
60	Santa Fe Railway	Pullman, 1924	Postal Car
122	Southern Pacific	American Standard, 1900	Business "Sacramento"
175	San Diego & Arizona Eastern	Pullman, 1915	Combination
204	Union Pacific	Pullman, 1922	Rules Examiner Car
542	Los Angeles & Salt Lake (UP)	Pullman, 1926	
552	Denver & Rio Grande Western	Pullman, 1891	Combination
692	Oregon Short Line (UP)	Pullman, 1911	
743	Denver & Rio Grande Western	Barney & Smith, 1910	Baggage
745	Denver & Rio Grande Western	ACF, 1929	Baggage
1530	Union Pacific	Pullman, 1924	Dormitory/Club
1999	Santa Fe Railway	Pullman, 1930	Horse Express

Fleet No.	Principal Owner	Builder, Year	Remarks
2055	Santa Fe Railway	Pullman, 1930	Baggage/Postal
2065	Union Pacific	Pullman, 1914	Postal Car
2419	Santa Fe Railway	Ohio Falls, 1879	Combination
2543	Santa Fe Railway	ACF, 1911	Combination
2602	Santa Fe Railway	Pullman, 1931	Combination
3010	Santa Fe Railway	Pullman, 1927	Chair Car
3209	Santa Fe Railway	Pullman, 1910	Parlor/Observation
89631	U.S. Army Transportation Corps	St. Louis, 1950	Troop Kitchen
89647	U.S. Army Transportation Corps	St. Louis, 1950	Troop Kitchen
Corydon	Pullman Company	Pullman, 1917	7 Compartment/2 Drawing Room

Steam Railroad Maintenance of Way Equipment

Fleet No.	Principal Owner	Builder, Year	Remarks
MW1354	Southern Pacific		Supply Car
MW7090	Southern Pacific	Industrial Works, 1912	Derrick
MW7091	Southern Pacific	Southern Pacific, 1912	Tender for MW7090
189783	Santa Fe Railway	Standard, 1907/Rblt. 1932	Fuel/Water for 199774
190548	Santa Fe Railway	ACF, 1913/Rblt. 1947	Wheel Car
193673	Santa Fe Railway	Santa Fe, 1923	Bunk Car
199774	Santa Fe Railway	Industrial Works, 1909	Derrick
905219	Union Pacific	Bettendorf, 1928	Flat Car

Internal Combustion Locomotives

Fleet No.	Principal Owner	Builder, Year	Remarks
12	Southern California Edison	Plymouth, 1941	Gas-Mechanical
E80	American Potash & Chemical	General Electric, 1941	Diesel-Electric
E513	American Potash & Chemical	Baldwin, 1956	Diesel-Hydraulic
1802	Southern Pacific	Alco, 1952	S4 Diesel-Electric
7441	U.S. Air Force	General Electric, 1942	Diesel-Electric
8550	U.S. Air Force	General Electric, 1944	Diesel-Electric

Steam Railroad Interurban and Freight Cars and Cabooses

Fleet No.	Principal Owner	Builder, Year	Remarks
(1)	Pacific Electric	Standard, 1924	Box Cars (5)
205	Tonopah & Tidewater	Seattle Car & Mfg., 1906	Flat Car
453	General American Transportation (GATX)	, 1930	Wine Tank Car
570	Southern Pacific	Southern Pacific, 1924	Caboose
813	Richfield Oil (ROX)	North American Car, 1917	Tank Car
D918	Santa Fe Railway	Santa Fe, 1929	Drover's Caboose
1421	Santa Fe Railway	ACF, 1923	Caboose
1651	Standard Brands (SBIX)	Fleischmann, 1928	Vinegar Tank Car
1962	Pacific Electric	Pacific Electric, 1939	Caboose
1970	Pacific Electric		Caboose
1971	Pacific Electric		Caboose
1973	Pacific Electric	Lehigh Valley, 1926	Caboose
1985	Pacific Electric	, 1905	Caboose
2721	Pacific Electric	Standard, 1924	Box Car
8875	Santa Fe Railway	ACF, 1910	Refrigerator Car
9210	Union Tank Car Co. (UTLX)	Union Tank, 1937	Tank Car
20305	Pacific Fruit Express (PFE)	Pullman–Standard, 1947	Refrigerator Car
21028	Santa Fe Railway (SFRD)	Standard, 1923	Refrigerator Car
25480	Santa Fe Railway	Standard, 1923	Stock Car
28504	Union Pacific	, 1925	Gondola
43535	Pacific Fruit Express	Pullman–Standard, 1937	Refrigerator Car
49131	Santa Fe Railway	Pullman, 1913	Box Car
70529	General American Transportation (GATX)	, 1941	Wine Tank Car
85727	Union Pacific	Pullman, 1926	Hopper
1761R	Santa Fe Railway	ACF, 1929	Caboose
176695	Santa Fe Railway	, 1943	Gondola
183206	Union Pacific	, 1936	Box Car
(2)	U.S. Navy	General American, 1942	Box Cars (7)
61-02836	U.S. Navy	, 1945	Flat Car

Trolley Buses

Fleet No.	Principal Owner	Builder, Year	Remarks
530	Municipal Railway of San Francisco	Marmon–Herrington, 1948	TC-40
536	Municipal Railway of San Francisco	Marmon–Herrington, 1948	TC-40
614	Municipal Railway of San Francisco	Twin Coach, 1949	44-TTW-45
633	Seattle Metro	Twin Coach, 1940	GWFT
656	Seattle Metro	Pullman, 1943	44CX
8001	Los Angeles Transit Lines	Brill, 1946	TC44

(1) Numbers 2704, 2721, 2729, 2731 and 2737.
(2) Numbers (all prefix 61-) 02479, 02480, 02481, 02483, 02484, 02489 and 02494.

California • Rio Vista Jct.

California Railway Museum. On State Route 12 between Fairfield and Rio Vista in Solano County. Owned and operated by the Bay Area Electric Railroad Association, Box 3694, San Francisco, CA 94117. Standard Gauge.

THIS LARGE, well-run museum has deep roots. The initial impetus for its creation was the impending destruction of a surviving car from the Napa Valley interurban line. In April 1945 a group was formed to buy it and then, bitten with the collection bug, spent the next few years surveying the remaining California trolley systems, arranging special trips on historic cars and raising money to buy them for the collection.

As interest grew, it became imperative to formalize the group's aims. The present Association was set up at the end of 1946 and for the next 13 years this purely voluntary organization managed to buy cars and arrange temporary storage for them. But the cost of moving cars from place to place was a continual drain on finances, while the destruction of the Napa Valley car by vandals proved to be the last straw. A feverish attempt was made to locate a permanent home.

The present site, beside the Sacramento Northern's former interurban main line, was located in 1960. It was subsequently purchased outright, but the cost was so heavy that progress was inhibited and money scarce. Through no fault of their own, therefore, it was not until January 1966 that the members were able to first run a trolley under its own power. Satisfied that operations were on a firm footing, the museum finally opened to the public in September 1966.

The extensive collection specialises almost entirely in trolleys of the Western U.S., though there is a car from Saskatoon, Canada, and an open car from Black-

CALIFORNIA RAILWAY MUSEUM. The outer end of the museum line, beyond "South Park" junction where the loop comes together, parallels the old Sacramento Northern line to the San Francisco bay area, now itself leased to the museum. *East Bay Street Railways #987 heads south under catenary. Harre W. Demoro*

CALIFORNIA RAILWAY MU-SEUM. The beginnings of the magnificent shops, seen under construction in 1975. *Sacramento*

Northern Birney car #62 is at right, while the car in shadow is one of the ex-New York elevated cars of 1885. *A.D. Young*

pool, England. The oldest cars are two 1888 rapid transit cars built for New York's Manhattan Elevated Railway Company. Among the first to be fitted in the 1890s with the newly invented multiple-unit electrical control system (the heart of all subsequent rapid transit and Light Rail operations) these antique cars owe their survival to the Second World War, and their transfer from New York to the Richmond Shipyard Railway in the Bay area. Operated on that line until 1945, the cars were then privately preserved, being transferred to the present museum's founding group in 1965.

Since the museum's future expansion plans include the collection of all kinds of railroading artifacts, there are now a number of interurban express freight cars, electric freight locos and maintenance-of-way cars, together with steam locos and steam passenger cars. Steam operation is a feature of special events at the museum.

The visitor to Rio Vista should hardly need reminding that San Francisco's famous cable cars are a scant 50 miles away. Don't let the fact that the system has run almost continuously since 1873 mislead you; it is as much a vital component in San Francisco's overall transit network as it is a series of tourist lines. The relationship between the museum and San Francisco's MUNI has traditionally been cordial, and in recent

CALIFORNIA RAILWAY MU-SEUM. *Sacramento Northern* Birney #62 takes the return track at South Park to return to the loading area. The tall building at center was a former SN substation, which was dismantled and reassembled at this site; it now houses a former *BARTD* solid state converter, used during its early testing. *Harre W. Demoro*

CALIFORNIA RAILWAY MUSEUM. Landscaping is a feature of the two California museums. Here San Francisco "Iron Monster" #178 awaits dispatch from Laflin station. The wooded grove to the right leads to the picnic area and duck pond.   A.D. Young

CALIFORNIA RAILWAY MUSEUM. Once only a shed in a grove, *Petaluma & Santa Rosa #63* has been made back into an operating interurban car with trucks and equipment salvaged from other rolling stock.
Harre W. Demoro

years has become even closer. One of Rio Vista's San Francisco cars was back in its native city on loan in 1981 and 1982, running cheek-by-jowl with two other MUNI-owned historic trolleys. The contrast between these and the very latest reincarnation of the trolley concept, namely the beautiful new Light Rail system, is most marked, and a visit to both Rio Vista and to San Francisco is to see more than 100 years of the trolley story in completely operating form.

At Rio Vista, recent years have seen work concentrated on completing the huge new repair shop and an impressive facility has taken shape. Landscaping, too, has been a major priority, and the area boasts picnic grounds, a charming duckpond well filled with ducks, beautiful trees and shrubs. All have a neat and tidy appearance. There is an excellent parking lot and a most impressively stocked bookstore.

Trackage extends 1½ miles on a loop track around the museum, together with a terminal spur running some distance to the south, with plans for further extension. As at Orange Empire, special events can produce the spectacle of several cars running over different routes, together with a chance to ride a steam train. With the acquisition of more railroad exhibits, the museum is fast becoming a comprehensive regional museum of rail transport.

CALIFORNIA RAILWAY MUSEUM. A particular delight for visitors is the Blackpool, England, "boat" tram, seen on the inner portion of the museum's teardrop-shaped loop.   *Harre W. Demoro*

Fleet No.	Principal Owner	Builder, Year	Remarks
City and Suburban Cars			
12	Saskatoon, Alberta (Canada)	St. Louis, 1915	Stone & Webster Design
35	Pacific Gas & Electric (Sacramento)	American, 1914	California
41	Pacific Gas & Electric	American, 1918	Birney Safety
62	Sacramento Northern (Chico)	American, 1920	Birney Safety
178	Municipal Railway of San Francisco	Bethlehem, 1923	Type K
182	Key System	Bethlehem, 1937	Articulated
186	Key System	Bethlehem, 1937	Articulated
271	Key System/Lehigh Valley Transit	St. Louis, 1901	
317	Presidio & Ferries/United Railroads	Hammond, 1895	
352	Key System (East Bay Street Railway)	St. Louis, 1912	
578	Municipal Railway of San Francisco/MSRy.	Hammond, 1896	California
601	Blackpool Corporation (England)	English Electric, 1934	Open "Boat" Car
987	Key System	Key System, 1927	
1003	Municipal Railway of San Francisco	St. Louis, 1939	Streamliner "Magic Carpet"
1016	Municipal Railway of San Francisco	St. Louis, 1951	PCC
1043	San Diego Electric/Third Avenue Ry.	Brill, 1908	Convertible
1153	Municipal Railway of San Francisco	St. Louis, 1945	PCC/Orig. St. Louis Public Service
1190	Municipal Railway of S.F./Toronto Trans.	St. Louis, 1947	PCC, Orig. Kansas City
Interurban Cars			
52	Peninsular Railway	American, 1903	
61	Peninsular Railway	American, 1903	Trailer
63	Petaluma & Santa Rosa	Holman, 1904	Combine
111	Cincinnati & Lake Erie	Cincinnati, 1930	High-Speed Lightweight
200	Tidewater Southern	Jewett, 1912	
202	Indiana Railroad	Kuhlman, 1926	Lightweight
332	Southern Pacific (I.E.R.)/Pac. Electric	ACF, 1911	
400	Bamberger	Niles, 1910	Trailer
751	Salt Lake & Utah	Niles, 1915	Observation-Lounge, Trailer
1001	Oregon Electric	Niles, 1910	Parlor "Champoeg"
1005	Sacramento Northern	Holman, 1912	Combine
1019	Sacramento Northern	Hall Scott, 1913	Trailer
1020	Sacramento Northern	Hall Scott, 1913	Trailer
Bidwell	Sacramento Northern	Niles, 1906	Parlor/Obs./Diner
Electric Locomotives			
7	Central California Traction	Brill, 1929	Box Motor
652	Sacramento Northern	General Electric/Alco, 1928	Steeple Cab
654	Sacramento Northern	General Electric/Alco, 1930	Steeple Cab
1001	Key System (Oakland Terminal)	Oakland Traction, 1910	Steeple Cab
1215	Key System	Key System, 1926	Shop Switcher
Maintenance of Way Cars			
C-1	Municipal Railway of San Francisco	Pacific Car, 1923	Motor Flat/Tower
0109	Municipal Railway of San Francisco	Hammond, 1900	Rail Grinder
0130	Municipal Railway of San Francisco	United RRs of S.F., 1907	5-ton Crane
602	Sacramento Northern	Holman, 1910	Bunk Car
1011	Key System	Oakland Traction, 1906	Wrecker
1014	Key System	Hammond?, 1897	Wrecker
1201	Key System	Carter Brothers, 1895	Line Car
1218	Key System	Key System, 1929	Motor Flat/Tower
Rapid Transit Cars			
844	Richmond Shipyard/Manhattan Elevated	Gilbert, 1886	
889	Richmond Shipyard/Manhattan Elevated	Gilbert, 1886	
Steam Locomotives			
3	Robert Dollar Lumber	Alco, 1927	2-6-2T
94	Western Pacific	Alco, 1909	4-6-0
334	Western Pacific	Alco, 1929	2-8-2
2978	Robert Dollar Lumber	Lima, 1918	B Shay
Steam Passenger and Baggage Cars			
653	Western Pacific	Pullman, 1931	Observation/Lounge
1772	Santa Fe Railway		Baggage
	Pullman Co.	Pullman, 1916	Sleeper, *Circumnavigator's Club*
Steam Railroad Maintenance of Way Equipment			
7030	Southern Pacific	Industrial, 1920	Derrick

Internal Combustion Locomotives

30	Central California Traction Co.	General Electric, 1947	Diesel-Electric
502	Visalia Electric	General Electric, 1946	44-ton Diesel-Electric

Interurban and Steam Railroad Freight Cars and Cabooses

19	Central California Traction Co.	, 1910	Caboose
023	McCloud River Railroad	,1899	Caboose (Great Northern X443)
0293	Western Pacific	ACF, 1936	Box Car
530	The Pacific Lumber Co.	The Pacific Lumber Co., 1977	Logging Flat
1017	Central California Traction Co.	, 1910	Flat Car
1582	Western Pacific	ACF, 1912	Tender
2001	Central California Traction Co.	, 1910	Box Car
3001	Central California Traction Co.	, 1913	Box Car
4001	Richmond, Fredericksburg & Potomac	, 1929	Box Car
6113	Western Pacific	Mt. Vernon, 1917	Box Car
8542	Western Pacific		
11324	United States Army	, 1943	Tank Car (no tank)
28124	Minneapolis & St. Louis	, 1920	Box Car
29502	Union Refrigerator Transit	URTX, 1954	Refrigerator
(1)	Western Pacific	Pullman-Standard, 1951	Box Car
63383	Denver & Rio Grande Western	, 1927	Box Car
74583	Pacific Fruit Express	, 1922	Refrigerator
79801	General American Transportation Co.	, 1920	Tank Car
61-0200	United States Navy		Box Car

(1) Numbers 57044, 57092 and 57099

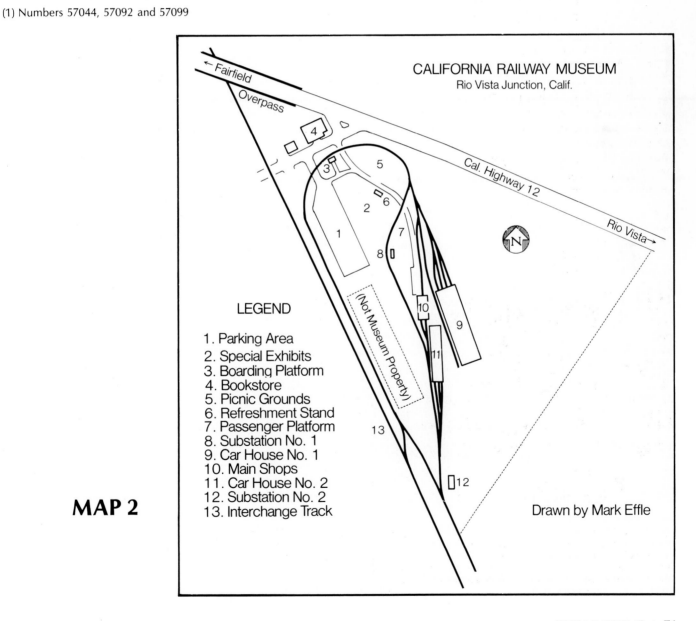

CALIFORNIA RAILWAY MUSEUM
Rio Vista Junction, Calif.

LEGEND

1. Parking Area
2. Special Exhibits
3. Boarding Platform
4. Bookstore
5. Picnic Grounds
6. Refreshment Stand
7. Passenger Platform
8. Substation No. 1
9. Car House No. 1
10. Main Shops
11. Car House No. 2
12. Substation No. 2
13. Interchange Track

MAP 2

Drawn by Mark Effle

Connecticut • Branford

Branford Electric Railway. On River Street, East Haven. Use Connecticut Turnpike exit 51 eastbound, exit 52 westbound, then follow signs from East Haven Green to River Street. Owned and operated by the Branford Electric Railway Association, 17 River Street, East Haven, CT 06405. Standard gauge.

INSPIRED BY the pre-war success of the Seashore and Warehouse Point groups, the BERA was established in August of 1945. Its most active member, one Wadsworth G. Fyler, had for some time been the galvanising force behind the Association and even before war's end had been keeping an eye open for suitable Connecticut locations at which to establish an operating electric trolley museum.

His options were narrowed down to a short list of three, of which the present site ultimately became the

BRANFORD TROLLEY MUSEUM. Open-bench cars have been the mainstay of summer operations of this museum for over three decades. *Connecticut Company #1414* is at the then-end of the line, just short of the trestle beyond Riverside (see map), in September 1958. Significant track improvements and extension have been accomplished in the intervening years.   *Jim Walker*

practical choice when it was sold to the BERA by the Connecticut Company for $3,500. This was a very generous gesture, since the price was virtually a giveaway. It has been said that the Company could have realised $15,000 by selling the line to scrap merchants.

The Connecticut Company continued trolley operations on the line until March 8, 1947, and on the next day the BERA took possession with great jubilation, heralding its new acquisition (rightly) as the world's only operating trolley museum. Their double-track line of route was the final leg of a line which led back to downtown New Haven, but with the advantage of private right-of-way, away from roads and vandals. The 1½-mile stretch runs through woodland and tidal marshes almost to the sea at Short Beach.

Since the museum was established on a functioning trolley line, and since the Connecticut Company obligingly left in both track and electrical connections to the rest of its system for over a year, most of Branford's cars of local origin, plus others from New York, New Jersey and Washington, D.C., were easily and cheaply delivered under their own power from a central storage location at Connecticut's James Street carhouse in New Haven.

But with the final severing of the connection in 1948, Branford was on its own, and the ensuing few years were very shaky. The tracks were functional, but in very poor shape and as an economy measure a start was made on single-tracking the line. Operation of the cars was still possible, using somewhat temperamental generating equipment, and the lack of connecting tracks did not prevent more cars from arriving at the museum. But the group's finances were parlous in the extreme. The museum was technically not open to the public, so that source of revenue could not be utilised, and the tracks sold for scrap did not realise a great deal of money. It was not until a scheme was devised by which 20-year interest-bearing bonds were issued by the Association that things began to improve and since then the museum has never looked back.

Lack of money did not deter the group from assessing its priorities and starting work. Covered accommo-

BRANFORD TROLLEY MUSEUM. Though the Farm River Road complex is a lively and bustling area, the onward route to Short Beach is rural and bucolic. Here is *Third Avenue Railway System* #629 on a return trip from Short Beach. This car spent the years 1949 to 1967 in Vienna, Austria, along with 24 of its sisters; they were sent there under the terms of the Marshall Plan. *A.D. Young*

dation was an urgent necessity and as early as 1948 the first barn and yard area were readied for service. Now there are five barns jammed full of cars, enabling practically all the exhibits to be housed under cover. Their car fleet is unbelievably diverse and spans a great period of time. Originally intended to represent Connecticut, Rhode Island, New York and New Jersey, the collection today is comprehensive enough to tell the story of the electric trolley's evolution from the early 1890s through the 1950s in all its forms, with particular attention to rapid transit vehicles, of which BERA has a goodly number.

The visitor first encounters Branford's trolleys at the Sprague Building on East Haven's River Street. A memorial to Frank Sprague, the man who perfected the electric trolley and invented the multiple-unit electric train, the building provides parking, small exhibit displays, a gift shop and a ticket office, plus the other necessary facilities. The trolley stands outside in the street, waiting for its passengers.

Once you are on board, the car transports you over an impressive wooden trestle spanning the tidal East Haven River, and then enters the private trackage of the museum, passing suburban back yards on the way to the carbarn complex at Farm River Road. This is the hub of the museum and passengers can alight here to inspect the barns, shops and other facilities in a setting reminiscent of any country trolley junction of sixty years ago. Then the route settles down to an easy meander through woodland and tidal marsh over to Short Beach and the smell of the sea. Much effort has been expended over the years to get the remaining single track into first-class order, and for some time now, Branford's tracks have been among the best at any trolley museum, in spite of the added encumbrance of three wooden trestles on the line with all the associated problems they bring.

Restoration and maintenance are a vital element of this museum's work, and on a number of occasions a pageant of restored trolley cars is operated. Literally dozens of cars participate, and a pageant day is perhaps one of the most rewarding a visitor could choose for a trip to this museum, for the sight of so many restored cars is breathtaking, as is the pride of the museum at being able to muster them all for operation.

Behind the scenes, the museum has been especially active in the ARM and its experience has been of great help to others. Operations are not just confined to summer months, since there are occasional Santa Claus runs at Christmas and on occasional snowy days demonstrations of trolley snowplows at work.

BRANFORD TROLLEY MUSEUM. The collection covers a wide geographical range. *Montreal & Southern Counties #9 sits next to Johnstown (Penna.) Traction Co. #356 in front of one of the carbarns.* *Mark Effle*

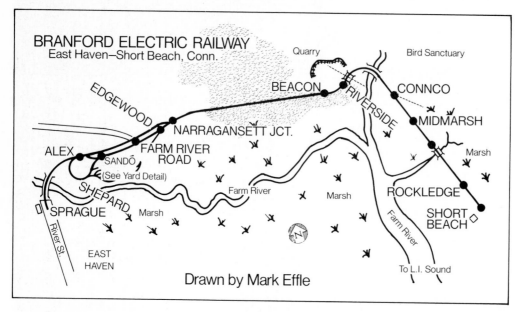

BRANFORD ELECTRIC RAILWAY
East Haven—Short Beach, Conn.

Quarry
Bird Sanctuary
BEACON
#RIVERSIDE
CONNCO
EDGEWOOD
MIDMARSH
NARRAGANSETT JCT.
ALEX
FARM RIVER ROAD
SANDO
(See Yard Detail)
Marsh
SHEPARD
Farm River
Marsh
ROCKLEDGE
SPRAGUE
Marsh
SHORT BEACH
Farm River
River St.
EAST HAVEN
To L.I. Sound

Drawn by Mark Effle

MAP 3

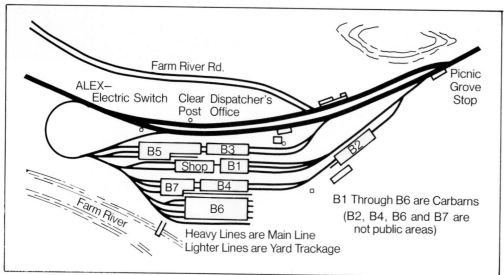

Farm River Rd.

ALEX—
Electric Switch
Clear Post
Dispatcher's Office
Picnic Grove Stop

B5
B3
B2
Shop
B1
B7
B4
B6

Farm River

B1 Through B6 are Carbarns
(B2, B4, B6 and B7 are not public areas)

Heavy Lines are Main Line
Lighter Lines are Yard Trackage

MAP 4

BRANFORD TROLLEY MUSEUM.
A notable feature of Branford's trackage is the presence of several trestles over tidal creeks. Here *Brooklyn-Manhattan Transit* convertible car #4573 is posed over one of the water crossings at low tide.   *A.D. Young*

BRANFORD TROLLEY MUSEUM.
A conductor's view of the double-track section of the line is at Farm River Rd. crossing. The switch is the main lead to some of the car-barn tracks.   *Mark G. Effle*

Fleet No.	Principal Owner	Builder, Year	Remarks
City and Suburban Cars			
3	Metropolitan St. Ry. (New York)	Stephenson, 1893	Horse Car
8	Red Arrow Lines (Philadelphia)	Brill, 1941	Brilliner
11	Toronto Transportation Commission	TTC, 1933 (replica)	Open Horse Car
23	Red Arrow Lines (Philadelphia)	St. Louis, 1949	PCC Suburban
34	Lynchburg, Vir./5-Mile Beach	Jackson & Sharp, 1899	9-bench Open
61	Rhode Island Company	Jones, 1893	
71	Goteborg Sparvagar (Sweden)	ASEA, 1912	
193	Connecticut Company	Jewett, 1904	
220	Third Avenue Ry. (New York)	Laclede, 1892	ex-Cable Car
316	Union Street Ry. (New Bedford)	American, 1895	
356	Johnstown Traction Co. (Pennsylvania)	St. Louis, 1926	

Fleet No.	Principal Owner	Builder, Year	Remarks
357	Johnstown Traction Co. (Pennsylvania)	St. Louis, 1926	
500	Connecticut Company	Brill, 1904	Parlor Car
614	Connecticut Company	Brill, 1901	15-bench Open
629	Third Avenue Railway (New York)	Third Ave. Ry., 1939	
650	Capital Transit Co. (Washington, D.C.)	Brill, 1912	Center Entrance Semi-Conv.
830	Third Avenue Railway (New York)	Brill, 1908	
850	New Orleans Public Service	Perley Thomas, 1922	
865	Connecticut Company	Wason, 1905	
884	Third Avenue Railway (New York)	Brill, 1909	Convertible
923	Connecticut Company	Jones, 1906	15-bench Open
948	Georgia Power Co. (Atlanta)	Cincinnati, 1926	
1001	Brooklyn & Queens Transit (New York)	St. Louis, 1936	PCC
1199	Connecticut Company	Stephenson, 1906	
1330	Connecticut Company	Osgood Bradley, 1910	
1339	Connecticut Company	Osgood Bradley, 1910	
1403	Montreal Tramways	Ottawa, 1914	
1414	Connecticut Company	Osgood Bradley, 1911	15-bench Open
1425	Connecticut Company	Osgood Bradley, 1911	15-bench Open
1602	Connecticut Company	Wason, 1911	
1706	Toronto Railway Co.	Toronto Railway, 1913	Convertible
1792	Nassau Electric (New York)	Laclede, 1899	
1802	Connecticut Company	Wason, 1917	
1972	Montreal Tramways	Can Car & Fdy., 1929	
2001	Montreal Tramways	Can Car & Fdy., 1929	
2350	Connecticut Company	Osgood Bradley, 1922	Birney Safety Car
2431	Public Service of New Jersey	Cincinnati, 1913	
2898	Toronto Transportation Commission	Ottawa, 1923	Peter Witt
3000	Connecticut Company	Wason, 1922	Double-truck Birney Safety
3323	Boston Elevated Railway	Pullman, 1946	PCC
4573	Brooklyn-Manhattan Transit	Laconia, 1906	Convertible
5706	Boston Elevated Railway	Brill, 1924	Type 5A, Semi-Convertible
8111	Brooklyn-Manhattan Transit	St. Louis, 1923	Peter Witt

Interurban Cars

9	Montreal & Southern Counties	Grand Trunk Ry., 1911	Combine
116	Cincinnati & Lake Erie	Cincinnati, 1930	High Speed Lightweight
250	Fairmont & Clarksburg (W. Va.)	Jewett, 1904	
302	Union St. Ry. (New Bedford)	Jones, 1907	Mail Car
709	Chicago, North Shore & Milwaukee	Cincinnati, 1924	
1575	Rhode Island Company	Rhode Island, 1912	Box Motor
9421	South Brooklyn Railway	Middletown, 1903	Box Motor
9425	South Brooklyn Railway	Middletown, 1903	Box Motor

Electric Locomotives

4	Brooklyn Rapid Transit	Brooklyn, 1907	
12	Cornwall St. Ry. (Ontario)	Baldwin, 1917	Steeple Cab
62	Interborough Rapid Transit (NYC)	Pressed Steel, 1906	Switcher
5002	Montreal Tramways	Montreal Tramways, 1918	Steeple Cab
Amy	Abendroth Foundry	General Electric, 1902	
—	Lonsdale Bleachery (Rhode Island)		
5002	Montreal Tramways	Montreal Tramways, 1912	Switcher

Maintenance of Way Cars

W-3	Montreal Tramways	Differential, 1929	Crane
5	Montreal Tramways	Peckham, 1910	Rotary Snowplow
10	Brooklyn Rapid Transit	Taunton, 1898	Blade Snowplow
25	Ottawa Electric Railways	Ottawa, 1923	Line Car
S-36	Toronto Transportation Commission	Russell, 1921	Snow Sweeper
59	Yonkers, New York	McGuire-Cummings, 1914	Snow Sweeper
0245	Connecticut Company	Russell, 1916	Snowplow
1504	Rhode Island Company	Rhode Island, 1904	Emergency Car
2624	Philadelphia Rapid Transit	Philadelphia Rapid Transit, 1908	Coal Car
3715	United Railway & Electric (Baltimore)	United Ry. & Electric, 1913	Crane
9137	South Brooklyn Railway	Middletown, 1903	Rail Crane
9161	South Brooklyn Railway	Baltimore Steel, 1904	Gondola
9799	Brooklyn Rapid Transit	Taunton, 1898	Wedge Snowplow
9832	Brooklyn Rapid Transit	Brill, 1915	Snow Sweeper
Brick	Johnstown Traction Co.	Johnstown Traction Co., 1945	Flat

Fleet No.	Principal Owner	Builder, Year	Remarks
Rapid Transit Passenger and Maintenance of Way Cars			
G	Interborough Rapid Transit	Gilbert & Bush, 1878	Money Collection Car
M-1	Interborough Rapid Transit	Wason, 1878	Flat Car
M-8	Interborough Rapid Transit	Wason, 1878	Flat Car
53	Interborough Rapid Transit	Pressed Steel, 1960	Hose Car
95	Interborough Rapid Transit	Magor, 1914	Utility Hopper
197	Kings County Elevated	Pullman, 1888	Elevated Car
503	Hudson & Manhattan tubes	ACF, 1928	Subway Car
659	Brooklyn Rapid Transit	Jewett, 1901	Elevated Car
824	Interborough Rapid Transit	Pullman, 1881	Instruction Car
999	Brooklyn Rapid Transit	Brooklyn Hts. RR, 1905	Instruction Car
1227	Brooklyn Rapid Transit	Osgood Bradley, 1903	Elevated Car
1349	Brooklyn Rapid Transit	Cincinnati, 1-05	Elevated Car
1362	Brooklyn Rapid Transit	Jewett, 1905	Elevated Car
1689	Independent Subway, New York	ACF, 1940	Subway Car
2775	New York Transit Authority	Pressed Steel, 1922	Subway Car
3344	Interborough Rapid Transit	Wason, 1904	Private Car
3662	Interborough Rapid Transit	ACF, 1907	Subway Car
4280	Chicago Rapid Transit	Cincinnati, 1922	Elevated Car ·
Steam Railroad Freight Cars and Cabooses			
12	Long Island Railroad	ACF, 1927	Caboose
516	Lehigh & New England	ACF, 1914	Caboose
58072	General American Tank	GATX, 1926	Tank Car

Connecticut • Warehouse Point

Connecticut Electric Railway Association, Inc. Twelve miles north of Hartford near East Windsor on route 140, ½ mile east of the Bridge Street exit (#45) of I-91. Write to P.O. Box 360, East Windsor, CT 06088. Standard gauge.

ON OCTOBER 28, 1940, Roger Borrup, Henry R. Steig and Richard E. Whittier signed the incorporation papers of the Connecticut Electric Railway Association, and in doing so created the legal framework for North America's second trolley museum. Their objective was to re-create an electric trolley line by operating passenger cars, freight and maintenance vehicles and by erecting buildings and other associated plant which commonly were a part of a trolley system. In addition they intended to assemble educational exhibits and literature to create an environment in which the visitor would be able to hear, see, feel, touch and smell a typical New England trolley line.

Many of the founders were Connecticut members of the original 1939 Seashore group, concerned at the selection of a Maine location too far for them easily to devote every weekend to museum work. They, in turn, had begun to look for a location closer to home and,

with the finding of the present site in 1940, incorporation was a matter of course. It is arguable that Warehouse Point rather than Seashore was the first museum, since formal incorporation occurred many months prior to that of Seashore. However, the Seashore group had bought its first car in 1939, two years before Warehouse Point, and it has commonly been accepted that this gave Seashore priority as number one.

The project was initially conceived by the Connecticut Valley Chapter of the National Railway Historical Society; another nationwide enthusiast group first founded in the 1930s and flourishing to this day. For legal reasons, however, the museum was incorporated as a separate entity (the NRHS by-laws at that time did not allow chapters to own equipment) and has remained so, though relations between it and the local NRHS chapter remain close.

From the outset this was an active group and 1941 was a year of hard work. An unbroken three-mile stretch of the Rockville Branch of the abandoned Hartford and Springfield Street Railway was purchased, running between Warehouse Point and Broad Brook. Since the track had been torn up in 1926, track, poles, wires and cars had also to be purchased, and this was a task pursued vigorously. Such was the rate of progress that this was the first amateur trolley museum to open to the public, doing so once the first car arrived at the site in August 1941. But the war curtailed any further activity and it was not until 1945 that track and car purchase resumed.

Though money was always tight, the relationship with the local NRHS chapter was of material help in the early post-war years. Trolley and train riding was an important part of the chapter's activities, and the frequent railfan trip schedules sponsored by the chapter ensured that there was always some money invested by the chapter into the museum on a regular basis. This enabled continuity of effort in the museum to be taken for granted, and as a result Warehouse Point, with its firm policy of collecting mainly local exhibits (enunciated from the beginning) was able to maintain that policy when the majority of New York and New England's remaining trolleys were scrapped in the '40s and '50s.

Since then the collection has been enlarged by a good selection of cars from Montreal, and representative samples of car types from other regions. Cars from New Orleans, Cleveland, Chicago (rapid transit and interurban), the Illinois Terminal and Northern Ohio therefore can be seen, too, as a contrast to the native New England cars.

An important decision, taken early in the museum's life, saw the institution become very active in the collection of paper artifacts relating to the trolley. Today the Warehouse Point museum has an unrivaled collection of historical material on New England's

trolleys, most of it presently on loan to the University of Connecticut. An important by-product of this interest in trolley paper has been the Connecticut Valley Chapter's magazine, *Transportation,* which for many years has been one of the best sources for material on New England trolley history. It offers reprints of historic railroad material and books by the museum.

The first car ran under its own power on April 11, 1954 (two cars to be precise) but trouble with the generator prevented regularly scheduled service from starting until 1955, on a mere 1,200 feet of track. In the years since then, extensions have regularly been made, and now almost half the originally purchased right-of-way has been brought into use. The track crosses two township roads at grade (protected by gates) and there

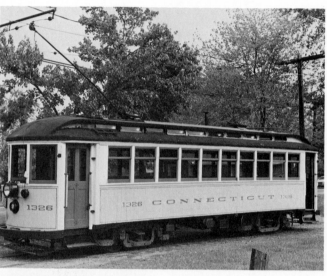

CONNECTICUT ELECTRIC RAILWAY ASSOCIATION. Wood-sheathed sides and a clerestory roof are hallmarks of many *Connecticut Company* cars. Note the extra headlight on #1326, a museum safety precaution.

William E. Wood

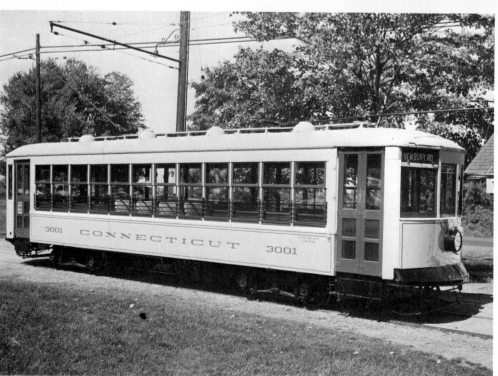

CONNECTICUT ELECTRIC RAILWAY ASSOCIATION. This delightful double-truck Birney car of the *Connecticut Company,* painstakingly restored, sits by the museum station for an official portrait. On sizzling summer afternoons, however, the New England public prefers the breezes of a ride aboard a classic open-bench car.

William E. Wood

CONNECTICUT ELECTRIC RAILWAY ASSOCIATION. This is one of the museums which has gone far afield to round out its collections of different types of rolling stock. (TOP) New Orleans #836 was regauged to railroad standard. It stands at the outer end of the operating line. (BOTTOM) Two of Chicago's "Cincinnati" elevated cars head toward the carbarn leads after a three-mile round trip. A wooden high platform is used for passenger loading.　　*BOTH: William E. Wood*

is a turnout, but in the main this is a straight single-track line through wooded country.

There is an attractive station building on the site and some substantial carbarns. Many older cars have been thoroughly restored and the standard of routine maintenance is high. The collection of operable open cars, so beloved by the visitors, is presently unsurpassed by any other museum. The original New England opens, though, have been augmented by an open sightseeing car from Montreal and a couple of American-built Brazilian opens; the South American cars are part of the ARM shipment of 1965. Still, it is appropriate that New England opens are operable at the museum, since open cars are the ones best remembered in the region. Indeed this museum, with so many cars of local origin, has managed to fulfill its original purpose stated more than 40 years ago, of re-creating on its one and one-half

miles of track the essence of the New England rural trolley. And isn't that what it's all about?

As a not-for-profit corporation, the museum nowadays finances all operating charges and vehicle acquisitions from the farebox. Volunteer labor is exclusively employed for operation, maintenance and management, but large-scale projects, such as grading, erection of buildings and some restoration projects are currently put out to contract.

On a typical busy Sunday between three and five cars are in use on the line, ensuring a schedule that dispatches a car from the terminal every 7½ minutes. This is a respectable performance, one that most of the nation's busiest urban lines would have been happy to maintain. The museum too takes justifiable pride in the fact that it can handle more than 3,000 passengers in any given afternoon on that schedule without effort.

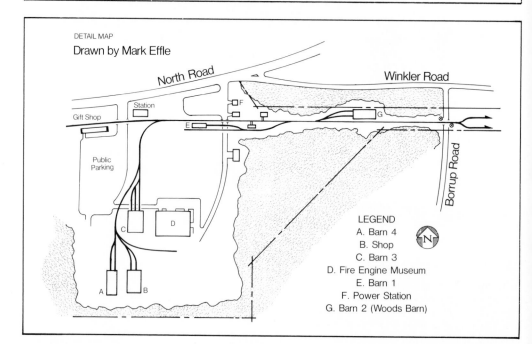

MAP 5

CONNECTICUT ELECTRIC RAILWAY
near Warehouse Point, Conn.

MAP 6

DETAIL MAP
Drawn by Mark Effle

LEGEND
A. Barn 4
B. Shop
C. Barn 3
D. Fire Engine Museum
E. Barn 1
F. Power Station
G. Barn 2 (Woods Barn)

CONNECTICUT ELECTRIC RAIL-WAY ASSOCIATION. Winter spectaculars, held at a number of museums in the coldest part of the year, can indeed be spectacular—if you can get the line clear enough to run the cars! This *Gardner & Templeton Street Railway* snowplow, #12, prepares to do its duty. *William E. Wood*

CONNECTICUT ELECTRIC RAILWAY ASSOCIATION. A prized exhibit at the Warehouse Point museum is this extraordinary, yet practical, steeped sightseeing car, used (with others of its class) on tourist services in Montreal until the demise of that rail system in the late 1950s.   *William E. Wood*

Fleet No.	Principal Owner	Builder, Year	Remarks
City and Suburban Cars			
4	Montreal Tramways	Montreal Tramways, 1924	Open Observation Car
28	Bristol & Plainville Tramway Co.	Wason, 1907	28-foot Wooden, Closed
36	Five Mile Beach (New Jersey)	Brill, 1895	9-bench Open Car
65	Connecticut Company	Wason, 1906	Closed
169	Nassau Electric (New York)	St. Louis, 1894	Closed
355	Connecticut Company	Brill, 1902	15-bench Open Car
451	Illinois Terminal Railway	St. Louis, 1949	PCC, Double End
771	Connecticut Company	Jewett, 1904	Closed
836	New Orleans Public Service	Perley Thomas, 1922	
840	Connecticut Company	Jones, 1905	15-bench Open Car
1201	Shaker Heights Rapid Transit	Kuhlman, 1914	Center Entrance
1326	Connecticut Company	Osgood Bradley, 1910	
1850	Rio de Janeiro Tramway, Light & Power	St. Louis, 1912	13-Bench Open Car
1887	Rio de Janeiro Tramway, Light & Power	St. Louis, 1912	13-bench Open Car
2056	Montreal Tramways/Springfield, Mass.	Wason, 1927	Lightweight
2600	Montreal Tramways	Can Car & Fdy., 1929	Lightweight
3001	Connecticut Company	Wason, 1922	Double Truck Birney Safety
3003	Boston Elevated Railway	Pullman Standard, 1940	PCC
3333	Boston Elevated Railway/MTA	Pullman Standard, 1945	PCC Double End (ex-Dallas)
5645	Boston Elevated Railway	Laconia, 1923	Type 5A, Semi-Convertible
5777	Boston Elevated Railway	Osgood Bradley, 1923	Type 5A, Semi-Convertible
Interurban Cars			
10	Springfield Terminal Railroad (Vermont)	Wason, 1901	Combine
16	Springfield Terminal Railroad (Vermont)	Wason, 1926	Combine
25	Connecticut Company	Connecticut, 1910	Express
162	Chicago, North Shore & Milwaukee	Brill 1915	
710	Chicago, North Shore & Milwaukee	Cincinnati, 1924	
1500	Everett-Moore Syndicate (Ohio)	Niles, 1911	Private Car "Northern"
2022	Connecticut Company	Wason, 1911	Express
2023	Connecticut Company	Connecticut Co., 1910	Express

Fleet No.	Principal Owner	Builder, Year	Remarks
Maintenance of Way Cars			
W-1	Montreal Tramways	Montreal Tramways, 1912	Crane
010	Capital Transit (Washington, D.C.)	McGuire-Cummings, 1899	Snow Sweeper
12	Gardner & Templeton Street Ry.	Brill, 1915	Snowplow
0309	Connecticut Company	Brill, 1902	Work Car
Electric Locomotives			
—	Taftville Cotton Mills (Connecticut)	General Electric, 1894	"Black Maria"
18	Auburn & Syracuse (New York)	Baldwin, 1918	
S193	Ponemah Mill	Ponemah Mills, 1905	Locomotive/Line Car
Rapid Transit Cars			
4262	Chicago Elevated/CTA	Cincinnati, 1922	Elevated Car
4436	Chicago Elevated/CTA	Cincinnati, 1924	Elevated Car
4409	Chicago Elevated/CTA	Cincinnati, 1924	Elevated Car
4605	Chicago Elevated/CTA	Cincinnati, 1924	Elevated Car
Steam Locomotives			
3	Middle Fork Railroad	Climax, 1910	Climax Type B
3	Hartford Electric Light Co.	Porter, 1916	0-4-0 Saddle Tank
5	Hartford Electric Light Co.	Alco/Cooke, 1920	0-4-0 Saddle Tank
5	Stanley Works (Connecticut)	H.K. Porter, 1934	0-4-0 "Fireless Cooker"
Electric Railroad Commuter Cars			
4153	Long Island Railroad	Pennsylvania RR, 1930	MP 54-A1 (Multiple Unit)

Illinois • South Elgin

RELIC—The Fox River Line. Entrance is on Illinois Route 31 at South Elgin, a short distance south of the Northwest Tollway (I-90) and about 35 miles west of the Chicago Loop. Owned and operated by Relic, P.O. Box 752, South Elgin, IL 60177. Standard gauge.

THE RIGHT-OF-WAY at this museum is that of the Aurora, Elgin and Fox River, which ceased passenger operation in 1935. Sporadic electric freight service continued until 1946 and, until the mid-70s, three miles of this line were still in use to connect the Illinois Central Railroad with the South Elgin State Hospital, enabling the hospital to receive rail-shipped coal to fire its boilers.

The line of route south from the hospital to the museum entrance ran at the side of the road in a fashion more commonly seen 60 years ago on New England's rural trolley lines. At that point the AE&FR forsook the highway to run for some distance on a scenic wooded right-of-way alongside the Fox River. It is this stretch which forms the basis of the present trolley operation.

The Fox River line had been a subsidiary of the Chicago, Aurora and Elgin, a wonderful interurban giving communities west of Chicago a frequent high-speed service into the Loop. The CA&E ceased passenger operations in 1957, and was closed down altogether in 1959. At that time, a group which had bought some CA&E cars came to an agreement with the then-owners of the AE&FR tracks. In essence, the agreement allowed the group to run its own cars along the line at weekends, and to do so legally the group had to be formally incorporated as a business. This was formed as the Railway Equipment Leasing and Investment Corporation. The arrangement worked well for years and as time passed, Relic purchased the right-of-way. Since the hospital switched from coal to other fuels, the line no longer has freight service to worry about.

In 1959, the first mile from the entrance to Coleman Road was wired, together with storage tracks and, with the purchase of a rotary converter, service started on a regular basis in 1965. Though the collection's nucleus was of local interurban cars, it was quickly found that the public preferred to ride open cars on the scenic run. So the operators quickly jumped at the opportunity to participate in the mass purchase of Brazilian opens in 1965, and now has two on the property, of

RELIC — The Fox River Line. Near the south end of the museum line a portion of the former *Aurora, Elgin & Fox River* interurban, this Rio de Janeiro open-bench car passes under the steelwork on a railroad bridge.   *RELIC*

RELIC — The Fox River Line. The oldest of the museum's *Chicago, Aurora & Elgin* interurbans, wooden car #20, poses at the display and yard area.   *Jim Walker*

which one provides the backbone of present-day operations.

While the collection of local interurban cars is still the main attraction for the historically minded, Relic has survived the years by catering primarily to weekend day trippers from the Chicago area, and has become a lovely tourist trolley line in the process. Interest is kept at a high level by promotion of various special events in which the trolleys play a central role, and its flea market (held annually) is something special. The next priority is to get the cars under cover, and work is proceeding.

Fleet No.	Principal Owner	Builder, Year	Remarks
City and Suburban Cars			
362	Johnstown Traction Co.	St. Louis, 1926	
441	Rio de Janeiro Tramway, Light & Power Co.	Brill, 1910	10-bench Open
1719	Rio de Janeiro Tramway, Light & Power Co.	Brill, 1910	13-bench Open
Interurban Cars			
20	Chicago, Aurora & Elgin	Niles, 1902	
316	Chicago, Aurora & Elgin	Jewett, 1913	
317	Chicago, Aurora & Elgin	Jewett, 1913	
756	Chicago, North Shore & Milwaukee	Pullman, 1930	
Maintenance of Way Cars and Equipment			
11	Chicago, Aurora & Elgin	Brill, 1910	Line Car
C-150	Philadelphia Rapid Transit	Brill, 1923	Snow Sweeper
Electric Locomotive			
L-202	Chicago Transit Authority	Chicago City Ry., 1908	Steeple Cab
Rapid Transit Car			
4451	Chicago Transit Authority	Cincinnati, 1924	Elevated Car
Interurban and Steam Railroad Freight Cars and Cabooses			
C	Chicago, Aurora & Elgin	Pullman, 1927	Flat Car
130	Soo Line	Missouri Car & Foundry, 1887	Caboose
25010	Swift Refrigerator Lines	GATX, 1954	Refrigerator
25032	Swift Refrigerator Lines	GATX, 1954	Refrigerator

Illinois • Union

Illinois Railway Museum. On Olson Road at Union, Illinois, 65 miles northwest of Chicago. Owned and operated by the Illinois Railway Museum, P.O. Box 431, Union, IL 60180. Standard gauge.

ONE OF THE COUNTRY'S largest operating trolley museums in terms of both vehicles and trackage, this huge organization has grown to maturity in a very short time. With roots in a number of Chicago area groups, the IRM has from the beginning catered to many interests. Second only to the New York area in richness of urban transportation facilities, Chicago could boast an incredible number of streetcar and interurban systems, while its near neighbor, Milwaukee, was of almost equal richness in transit.

The Chicago area still boasts passenger railroad service to all parts of the U.S., the nation's best-run and most comprehensive railroad commuter system, and a dense network of electric subway and elevated lines. Moreover, the area is home to America's last operating interurban, the shortly-to-be-modernized South Shore line to Gary, Michigan City and South Bend, Indiana. Small wonder, then, that the IRM, in covering all interests, has so diverse a collection.

Established in 1953 as the Illinois Electric Railway Museum by a group of ten railfans, the museum's original intention was to establish and maintain an operating electric railway museum in the Chicago area. To that end, the museum from the first was in search of suitable sites to establish itself. In the interim, a yard was hired from the Chicago Hardware Foundry in North Chicago, and the growing collection was stored there. The location was chosen because Frank J. Sherwin, president of the company, was a railfan himself. Sherwin owned nine pieces of equipment, which he later donated to the museum.

Over the next few years, the group was exceptionally active in acquiring exhibits, principally from the area, since the Chicago and Milwaukee streetcar systems and the Chicago, Aurora and Elgin, the Chicago North Shore and Milwaukee, and the downstate Illinois Terminal interurbans all ran down their operations between 1955 and 1963.

The Union site was located as early as 1958 and a strip of 5.7 miles of the old Elgin and Belvidere Electric Railway was negotiated for, but it wasn't initially felt to be the most promising choice owing to its distance from Chicago. As years went by other sites were exam-

ILLINOIS RAILWAY MUSEUM. *Chicago Surface Lines'* "red Pullman" #144 is a favorite with visitors, and exhibits beautiful woodwork and handsome design. It pauses near the terminal area; behind are steam railroad baggage and freight cars. Note the landscaping and graded walkway.

ILLINOIS RAILWAY MUSEUM. This photograph has all the flavor of an interurban station which has been captured by the museum in its placement of depot, paving and overhead structure. Passengers are taking their seats inside North Shore car #714.

BOTH: A.D. Young

ined, but were also found wanting. In the meantime cars kept right on coming to the foundry yard.

One of the alternatives considered was the Batavia branch of the Chicago, Aurora and Elgin. Another was the East Troy line, now the home of the East Troy Trolley Museum. All the while taxes were continuing to be paid on the Union right-of-way, and efforts continued to get clear title to it by the payment of back taxes to the local authorities. The problem with Union was the need for considerable grading, since the line had closed decades before and the right-of-way was less than perfect.

Thus no decision was made on a site for some years, and with deadlock and disagreement on a permanent location for the museum, the question of museum policy soon became a live issue, resulting (in 1962) in a change of name to the present Illinois Railway Museum. The change was explained as a public relations move rather than a change in emphasis away from electric trolleys, but it turned out to be the catalyst that finally prompted movement on the site question. Widening the collection policy to include steam railroad and other transportation modes made the solving of the site problem of extreme importance.

Towards the end of 1962 a committee was set up to develop plans for a gradual transfer of the collection from the Foundry Yard to Union. The membership was assured that this development in no way implied a final commitment to the Union site but rather a job that had to be done whatever site was ultimately picked since the foundry would be available to them only for a limited time.

Cars continued to pour in, most notably a large interurban fleet from the now-closed North Shore line. Pressure mounted for a decision to be made on the site throughout 1963 and, with the machinery of transfer out of the foundry yard already in motion, Union was ever more firmly in the Museum's ownership, while other sites seemed as far off as ever. A promise had been made that the foundry site would be vacated by June 1964 and as that date grew closer, the issue came to a head.

On March 28, 1964, the Museum board felt no useful purpose could be served by further delaying the decision and the Union site was decided on. The move from the foundry was completed by the end of August and other possible sites, still under consideration at the beginning of March, were shelved.

After years of indecision, the speed with which the Union site was made habitable was startling. By September 1964, 3,000 feet of track had been laid, 42 cars had been moved to Union and IRM was in business to stay.

Nevertheless, the Museum board became uneasy at the lack of a regular income. Thousands of people had come to visit the foundry yard, even while the transfer to Union was being made, because the museum was the first and only railroad museum in Chicago, the nation's largest railroad and trolley center. The work at Union had to be continued since no one else but the membership could continue to provide Chicago with that kind of historical attraction. Poles and wire had to be erected and cars running for the 1965 season, the first at the Union site. To do that, the financial crunch had to be dealt with.

An imaginative approach to solving the money problems was the issuance by the museum of $100 5% bonds with a 10-year maturity. The problem was further eased, later in 1965, with the establishment of a gift shop under the control of a manager. But the site was in such bad shape that the 1965 operational target could not be met. Most of the year was taken up in repairing the years of damage and erosion to the track bed, the fills and culverts. It was not until July 17, 1966, that electrical operation was first achieved, and scheduling of cars was a little erratic for a time even after that.

But, since the 1967 season, Union has never looked back. Steam operation was added in October and mixed electric and steam runs have continued on a scheduled basis ever since. The work done since 1967 at the museum has been prodigious. While the bulk of the trolley fleet comes from the tri-state area of Illinois, Wisconsin and Indiana, the collection is comprehensive enough to illustrate design and functional evolution in trolley cars from the 1890s to the 1940s, and can do the same for interurban and elevated car designs. The collection range then would identify this as an archetypical "first generation" trolley museum except that, since arriving at Union, its scope and ambition has always been broader.

Its success at broadening its range has led to a snowball effect. While in the early days the members had to laboriously seek out exhibits to add to the collection, the conversion to a successful transportation museum of comprehensive scope has attracted many potential donors who have over the years generously showered the museum with unique exhibits.

Today there is a large operational collection of mainline and diesel locomotives and a complete 1930s streamline passenger train. Moreover, the museum can boast some of the largest electric vehicles in the country in the form of its recently acquired North Shore *Electroliner*, South Shore *Little Joe* and Pennsylvania

ILLINOIS RAILWAY MUSEUM. Home at last! After the demise of the North Shore interurban line between Chicago and Milwaukee, both *Electroliner* articulated trains were sold for use on the Red Arrow suburban line in Philadelphia. When retired from that use, they were put up for competitive bid and the museum successfully retrieved one set. This view was taken soon after its arrival—still in its Red Arrow livery.

A.D. Young

ILLINOIS RAILWAY MUSEUM. *Illinois Terminal* suburban light-weight #415 shows off its clean 1920s styling on the museum's large new loop. The blanked-off portion above the windows and below the letterboard covers up an area which once sported beautiful colored art glass.

A.D. Young

Railroad *GG1* locomotive. These behemoths run on the same tracks as the trolleys and on members' days (and certain other occasions) service is intermingled with those having compatible electrical systems. So if you don't want to ride the trolley, step back and let it go by, for a train will follow close behind!

If *that* isn't enough for you, the IRM operates the continent's largest working trolley coach line, and has done so since the first runs were made in September 1973. The trolley coaches, too, are an example of the snowball effect a successfully operating museum can initiate. It is doubtful if the original owners would have donated them to a purely electric trolley museum, or one without facilities to keep them properly. But since Union was known as a museum of transportation, the trolley buses were a natural extension to the collection range, operating as they do over the museum's considerable network of internal roads.

The right-of-way continues to be extended. A new loop was recently added and, in due course, the present two miles of track will be extended to the full 5.7 miles owned. This will make the IRM only the second museum in the country to have a long stretch of open track on which to exercise its powerful and speedy interurban cars, an important feature for a museum which has always stressed the richness and depth of its interurban collection. Though the track is mainly single, there are two passing sidings, one of considerable length—a major operational convenience. The

ILLINOIS RAILWAY MUSEUM. Some years ago, the museum began to ballast its track for heavy duty. *Illinois Terminal* Class B locomotive #1565 stands at one end of the line prior to a test trip. It is forecast that 1983 will see the opening of an extension for a further one-half mile beyond this point. *A.D. Young*

enormous carbarn area, always open to public view, is a hive of activity and IRM now has one of the newest and best-equipped shops in the country.

Future plans call for the building of an administrative complex, a large part of which will be given over to the housing of the museum's paper collection and its many thousands of photographs. Ultimately this material will help transform the museum into a major research center for those studying the history of transportation. It is to be hoped that day isn't too far distant.

ILLINOIS RAILWAY MUSEUM. It is remarkable that many of the large trolley museum barns are far more commodious and substantial than the majority of those on America's small town trolley systems. *Illinois Terminal #277 and Chicago PCC #4391 bask in the late afternoon sunshine.*

A.D. Young

ILLINOIS RAILWAY MUSEUM. Beautifully restored *Chicago, North Shore & Milwaukee* combine #251 sits by the station platform. This car is a tribute to the amateur museum movement and its restorers, for this very difficult "paintliner" paint job (the effect of stainless steel fluting on flat panels originated by the North Shore's Highwood Shops) has been superbly reproduced. It is so well done that it is impossible to tell that the car sides are not fluted until one actually touches the car!

A.D. Young

Fleet No.	Principal Owner	Builder, Year	Remarks
City and Suburban Cars			
14	Fitchburg & Leominster (Mass.)	Wason, 1905	13-bench Open
68	Philadelphia Suburban (Red Arrow)	Brill, 1926	Center Entrance Suburban
68	Sand Springs Railway (Oklahoma)	Cincinnati, 1918	Lightweight
101	Illinois Terminal	American, 1921	Center Entrance Suburban
141	Chicago & West Towns	McGuire-Cummings, 1924	
144	Chicago Surface Lines	Pullman, 1908	
170	Illinois Terminal (Galesburg, Ill.)	American, 1921	Birney Safety
354	Chicago & Milwaukee Electric	St. Louis, 1927	Double Truck Birney Safety
415	Illinois Terminal	St. Louis, 1924	Suburban
966	Milwaukee Electric	St. Louis, 1927	
972	Milwaukee Electric	St. Louis, 1927	

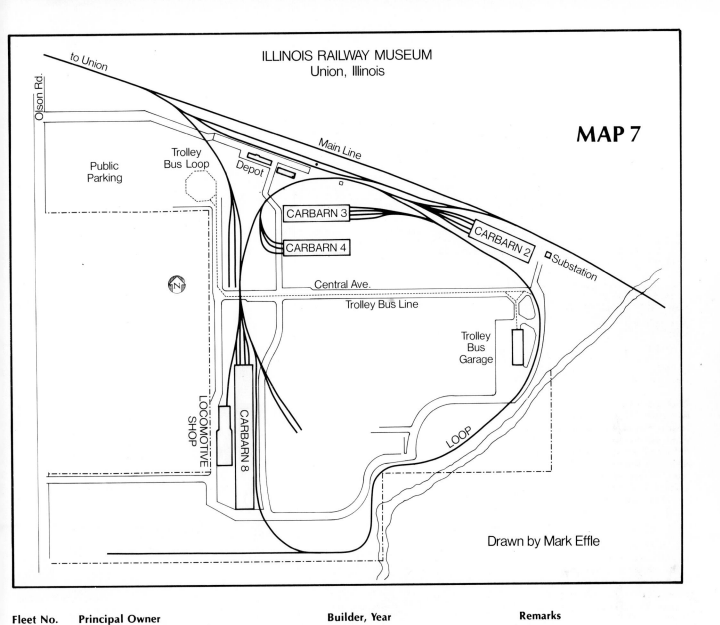

ILLINOIS RAILWAY MUSEUM
Union, Illinois

MAP 7

Drawn by Mark Effle

Fleet No.	Principal Owner	Builder, Year	Remarks
1183	Muni. Ry. San Francisco/Toronto/Kansas City	St. Louis, 1946	PCC
1374	Chicago Surface Lines	St. Louis, 1906	
1467	Chicago Surface Lines	Chicago UT, 1899	
2843	Chicago Surface Lines	Jewett, 1903	
2846	Chicago Surface Lines	South Chicago City Ry., 1907	
3142	Chicago Surface Lines	Brill, 1923	
4001	Chicago Surface Lines	Pullman, 1934	Experimental pre-PCC
4391	Chicago Transit Authority	St. Louis, 1948	PCC
9020	Chicago Surface Lines	Chicago Surface Lines, 1921	Trailer Car

Interurban Cars

Fleet No.	Principal Owner	Builder, Year	Remarks
M15	Milwaukee Electric Lines (TMER&L)	TMER&L, 1920	Box Motor
28	Michigan Electric	St. Louis, 1913	Combine
65	Indiana Railroad	Pullman, 1931	High Speed Lightweight
160	Chicago, North Shore & Milwaukee	Brill, 1915	
213	Chicago, North Shore & Milwaukee	Cincinnati, 1919	Box Trailer
218	Chicago, North Shore & Milwaukee	Cincinnati, 1922	Box Motor
229	Chicago, North Shore & Milwaukee	Cincinnati, 1922	Box Motor
233	Illinois Terminal	St. Louis, 1906	Office Car
234	Illinois Terminal	Danville Car Co., 1910	Open Platform Observation
237	Chicago, North Shore & Milwaukee	Cincinnati, 1923	Box Motor
251	Chicago, North Shore & Milwaukee	Jewett, 1917	Combine "Silverliner"
253	Chicago, North Shore & Milwaukee	Jewett, 1917	Combine "Silverliner"
277	Illinois Terminal	St. Louis, 1914	Combine

Fleet No.	Principal Owner	Builder, Year	Remarks
309	Chicago, Aurora & Elgin	Hicks, 1908	
321	Chicago, Aurora & Elgin	Jewett, 1918	
431	Chicago, Aurora & Elgin	Cincinnati, 1927	
504	Illinois Terminal	ACF, 1910	Sleeping Car *Peoria*
504	Chicago, South Shore & South Bend	St. Louis, 1925	Box Trailer
518	Illinois Terminal	St. Louis, 1911	Trailer
714	Chicago, North Shore & Milwaukee	Cincinnati, 1926	
749	Chicago, North Shore & Milwaukee	Pullman, 1928	
801	Chicago, North Shore & Milwaukee	St. Louis, 1941	Electroliner
1129	Milwaukee Electric	TMER&L, 1924	
1135	Milwaukee Electric	TMER&L, 1924	Parlor Car *Menominee*

ILLINOIS RAILWAY MUSEUM. *Chicago Surface Lines* #1374's restoration, though now well advanced, has been fraught with difficulty from the beginning. It is worthwhile reviewing its saga, though it is no more or less problematic than most such restorations. To those actually doing the job, the car is now a repository of years of work, sweat, hopes, dreams and problems.

When restoration first began, the car was in poor physical condition due to years of use as a salt spreader. Salt had eaten away much metalwork and damaged large portions of the wooden framing. What logic suggested should be done first, an enlightened psychological sense denied. To help encourage new volunteers and promote good public relations as well, it was decided to clean and paint the car first, regardless of its condition, and to fix the roof. Thus the museum visitor had a presentable car to look at rather than a seeming wreck.

From then on the real work could start. A new floor had to be put in, and new car sides had to be installed (reproducing as nearly as possible the original curvature of the original sides). The roof required 152 patches to make it fit for continued use. To add stringers and canvas took no less than two years, including ventilators. As often happens in these projects, many needed parts were missing and could not be manufactured and so it was a stroke of luck when the body of sister car #1333 was discovered out in Wisconsin, with almost all the missing body parts needed! But, even with all the body parts correctly installed on the car, long years lay ahead. It took all of one season to remove the side and center rail and to install new parts and re-sheet with new wood (which of course had to be primed with petroleum and white lead or fish oil). It took no less than 20 months to remove, restore and refit the interior woodwork and fittings and it cost $5,000 to acquire custom-made rattan to reupholster the seats (eight rolls were needed to do the job). No less than 1,000 custom-made springs were required for the seat cushions and it is impossible to estimate just how much time and money would have been needed to correctly reproduce the metal seat frame pattern had not the Wisconsin derelict been fitted with more than enough for the purpose. It would be tedious to continue, but Chicago #1374, for all its complexities, is not in reality much different than any other car in need of sound restoration. And, one would do well to remember we have only talked of body work. Restoring electrical and mechanical parts to museum operating condition can be just as difficult and time-consuming, and needing as much good luck and detective skills as anything encountered on the body side of things. *A.D. Young*

Fleet No.	Principal Owner	Builder, Year	Remarks
Electric Locomotives			
4	Commonwealth Edison	Alco/General Electric, 1911	Steeple Cab
14	Cornwall Street Ry. (Ontario)	Baldwin/West., 1929	
30	Iowa Terminal	McGuire-Cummings, 1915	Steeple Cab
803	Chicago, South Shore & South Bend	General Electric, 1949	"Little Joe"
1565	Illinois Terminal	Illinois Terminal, 1910	Class B Box Cab
4939	Pennsylvania Railroad	General Electric, 1943	GG1
Maintenance of Way Cars			
X-4	Chicago Surface Lines	Chicago Surface Lines, 1946	Crane
E-223	Chicago Surface Lines	McGuire-Cummings, 1908	Snow Sweeper
F-305	Chicago Surface Lines	Chicago Surface Lines, 1930	Snowplow
604	Chicago, North Shore & Milwaukee	Chicago & Milwaukee Elec., 1914	Line Car
1702	Illinois Terminal	Illinois Terminal, 1922	Line Car
Rapid Transit Passenger and Maintenance of Way Cars			
1024	Northwestern Elevated	Pullman, 1898	Open Platform
1198	Illinois Central	Pullman, 1926	Commuter Car
1268	Northwestern Elevated	ACF, 1907	Control Trailer
1380	Illinois Central	Pullman, 1926	Commuter Car Trailer
1754	Northwestern Elevated	Jewett, 1906	Elevated Car
1797	Chicago Elevated Railway	ACF, 1907	Elevated Car
1808	Chicago Elevated Railway	ACF, 1907	Elevated Car
2872	Metropolitan West Side	Pullman, 1906	Elevated Car
2888	Metropolitan West Side	Pullman, 1906	Elevated Car
4146	Chicago Elevated Railway	Cincinnati, 1915	Elevated Car
4253	Chicago Transit Authority	Cincinnati, 1922	Tool Car
4410	Chicago Transit Authority	Cincinnati, 1924	Elevated Car
4412	Chicago Transit Authority	Cincinnati, 1924	Elevated Car
Trolley Buses			
84	Chicago Surface Lines	American, 1930	Brill T-40
192	Chicago Surface Lines	Brill, 1937	T-40S
193	Chicago Surface Lines	Brill, 1937	T-40S
239	Des Moines Railways	Brill, 1948	Brill TC-44
269	Milwaukee & Suburban	St. Louis, 1941	STL 44
435	Dayton City Transit	Pullman, 1947	45W-S102-45CX
441	Milwaukee & Suburban	Marmon-Herrington, 1948	TC-44
874	Cleveland Transit	Pullman, 1948	44CX (ex-Providence, R.I.)
9553	Chicago Transit Authority	Marmon-Herrington, 1951	TC-48
9631	Chicago Transit Authority	Marmon-Herrington, 1951	TC-48
9763	Chicago Transit Authority	Twin Coach, 1949	58 DWTT (Articulated)
Steam Locomotives			
5	J. Neils Lumber Co.	Lima, 1929	3-truck Shay
5	Commonwealth Edison	Baldwin, 1922	0-6-0
7	Public Service Co.	Baldwin, 1926	0-6-0T
7	American Creosote Works	Vulcan, 1917	0-4-0T
26	Graysonia, Mashville & Ashdown	Baldwin, 1926	2-6-0
34	Lake Superior & Ishpeming	Baldwin, 1916	2-8-0
80	Northwestern Steel & Wire		0-8-0
99	Louisiana & Arkansas	Baldwin, 1919	2-8-0
101	Tuskegee	Baldwin, 1926	2-6-2
207	Lehigh & New England	Baldwin, 1936	0-6-0
265	Milwaukee Road	Alco, 1944	4-8-4
428	Union Pacific	Baldwin, 1901	2-8-0
1630	St. Louis & San Francisco	Baldwin, 1918	2-10-0
2050	Norfolk & Western	Alco, 1923	2-8-8-2
6323	Grand Trunk Western		4-8-4
8080	Grand Trunk Western		0-8-0
Steam Railroad Passenger Cars			
10	Nevada Northern	Pullman, 1889	Private Car *Noa*
67	Soo Line	Pullman, 1906	Coach
90	Chicago, Burlington & Quincy	Pullman, 1906	Office Car
99	Chicago Great Western	Pullman, 1905	Business Car
122	Milwaukee Road		Diner
481	Chicago, Burlington & Quincy	Pullman, 1948	Lightweight Sleeper
556	Delaware, Lackawanna & Western	Pullman, 1914	Coach
561	Delaware, Lackawanna & Western	Pullman, 1914	Coach

Fleet No.	Principal Owner	Builder, Year	Remarks
567	Delaware, Lackawanna & Western	Pullman, 1914	Coach
1131	Chicago & Northwestern	Pullman, 1899	Baggage/Railway Postal
1236	Chicago & Northwestern	Pullman, 1906	Baggage/Railway Postal
1304	Chicago & Northwestern	Pullman, 1908	Baggage/Railway Postal
1504	Atchison, Topeka & Santa Fe	Pullman, 1914	Lounge Car
1923	Chicago, Burlington & Quincy	ACF, 1920?	Baggage/Railway Postal
2544	Atchison, Topeka & Santa Fe	Pullman, 1927	Combine
2555	Chicago, Rock Island & Pacific		Coach
2804	Illinois Central	Pullman, 1926	Coach
4618	Pennsylvania Railroad	Budd, 1949	Diner
5316	Grand Trunk Western	Pullman, 1912	Coach (ex-Parlor *Melanie*)
9695	Grand Trunk Western	Pullman, 1914	Railway Postal Car
—	Illinois Central	Pullman, 1942	Sleeper *King Cotton*
—	Pullman Co.	Pullman, 1910	Lounge/Obs. *Ingleholm*
Venus	Chicago, Burlington & Quincy	Budd, 1936	Power Car/Coach
Vesta	Chicago, Burlington & Quincy	Budd, 1936	Coach
Minerva	Chicago, Burlington & Quincy	Budd, 1936	Coach
Ceres	Chicago, Burlington & Quincy	Budd, 1936	Diner
Juno	Chicago, Burlington & Quincy	Budd, 1936	Parlor/Observation

NOTE: Above five units are the articulated lightweight train Nebraska Zephyr.

Internal Combustion Locomotives and Cars

Fleet No.	Principal Owner	Builder, Year	Remarks
M-35	Union Pacific	St. Louis, 1927	Gas-Electric Car
1792	Pullman	Davenport, 1928	Gas-Electric Locomotive
1951	Grand Trunk Western	Alco, 1957	RS-1 Diesel-Electric Locomotive
7563	United States Air Force	Davenport, 1941	Gas-Mechanical Locomotive
9952A	Chicago, Burlington & Quincy	EMD, 1940	E5A Diesel-Electric Locomotive
X201	American Association of Railroads	Buda, 1936	Rail Test Car
X202	American Association of Railroads	Buda, 1940	Rail Test Car

Interurban and Steam Railroad Freight Cars and Cabooses

Fleet No.	Principal Owner	Builder, Year	Remarks
X-81	Chicago & Illinois Midland	ACF, 1927	Caboose
1002	Chicago, North Shore & Milwaukee	ACF, 1927	Caboose
1003	Chicago, North Shore & Milwaukee	ACF, 1927	Caboose
1004	Chicago, North Shore & Milwaukee	ACF, 1927	Caboose
1021	General American Pfaudler Corp.	GATX, 1947	Milk Tank Car
1185	Chicago & Western Indiana	Haskell & Barber, 1913	Ballast Car
1313	United States Dept. of Defense	GATX, 1952	Tank Car
1772	Chicago & Western Indiana	, 1940	Flat Car
2034	Soo Line (Union Refrig. Transit)	GATX, 1931	Refrigerator
5315	Union Refrigerator Transit	GATX, 1941	Refrigerator
5348	Union Refrigerator Transit	GATX, 1941	Refrigerator
8715	Union Tank Car Leasing	ACF, 1937	Tank Car
10304	Chicago & Northwestern		Caboose
10494	Chicago & Northwesern	CNW, 1915	Caboose
12661	United States Dept. of Defense	GATX, 1952	Tank Car
14073	Chicago, Burlington & Quincy	CB&Q, 1903	Caboose
15030	Swift Refrigerator Lines	GATX, 1954	Refrigerator
20519	Chicago, Rock Island & Pacific	North American, 1927	Insulated Box Car
25004	Swift Refrigerator Lines	GATX, 1954	Refrigerator Car
25029	Swift Refrigerator Lines	GATX, 1954	Refrigerator Car
25041	Swift Refrigerator Lines	GATX, 1954	Refrigerator Car
26640	Union Refrigerator Transport	GATX, 1931	Insulated Box Car
33096	Soo Line	, 1913	Box Car
37190	Milwaukee Rd. (Union Refrig. Transp.)	GATX, 1948	Refrigerator
37226	Milwaukee Rd. (Union Refrig. Transp.)	GATX, 1948	Refrigerator
37241	American Beef Packers (Union Refrig.)	GATX, 1948	Refrigerator
37312	Milwaukee Rd. (Union Refrig. Transp.)	GATX, 1948	Refrigerator
40285	Illinois Central		Box Car
41146	Soo Line	Pullman, 1929	Box Car
54204	Grand Trunk Western	Pullman, 1929	Flat Car
60394	Atchison, Topeka & Santa Fe	, 1920	Stock Car
68229	Milwaukee Rd. (Union Refrig. Transp.)	GATX, 1954	Refrigerator
75524	Mid-States Packing (Union Refrig.)	GATX, 1954	Refrigerator
131650	Wisconsin Central	Pullman, 1914	Box Car
207051	Northern Pacific		Box Car
229100	Chicago, Burlington & Quincy	Rodgers, 1927	Ballast Car
220145	Chicago, Burlington & Quincy	Rodgers, 1927	Ballast Car

Indiana • Noblesville

Indiana Transportation Museum. Located in Forest Park, Noblesville, on Indiana Route 19, about 20 miles north of Indianapolis. Mailing address is Box 83, Noblesville, IN 46060. Standard gauge.

WHILE AN OPERATING demonstration interurban line is featured here, it is only one of the attractions offered by this small but growing regional transportation museum. Attractively sited in a park, this is a true "second generation" museum in its collection and display policies. Established in 1960, the museum has since collected not only trolley, interurban and railroad artifacts, but also the Hobbs, Indiana, Nickel Plate RR combination passenger and freight station, a collection of bicycles, radios, telegraph and telephone equipment—all of which had some connection with the state of Indiana.

A half mile of track has been in use since March 1973, and extensions are now being laid. Originally, a Chicago, North Shore and Milwaukee interurban provided service, but a restored Chicago rapid transit car was recently added. Until restoration of large exhibits is more advanced, work is being concentrated on the preparation of small exhibits as well as on the job of laying tracks and stringing overhead.

One of the best laid-out display areas in the country is at this museum, built around a livery stable and a blacksmith's shop, while an equally fascinating display in another building in given over to wooden railroad cars. A passenger train and freight train display is under development.

Thus the admission charge, which helps the museum finance its major programs, also gives visitors good value for their money. The North Shore car, the Singer electric locomotive (dating from 1898, it is perhaps the oldest electric locomotive to be preserved), rapid transit cars, and another locomotive are presently operable.

Once the main line is extended to the park entrance at Route 19, the museum will be able to pick up visitors at a reception/orientation center, and then run them through the park, at the same time showing off the paces of their interurban collection. Until that happens, this museum provides its visitors an interesting opportunity to see how such an institution grows.

Fleet No.	Principal Owner	Builder, Year	Remarks
City and Suburban Cars			
1	Indianapolis Street Railway	, 1868	Mule Car
153	Indianapolis Railways	Brill, 1932	Lightweight
Interurban Cars			
81	Terre Haute, Indianapolis & Eastern	Jewett, 1902	
172	Chicago, North Shore & Milwaukee	Cincinnati, 1919	
308	Chicago, Aurora & Elgin	Niles, 1906	
429	Union Traction Co.	St. Louis, 1925	Combine, *Noblesville*
437	Union Traction Co.	St. Louis, 1925	Combine, *Marion*
606	Indianapolis & Cincinnati Traction	Cincinnati, 1924	
Maintenance of Way Cars and Equipment			
14	Illinois Terminal	IT, 1930	Pushcar Tower Wagon
C-606	Chicago Transit Authority	Cincinnati, 1922	Line Car
Rapid Transit Cars			
4293	Chicago Rapid Transit	Cincinnati, 1922	Elevated Car
4454	Chicago Rapid Transit	Cincinnati, 1926	Elevated Car

Fleet No.	Principal Owner	Builder, Year	Remarks
Electric Locomotives			
1	Singer Sewing Machine	General Electric, 1898	Locomotive
4	Twin Branch RR, Mishawaka, Ind.	Baldwin/WH, 1928	Steeple Cab
55	Cedar Rapids & Iowa City	Detroit United, 1926	Steeple Cab
154	Evansville & Ohio Valley	General Electric, 1912	Steeple Cab
301	Cook's Brewery, Evansville, Ind.	General Electric, ?	Steeple Cab
Steam Railroad Passenger Cars			
03	Wheeling & Lake Erie	Pullman, 1888	Office Car
11	Delaware & Hudson	, 1891	Day Coach
45	Nickel Plate	ACF, 1907	Day Coach
71	Seaboard Air Line	Pullman, 1955	Lightweight Sleeper
801	Chicago, Burlington & Quincy	Budd, 1947	Lightweight Lounge/Baggage
2728	Louisville & Nashville	ACF, 1930	Diner (Cross Keys Tavern)
5243	Chesapeake & Ohio	Pullman, 1950	Lightweight Coach
8007	Pennsylvania RR	Pullman, 1938	Sleeper (Philadelphia County)
8020	Pennsylvania RR	Pullman, 1939	Sleeper (Magic Brook)
8222	New York Central	ACF, 1921	Baggage
Sandy Creek	New York Central	Pullman, 1948	Lightweight Obs.
Interurban and Steam Railroad Freight Cars and Cabooses			
X-66	Central Indiana	PRR, 1903	Flat Car
1039	Nickel Plate	Lafayette, 1881	Caboose
8099	Nickel Plate	, 1942	Box Car
10393	Lake Erie & Western	, 1903	Box Car
12219	Lake Erie & Western	, 1917	Box Car
18013	Nickel Plate	, 1917	Box Car
24019	Swift Refrigerator Line	GATX, 1953	Refrigerator
25011	Swift Refrigerator Line	GATX, 1954	Refrigerator
25023	Swift Refrigerator Line	GATX, 1954	Refrigerator
37191	Milwaukee Road (Union Refrig. Transit)	GATX, 1948	Refrigerator
37289	Milwaukee Road (Union Refrig. Transit)	GATX, 1948	Refrigerator
50571	Nickel Plate	?	Box Car
90876	Chesapeake & Ohio	C&O, 1926	Caboose

It is thought that 13 Chicago elevated cars of the same class as 4293 and 4454 are owned by the museum off the property, of which 4257, 4293, 4388 and 4453 are to be restored. The remainder are to be used as parts to rebuild the Indiana interurban cars which presently are bodies only.

In addition to the rail vehicles, twelve horse-drawn carriages are owned, including a surrey, some buggies, a cutter sleigh and a water wagon. In addition there are hay and grain wagons in the collection. Five of the vehicles were built by Studebaker.

Three bicycles from the 1880s and 1890s are in the collection together with nine motor trucks and fire engines from the inter-war period. They include Fords, a Stutz hook and ladder, a Stutz pumper and a Walker gas-electric milk delivery truck.

A complete hand-operated Indiana Bell telephone switchboard is owned, plus examples of design updates in such equipment. Operating telegraph equipment is located in the Hobbs, Indiana, railroad depot, which is now a part of the museum office. There is also an electric railroad substation, with both a rotary converter and a solid state rectifier to convert electric current from AC, as supplied, to DC suitable for running the electric vehicles on the line.

An archival collection is maintained, including correspondence, photographs and books relating to transportation.

MIDWEST ELECTRIC RAILWAY. There are a number of intermediate stops during the Old Threshers' Reunion. Throughout the event the cars are as busy as any might have been in the trolley's heyday. Southern Iowa Railway #9 takes on a large crowd. Note the horizon filled with tents, campers and trailers. A.D. Young

Iowa • Mt. Pleasant

Midwest Electric Railway. The trolley line is located just outside the grounds of the Midwest Old Settlers' and Threshers' Association's reunion in Mount Pleasant, southeast Iowa, 25 miles northwest of Burlington on US 34. The Railway and the Association can be contacted at Rural Route 1, Mt. Pleasant, IA 52641. Standard gauge.

IOWA IS RENOWNED as a prairie state and the big event of the year in its southland is the Old Threshers' Reunion, held annually over the Labor Day weekend at Mt. Pleasant. The reunion began in 1950, when local farmers with a love for old steam threshers founded the Association and, under its auspices, fired up their old machines in friendly competition. The

steam threshing contests remain the prime attraction but the meet has grown so huge that it is billed as the *Greatest Steam Show on Earth,* a description not so far from the truth.

There is a vast permanent exhibition hall jammed with old farm machinery and domestic paraphernalia. There is a small operating steam railroad; a collection of historic railroad vehicles; antique automobiles; and a complete replica of a 19th century farming village, typical of the midwest.

Iowa had a large interurban network, much of which continued in operation electrically until the mid-1950s. Thus, at a very late date, there remained in the state a number of historically interesting cars. The formation of the Iowa Railway Historical Society in that decade

prompted the purchase of some cars and arrangements were made with the Southern Iowa Railway, an electric freight line running between Centerville and Moravia, to operate the cars occasionally. Further cars were bought, but the accidental destruction of the line's electrical equipment and one of the cars by fire put an end to the arrangement. The line switched to diesel operation and the group had to find another home for its cars.

The Society and the Old Threshers got together in 1968 and the end result of that union was the creation of the present 1.1 mile loop of trolley track around the campgrounds adjacent to the Old Threshers' reunion. The trolleys are not just for museum display, however. They are there to fulfill a legitimate and pressing transportation need by servicing the tens of thousands who park or camp in the area, in some cases over half a mile from the main entrance. During the reunion the cars provide a service as busy and intensive as anything they ever did during their working lives. More than 50,000 people a day visit the reunion and, not surprisingly, the cars are quite busy. Dispatching is smooth and the crowd control skillful.

The first car ran in August 1971, but it was not until 1973 that the line was extended to form its present loop. It is visually very attractive, with several grades, fills and curves, set in pleasant rolling countryside. There are many individual car stops on the line, and passengers are constantly being picked up and set down. Five passenger cars and a snowsweeper are owned, two of which are Iowa vehicles, and another two the ever-popular open cars. More cars are planned to help cope with traffic, most of midwest origins.

Future plans call for the extension of the track into the reunion grounds proper, with the possibility of cre-

MIDWEST ELECTRIC RAILWAY. Car #2 was one of Ed Blossom's first restorations for the Magee museum (which see) and though it has survived 10 strenuous seasons on the Mount Pleasant pike, it is still lettered for the late Magee Shortline Electric Railroad. Well-filled, the car coasts around a curve at the far end of the line past the acres of campers during the 1981 season.   *A.D. Young*

MIDWEST ELECTRIC RAILWAY. Fully loaded Waterloo, Iowa, car #381 awaits the dispatcher's nod before pulling out of Yarmouth Station during the annual reunion operations.   *A.D. Young*

ating a "Toonerville" operation in which the trolley will meet all the trains. Outside the reunion period, car service is sporadic and a visitor should write ahead of time to ascertain when cars will be run. Regular working parties are conducted every three weeks throughout the year, however, to get the track and cars into shape for the heavy five days of the reunion, and during these times there is always some activity.

Fleet No.	Principal Owner	Builder, Year	Remarks
City and Suburban Cars			
1	Old Threshers (ex-Rio de Janeiro Power & Light #1718)	Brill, 1910	13-bench Open
2	Magee Shortway (ex-Rio de Janeiro Power & Light #1779)	Brill, 1911	13-bench Open
381	Waterloo, Cedar Falls & Nthn. (ex-Knoxville #379)	Perley Thomas, 1930	Lightweight
4476	Toronto Transportation Commission	St. Louis/CCF 1949	PCC
Interurban Cars			
9	Southern Iowa Railway	Barber, 1909 ?	Rebuilt 1922
320	Chicago, Aurora & Elgin	Jewett, 1914	
Maintenance of Way Cars and Equipment			
3	Waterloo, Cedar Falls & Northern		Snow Sweeper

Maine • Kennebunkport

Seashore Trolley Museum. On Log Cabin Road, Kennebunkport, off US 1, three miles north of Kennebunk. Owned and operated by the New England Electric Railway Historical Society, Box 220, Kennebunk, ME 04046. Standard gauge.

GRANDDADDY OF THEM ALL is the only phrase that adequately conveys this museum's role in the trolley museum movement. On April 19, 1939, a fan trip was scheduled over the lines of the Androscoggin and Kennebec Street Railway in Lewistown, Maine. Theodore Santarelli, Gerald Cunningham and John Amlaw were sitting in the rear of the fan-trip car, talking things over. Mr. Cunningham remarked that buses had been ordered for the Biddeford and Saco trolley operation and soon the open cars on those lines would be gone. What could be done? Could a car be saved, other than to be kept in someone's backyard? The group thought it was possible.

In due course a farewell fan trip was held on the Biddeford and Saco and more people plus a little money were rounded up dedicated to the idea of saving a Biddeford and Saco open car. By July 5, 1939, no less than twelve people had committed $150 to become charter members of the Seashore Electric Railway. The money was used to buy Biddeford and Saco open #31, which became the museum's first car. To avoid backyard preservation a safe spot was immediately sought.

Originally the car was to have been kept in the old Town House carhouse of the Atlantic Shore Line Railway, less than a mile from the present Seashore museum location. This move was vetoed at the suggestion of the carhouse owner, who feared vandalism and looting would be a problem, but suggested the group talk to a Mr. Clough who owned farm land nearby. Mr. Clough couldn't help, but his neighbor, Mr. Hill, could and an agreement was made after much shouting ensued—for poor Mr. Hill was hard of hearing. In essence, Mr. Hill agreed to rent land to the group, and for the next few years, they were all set.

By December 1941, three further cars in varying states of repair had been acquired, together with 300 feet of track which was laid to accommodate them. At the same time, incorporation as the New England Railway Historical Society was completed. Then came the war.

All development slowed for years, but financial help from the members ensured continuity and the promise of spectacular post-war development. Moreover, when gas rationing allowed, painting and car work did continue and the group emerged from the war in reasonable shape.

The years following were busy ones. Mr. Hill, after some years of receiving rent, was receptive to an offer to buy and the remainder of the 1940s saw the Seashore group purchasing further parcels of land to augment the original. Many cars were brought to the museum in those years while 300 feet of track were laid in 1948 with a further 500 in 1949. The year 1949, too, saw the start of the first carbarn. A huge forest fire had been fought off in 1947 and in that same year the south end of the main line was relocated.

One might be tempted to comment that these were all mundane and humdrum activities, but this kind of work was vital to the museum's future stability, for without a firm foundation, Seashore's expansion would be muted. To that end, the appointment of D. Ben Minnich as General Manager in 1953 was a milestone in the continuing maturation of the museum, for under his aegis electrical operation began and some huge land purchases were consummated. One of the most interesting was the deeding to the museum of five miles of the former Atlantic Shore Line Railway's right-of-way. In the years since then there have been constant purchases and exchange of land parcels so as to continue the work of consolidating the museum.

The original NEERHS charter had charged the museum with the building of an historical electric railway, representing a living display of the trolley industry's development, using local New England cars wherever possible. By 1948, however, only Boston of all the New England operators was still running cars (as it continues to do so today) and the Seashore museum had to look beyond its area to representative cars from other places. It succeeded beyond its wildest expectations.

Besides a good selection from New England and a superb Boston collection, making Seashore a fine museum of New England vehicles and practice, this is one of the few museums with a collection spanning the whole continent. There are cars from Dallas, Minneapolis, Los Angeles, Chicago, Pittsburgh and Milwaukee to name just a few. Utterly unique are the two single-truck Birney cars that constituted the all-time fleet of the Denver and South Platte Railway. There are not many museums that can boast of having taken over an entire trolley company's roster!

The first car ran under its own power on December 27, 1953, and thereafter the museum was permanently under wire, with daily public access beginning in 1954. In 1955 a second division was begun on 100 acres of land next to US 1, and in June of 1957, this new *Terminal* division began to offer daily passenger rides in the summer season. The old (and principal) location at Arundel shops, however, continued to be developed and ultimately the *Terminal* division (never physically connected) was abandoned after some years' use for open-air car storage.

By 1955 the museum claimed to have the largest group of preserved trolleys in the world. In 1982 it can still make that claim, with nearly 150 pieces of equipment in its ownership, including interurbans, rapid transit cars, snowplows, work cars, mail and express cars, locomotives, freight cars, buses and trolley coaches. One of the latest arrivals is an ex-Third Avenue Railway of New York car from Vienna. Part of a fleet shipped to Austria in 1949 under the Marshall Plan, Vienna #4216

was originally TARS #631 and is identical to the TARS car currently running at Branford.

The museum has responsibility for a staggering quantity of vehicles and, as might be expected, presentation of them to the visitor is quite sophisticated. Typical of the museum's approach is the carbarn display, given over entirely to showcasing the many vehicles painstakingly restored by the members. When one contrasts the dozens of restored cars in this barn, with the unrestored "junk" neatly stored out of the public eye on another part of the site, the magnitude and quality of the work done at this museum is brought home most forcefully. All these beautifully displayed cars are in operating condition, and are run a number of times a season in special pageants or parades, plus spells of regularly scheduled service.

An informative slide presentation on the museum is

on permanent display and, as at most museums, there is a gift shop. Here, however, you are probably in one of the largest in the country devoted to the sale of books and materials devoted to mass transit and the trolley. It is an integral part of the new visitors' center opened in August 1980. This 6,000-square-foot center is designed after a turn-of-the-century railroad station and is the museum's focal point; the first fruition of an immense development program.

Other phases of that program presently underway include a one-half-mile extension to the present main line, a terminal loop, a picnic area with nature trails and an ocean view, and the grading of an additional two miles of right-of-way, on which to exercise the interurban fleet. Yet another stage envisages the connection of the presently somewhat scattered barn area into one huge exhibit center with walkways for the

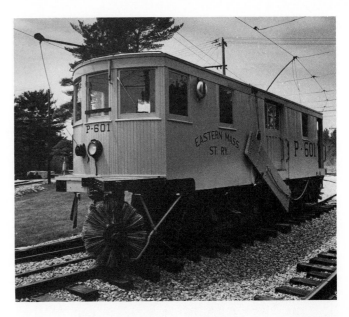

SEASHORE TROLLEY MUSEUM. *Eastern Massachusetts Street Railway* **#P-601 is a beautifully restored Russell snowplow. In later life it operated on New York's** *Third Avenue Railway System,* **and most recently in Toronto.**
Seashore Trolley Museum

SEASHORE TROLLEY MUSEUM. This museum is a busy and attractive place, full of cars and activity. #396 (at right) is a Boston car of 1896 vintage, used in the filming of the movie *The Cardinal* **during 1963 and loaned to Boston for various purposes on other occasions since then. To its left is** *Biddeford & Saco* **#31 (the** *first* **museum trolley, as discussed elsewhere), while directly along the track are two beautiful** *Connecticut Co.* **open cars about to take on a load of appreciative visitors. This view is taken from the Boston elevated railway tower at the entrance.**
Seashore Trolley Museum

SEASHORE TROLLEY MUSEUM. Blackpool #144, a 1924 British double-deck car, is not always to be seen since its British profile wheel treads don't quite match the somewhat larger tolerances of American open tracks. Thus its sojourns on the Seashore trackage have to be restricted to certain areas. All the same, the school kids on the balcony (upper deck) are having as good a time on the car as generations of Blackpool kids and summer visitors did years ago. *Seashore Trolley Museum*

SEASHORE TROLLEY MUSEUM. Visitors enjoy a close-up look inside the museum's Highwood display carbarn.

Seashore Trolley Museum

visitor, 40,000 of whom come to this remote Maine location in normal years.

The present line is 1½ miles long, threading its way through acres of carbarns, bursting with trolleys, freight and subway cars. The line enters the Maine wilderness a little beyond the barns.

Scheduled electric operations began in 1955 and since then a second line has been opened at the Arundel site to take passengers from the visitors' center down a branch route to the exhibits barn, where they can alight and glory in the finery of traction restored. In the development plan, this line is to be extended as a loop around the 80-acre core of the museum, taking in the visitors' center, restoration and maintenance shops, exhibits complex and the interurban diner—should be some trip! The interurban diner, by the way, is functional and serves a pretty good hamburger.

Through the years the museum has maintained its strictly amateur character in all areas except for repair.

There it has been for many years the practice to hire paid maintenance crews, usually from the museum's active membership. The shop facilities are superb and unique from a visitor's point of view since they are equipped with a viewing gallery from which to see work in progress without getting in anyone's way. The shop, its elderly machines and ancient trolley cars, all combine to transport the visitor back across time. It is a most effective exhibit.

Seashore's influence has been worldwide, inspiring many to emulate the American example. The best-known example has been the British **Tramway Museum Society** (now the **National Tramway Museum**) at Crich. This organisation has always credited the Seashore Museum as having given them the inspiration for their own activities, which began with car purchase in 1948, and formal incorporation in 1955. Indeed, the relationship between the two groups has always been quite close, since Seashore is the nearest transatlantic trolley museum to Crich.

On some occasions there have even been some hardy souls who have spent periods working at each other's museums. To emphasise that closeness, the Seashore Museum has a small collection of British double-deck cars, the first arriving almost 30 years ago. And with the small but representative collection of purely European trolleys, the museum is able to point up the contrast between U.S. and European practise most effectively.

LIBERTY BELL LIMITED

1030

1030

ALLENTOWN LIMITED

SEASHORE TROLLEY MUSEUM. A superbly restored 1931 lightweight interurban parlor car is painted in the colors of the Lehigh Valley Transit Company's *Liberty Bell* service. It was converted from a coach lounge in 1934 by original owner Indiana Railway, and was sold to LVT in 1941. #65, at the Illinois Railway Museum, is painted in the original IRR livery. IRR #55 became LVT #1030 and was rebuilt and modernized before entering service, and Seashore has kept it in that condition rather than tackle a rather substantial rebuilding. Moreover, as an LVT car, #1030 represents the last parlor (or club) car interurban service in the U.S. except for the North Shore line's *Electroliners,* which are in a special class by themselves. During World War II its interior appointments were converted to coach-type seating and it was removed from service in August 1951, a few days before the Liberty Bell service ended. Museum members bought #1030 from the scrap merchants and it was delivered to the museum early in 1952.   *Richard Brilliante*

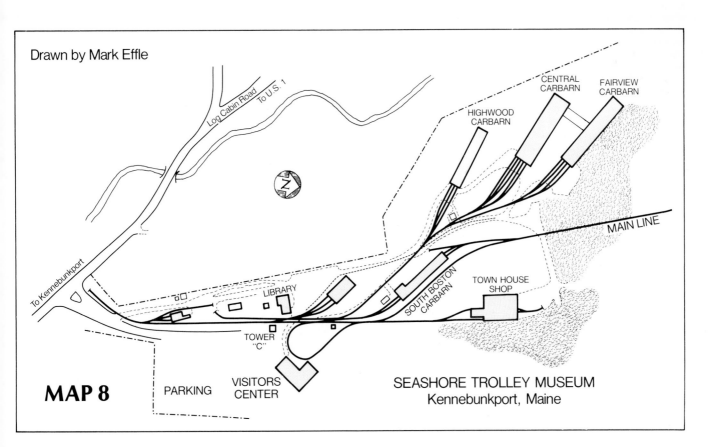

Drawn by Mark Effle

Log Cabin Road
To U.S. 1

N

To Kennebunkport

HIGHWOOD CARBARN

CENTRAL CARBARN

FAIRVIEW CARBARN

MAIN LINE

LIBRARY

SOUTH BOSTON CARBARN

TOWN HOUSE SHOP

TOWER "C"

MAP 8

PARKING

VISITORS CENTER

SEASHORE TROLLEY MUSEUM
Kennebunkport, Maine

Fleet No.	Principal Owner	Builder, Year	Remarks
City and Suburban Cars			
1	Denver & So. Platte (Colo.)/York Util. (Me.)	American, 1919	Birney
2	Denver & So Platte (Colo.)/York Util. (Me.)	American, 1919	Birney
2	Montreal Tramways	Montreal St. Ry., 1906	Observation
8	Brattleboro St. RR (Vermont)	Wason, 1917	
10	Union St. Ry. (New Bedford, Mass.)	Brill, 1880	Horse Car
12	Northern Mass. St. Ry./Fitchburn St. Ry.	Brill, 1886	Open Horse Car
24	Templeton St. Railway	Briggs, 1901	Convertible
31	Biddeford & Saco RR	Brill, 1900	12-bench Open
34	Union St. Ry. (New Bedford, Mass.)	Feigel, 1873	Mail Car (ex-Horse Car)
39	Cooperative Transport (Wheeling, W. Va.)	Cincinnati, 1924	
41	Middlesex & Boston St. Ry.	Stephenson, 1898	
48	Municipal Ry. of San Francisco/Cal Cable	Cal St. Cable RR, 1910	Cable Car
50	Mass. Northeastern St. Ry.	Laconia, 1902	
60	Manchester St. Ry. (New Hampshire)	Laconia, 1895	
62	Philadelphia & West Chester	Brill, 1925	Center-Entrance Sub'n
88	York Utilities (Sanford, Maine)	Wason, 1926	
105	Dunedin City Ry. (New Zealand)	Stansfield, 1903	Cable Grip Car
134	Nagasaki, Japan	Nippon Sharyo, 1911	
144	Blackpool Corporation, England	Blackpool, 1924	Open-Balcony Double Deck
225	Chicago Surface Lines	Pullman, 1907	
235	West End St. Ry. (Boston, Mass.)	Laconia, 1895	Presently Rail Grinder
279	Azienda Tranvia (Rome, Italy)	Tabanelli, 1924	
293	Liverpool Corporation, England	Liverpool, 1939	Double Deck
303	Connecticut Company (ex-615)	Brill, 1901	15-bench Open
396	Boston Elevated Railway	St. Louis, 1900	
434	Dallas Railway (Texas)	American, 1914	Stone & Webster "Turtle Roof"
475	Boston Elevated Railway	Newburyport, 1903	Presently Test Car
521	Los Angeles Railway	St. Louis, 1906	California Type
526	Leeds City Transport/ex-London	Union Const. & Fin., 1930	Double Deck
615	Biddeford & Saco (ex-Portland, Maine)	Wason, 1920	Birney
724	Boston Elevated Railway	Metropolitan, 1884	Orig. Horse Car
838	Connecticut Company	Jones, 1905	15-bench Open
861	Milwaukee Electric	St. Louis, 1920	
925	West End St. Ry. (Boston)	Jones, 1894	Parlor Car
957	Montreal Tramways	Ottawa, 1910	
966	New Orleans Public Service	Perley Thomas, 1924	
1059	West End St. Ry. (Boston)	Barney & Smith, 1895	Presently Rail Grinder
1160	Connecticut Company	Stephenson, 1906	
1176	Montreal Tramways	Montreal Tramways, 1943	
1177	Montreal Tramways	Montreal Tramways, 1943	
1267	Twin Cities Rapid Transit (Minneapolis)	Transit Supply, 1907	
1274	Glasgow Corporation, Scotland	Glasgow Corp., 1939	Double Deck
1391	Connecticut Company	Osgood Bradley, 1910	15-bench Open
1440	Pittsburgh Railways	St. Louis, 1942	PCC
1468	Connecticut Company	Osgood Bradley, 1911	15-bench Open
1700	Sydney Tramways (Australia)	Meadowbank, 1926	Compartment Car
2052	Montreal Tramways/ex-Springfield, Mass.	Wason, 1927	Lightweight
2652	Montreal Tramways	Canadian Car & Fdy., 1930	Lightweight
2710	Hamburger Hochbahn AG (Hamburg, W. Ger.)	Falkenreid, 1921	
3019	Boston Elevated Railway	Pullman, 1941	PCC
3083	Boston Elevated Railway	Pullman, 1945	PCC
3127	Boston Elevated Railway	Pullman, 1944	PCC
3221	Boston Elevated Railway	Pullman, 1946	PCC
3274	Boston MTA	Pullman, 1951	PCC
3340	Boston MTA/ex-Dallas	Pullman, 1946	Double End PCC
3342	Boston MTA/ex-Dallas	Pullman, 1946	Double End PCC
3400	Boston MBTA	Boston MBTA, 1971	Mock-Up of LRV
3412	Berlin Verkhers Betrieb.	, 1927	Center Entrance
4387	Eastern Massachusetts St. Ry.	Laconia, 1918	Semi-Convertible
4400	Boston Elevated Railway/ex-East. Mass.	Osgood Bradley, 1927	Suburban
4547	Brooklyn-Manhattan Transit (New York)	Jewett, 1906	Convertible
5055	Boston Elevated Railway	Brill, 1906	Type 2, Semi-Convertible
5060	Boston Elevated Railway	Brill, 1906	Type 2, Semi-Convertible
5071	Boston Elevated Railway	Brill, 1906	Type 2, Semi-Convertible
5734	Boston Elevated Railway	Brill, 1924	Type 5A, Semi-Convertible
5748	United Rys. & Elect. (Baltimore)	Brill, 1917	Semi-Convertible

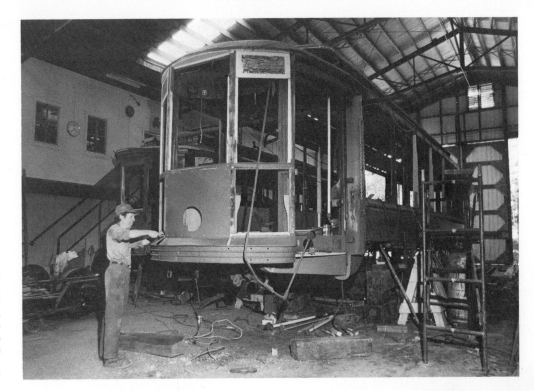

SEASHORE TROLLEY MUSEUM. Though the workshop is larger, more comfortable and better equipped than most, it doesn't mean that restoration work has become any less difficult or messy. Donald Curry, who has become recognized as an outstanding organizer of such efforts in the industry, installs a new dash panel on a semi-convertible car.
Seashore Trolley Museum

Fleet No.	Principal Owner	Builder, Year	Remarks
5821	Boston Elevated Railway	Brill, 1924	Type 5B, Semi-Convertible
6144	United Rys. & Elect. (Baltimore)	Brill, 1930	Peter Witt
6270	Boston Elevated Railway	Kuhlman, 1919	Center Entrance
6618	Philadelphia Rapid Transit	Brill, 1911	Nearside
City of Manchester	Manchester St. Ry. (New Hampshire)	Briggs, 1897	Parlor Car

Interurban Cars
8	Atlantic Shore Line (Maine)	Portland, 1893	Express Trailer
14	Portland-Lewiston Ry. (Maine)	Laconia, 1912	
38	Manchester & Nashua St. Ry. (New Hampshire)	Laconia, 1907	
40	Portland-Lewiston Ry. (Maine)	Laconia, 1915	
52	Aroostook Valley RR (Maine)	Brill, 1909	Express Motor
70	Aroostook Valley RR (Maine)	Wason, 1912	Combine
71	Aroostook Valley RR (Maine)	Wason, 1912	Combine
108	Portsmouth, Dover & York St. Ry. (N. Hamp.)	Laconia, 1904	Express/Mail (Now Line Car)
118	Cincinnati & Lake Erie (Ohio)	Cincinnati, 1930	High Speed Lightweight
149	Boston & Worcester St. Ry.	Osgood Bradley, 1915	
415	Chicago, North Shore & Milwaukee	Cincinnati, 1926	Diner
420	Chicago, North Shore & Milwaukee	Pullman, 1928	Parlor-Observ. Trailer
434	Chicago, Aurora & Elgin	Cincinnati, 1927	
454	Quebec Railway, Light & Power	Ottawa, 1930	
504	Montreal & Southern Counties	Ottawa, 1924	Express Motor
610	Montreal & Southern Counties	Ottawa, 1922	
621	Montreal & Southern Counties	Ottawa, 1930	
648	Cincinnati & Lake Erie	Cincinnati, 1930	Baggage/Express
755	Chicago, North Shore & Milwaukee	Standard, 1930	
797	Lake Erie & Northern Ry. (Ontario)	Preston, 1915	
1030	Lehigh Valley Transit	ACF, 1931	High-speed Lightweight
1280	Warwick Railway	Rhode Island, 1912	Express Motor
1304	British Columbia Electric Ry.	BCERy, 1946	Rebuilt on 1911 Car

Electric Locomotives
100	Sanford & Eastern Ry. (Maine)	Laconia, 1906	Steeple Cab
300	Oshawa Railway (Ontario)	Baldwin-Westinghouse, 1920	Steeple Cab
0514	Boston Elevated Railway	Boston Elevated, 1914	

Fleet No.	Principal Owner	Builder, Year	Remarks
Maintenance of Way Cars and Equipment			
B-2	Cornwall St. Ry. (Ontario)	Ottawa, 1926	Snow Sweeper
P-601	Eastern Mass. St. Ry./Toronto Transp.	Russell, 1920	Snow Sweeper
S-71	Eastern Mass. St. Ry.	Bay State, 1915	Line Car
T-116	Worcester Consol. St. Ry. (Mass.)	?	Flat Car Trailer
1	Claremont & Concord Ry.	Laconia, 1903	Flat Car Trailer
4	Claremont & Concord Ry.	C&C Ry. Shops	Line Car
6	Milwaukee Electric	?	Flat Car Trailer
7	Boston Elevated Railway	?	Flat Car Trailer
16	Providence, Rhode Island (Rhode Is. Co.)	Wason, 1905	Snowplow
038	Worcester, Mass.	Worcester, 1912	Motor Flat/Shop Switcher
0357	Connecticut Company	McGuire-Cummings, 1925	Flat Car
0504	Boston Elevated Railway	Industrial, 1901	Crane
0517	Boston Elevated Railway	Goldschmidt, 1913	Rail Grinder
2003	Boston Elevated Railway	?	Flat Car
2016	Boston Elevated Railway	Boston Elev. Shops, 1912	Motor Flat with Hoist
3234	Boston Elevated Railway	Goldschmidt, 1913	Rail Grinder
3246	Boston Elevated Railway	Industrial, 1916	Crane
3284	Boston Elevated Railway (ex-5970)	Laconia, 1918	Work Car
3603	Boston Elevated Railway	Boston Elev. Shops, 1923	Ramp Car Trailer
3608	Boston Elevated Railway	Differential, 1926	Side Dump Motor
3617	Boston Elevated Railway	Differential, 1927	Bottom Dump Motor
3622	Boston Elevated Railway	Differential, 1927	Side Dump Motor
5154	Boston Elevated Railway	St. Louis, 1908	Snowplow
Rapid Transit Cars			
0719	Boston Elevated Railway	Osgood Bradley, 1927	
3352	New York Transit Auth. (IRT)	ACF, 1905	
4137	Long Island Railroad	Pennsylvania RR, 1930	MP54 Commuter
Trolley Buses			
273	Halifax, Nova Scotia	Can/Car-Brill, 1950	T44A
336	Philadelphia Transportation Co.	Marmon-Herrington, 1955	TC49
376	City Transit Co. (Dayton, Ohio)	Pullman, 1942	
654	Delaware Coach Co. (Wilmington, Del.)	Mack, 1940	CR3S
713	Johnstown Traction Co. (Penna.)	Brill, 1941	40SMT
8361	Boston Metropolitan Transit Authority	Pullman, 1948	450-S-102-43CX
8490	Boston Metropolitan Transit Authority	Pullman, 1951	
Motor Buses			
31	Biddeford & Saco	Brill, 1947	
116	Mass. Northeastern Transp. Co.	ACF, 1929	Nancy Hanks
478	Eastern Massachusetts St. Ry.	ACF, 1934	H9
504	Portland Railroad (Maine)	General Motors, 1950	TDH 4807
2824	Boston Metropolitan Transit Authority	White, 1948	
3524	Eastern Massachusetts St. Ry.	General Motors, 1961	TDH 5301
None	?	Graham, 1924	Private Bus
Internal Combustion Cars and Locomotives			
3	Dragon Cement (Thomaston, Maine)	Plymouth/Fate Root Heath, 1929	
Interurban and Steam Railroad Freight Cars and Cabooses			
29	Long Island Railroad	Pressed Steel, 1926	Caboose
C40	Bangor & Aroostook	ACF, 1915	Caboose
097	Central Vermont/Luria	, 1929	Box Car
122	Central Vermont/Luria	, 1929	Box Car
1936	?	, 1954	Tank Car
2330	General American Transportation		Flat Car (ex-Tank)
6582	Bangor & Aroostook	, 1926	Refrigerator Car
7955	General American Transportation	GATX, 1930	Flat Car (ex-Tank)
12719	General American Transportation	GATX, 1948	Tank Car
*	Union Tank Car	, 1931	Box Car
31001	Union Tank Car	, 1954	Refrigerator
35038	Maine Central	Keith, 1919	Box Car
103002	Boston & Maine	Laconia, 1912	Caboose

*Numbers 26504, 26599, 26676, 26681, 26693

Maryland • Baltimore

Baltimore Streetcar Museum. Located on Falls Road, Baltimore. Owned and operated by Baltimore Streetcar Museum, Inc., P.O. Box 7184, Baltimore, MD 21218. 5'4½" gauge.

THIS SMALL "second generation" museum is unique in the whole movement in that it is devoted exclusively to telling the complete story of just one city's trolleys. At the same time it is one of only two trolley museums in North America to run its trolleys in an authentic urban setting, albeit in a pleasantly green area of town. Baltimore trolleys, as people remember them, were urban vehicles and this museum pays close attention to that fact.

The core of this unique collection was assembled nearly 60 years ago by Baltimore's United Railways and Electric Company, and was maintained by the city's trolley operators until 1953. At that time they were made available for disposal. The Maryland Historical Society was persuaded to become "caretaker" for the cars in 1954 while the search went on for a permanent site to house them. Eventually one was located and the cars moved there by 1962, together with those of the future National Capital Trolley Museum. But problems arose. Vandalism became a scourge. The homeowners adjoining the site objected. The lack of covered accommodation made the cars vulnerable to the weather.

The National Capital group withdrew to its present Wheaton site in 1965 and the remaining Baltimore group, now predominantly members of the Baltimore chapter of the National Railroad Historical Society, realised something must be done. That something was the formation of a new organisation and the Baltimore Streetcar Museum was established in 1966. The search

BALTIMORE STREETCAR MUSEUM. Looking down from atop the Chessie System bridge which crosses over the museum railway, it's an impressive view. The visitors' center is at left, with open-bench car #1164 loaded up for its next run. Behind is the three-track carbarn. The bus in the center is also part of the museum's collection. *Jim Walker*

BALTIMORE STREETCAR MUSEUM. It was a gala, if cold, day in January 1977 when the museum's outer loop opened for service. Eight Baltimore streetcars were brought out for this magnificent photograph. The trackage was an actual loop, the former 28th St. loop of the #15 line. Dismantling, moving and reassembly took almost two years and cost over $12,000. *E.G. Willis Photo/ Baltimore Streetcar Museum*

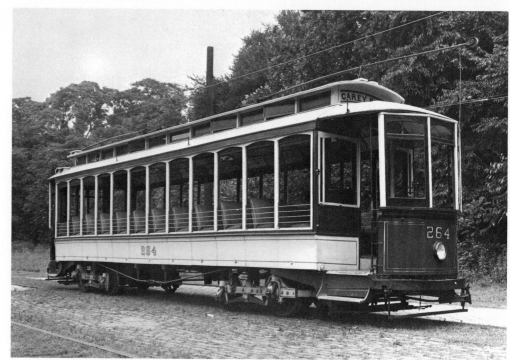

BALTIMORE STREETCAR MUSEUM. One of the classics in the collection is convertible car #264, built in 1900. It is shown with window panels removed and safety guard in place for summer use. It sits on maximum traction trucks.
E.G. Willis Photo/ Baltimore Streetcar Museum Library

for a site continued and the present Falls Road location, on abandoned Maryland and Pennsylvania RR property was the most suitable. An agreement was negotiated with a cooperative city of Baltimore and the cars finally moved to Falls Road in 1968.

The Baltimore museum group is unusual in the movement in that it owns no land. The city rented out the site for a nominal fee, built the carbarn and arranged the federal grant for construction of the visitors' center, one of the best in the country. Otherwise the museum itself has been responsible for everything, from track-laying to car restoration. First electric service began in July 1970 and has continued ever since with the exception of a part of the 1979 and 1980 seasons. In September 1979 the museum suffered massive flooding as a result of tropical storm "David" and it took months to repair the damage.

A nice touch in the trolley service is the museum's insistence that the trolley crews are as smartly turned out as the cars they operate. Many dress in authentic early day uniforms and those that can sport luxuriant moustaches and sideburns.

Six cars are presently in operating condition and others are under restoration. There is a further small reserve of Baltimore cars held by the museum which have yet to be worked on. The standard of restoration on the completed cars is very high and the museum with its parklike setting among greenery and buildings is a gem. As a result a visit to the Baltimore Streetcar Museum is a very satisfying experience.

BALTIMORE STREETCAR MUSEUM. The carhouse holds all the collection on site, which is all from the Baltimore streetcar system and all 5-foot 4½-inch gauge. On track #3 (left) is #1164, a 12-bench open car and #554, a Brownell-built single truck open. Track #2 (center) has on it #3828, built as an open platform car but closed in 1922 with folding doors and steps. The museum's newest car, on Track #1, is PCC #7407, built in 1944. The carhouse is 50' by 180'. A 1977 photograph.
E.G. Willis Photo/ Baltimore Streetcar Museum

Fleet No.	Principal Owner	Builder, Year	Remarks
City and Suburban Cars			
25	Baltimore City Passenger Railway	Poole & Hunt, 1859	Horse Car
264	United Railways & Electric	Brownell, 1900	Convertible
417	Baltimore City Passenger Railway	Brill, 1880	ex-Horse Car
554	Baltimore Traction	Brownell, 1896	9-bench Open
1164	United Railways & Electric	Brill, 1902	12-bench Open
3651	Baltimore Consolidated Railway Co.	Brownell, 1898	
3828	United Railways & Electric	Brill, 1902	
4533	United Railways & Electric	Brill, 1904	
4662	United Railways & Electric	Brill, 1904	
6119	United Railways & Electric	Brill, 1930	Peter Witt
7329	Baltimore Transit Co.	Pullman, 1939	PCC
7407	Baltimore Transit Co.	Pullman, 1944	PCC

Maryland • Wheaton

National Capital Trolley Museum. Entrance on Bonifant Road between Layhill Road and New Hampshire Avenue, north of Wheaton, MD, in the outer Washington suburbs. Mailing address is P.O. Box 4007, Colesville Branch, Silver Spring, MD 20904. Standard gauge.

THE EARLY HISTORY of this museum and the Baltimore Streetcar Museum are intertwined. Initially the joint groups had located a site just north of Baltimore where work could begin, but problems with vandals and hostile neighbors sabotaged the prospects of a secure future. With those problems in mind, the present Wheaton location was found.

Initially the groups were to continue their co-existence, since the Maryland location made a regional Baltimore and Washington, D.C., collection a natural and, of course, the major thrust of the collection at that time was cars from both cities. But the Baltimore element felt strongly that it wanted to keep its cars close to Baltimore and to achieve that end founded its own Baltimore Streetcar Museum in 1966. The split was, however, quite amicable.

The display philosophies of the two museums are remarkably similar despite the passage of years and both Maryland museums have well-defined character together with an impeccable appearance. If the Baltimore museum is exclusively urban, then the National Capital Museum is its country cousin, attractively situated in the Northwest Branch Regional Park north of Wheaton.

Originally it had been intended the museum would operate the O. Roy Chalk collection of Washington, D.C., cars, and insurance premiums for these cars were paid by the group from 1962. (Mr. Chalk had been head of D.C. Transit, the Washington streetcar company.) But after the first carhouse was completed in 1966, Mr.

NATIONAL CAPITAL TROLLEY MUSEUM. No other museum relies so much on its collection of foreign cars to hold down basic services. Here is a car and matching trailer from Vienna, Austria.
Robert H. Flack

NATIONAL CAPITAL TROLLEY MUSEUM. Dusseldorf #955 and Washington, D.C., PCC #1101 meet outside the carbarns. The marvelously neat and tidy appearance of the carbarn area is striking, while the building itself is unobtrusive, blending in well with the parkland. *Jim Walker*

Chalk said he had other plans for the cars and the arrangement was terminated. This presented quite a problem since by then the supply of U.S. trolley cars in ready-to-run condition had virtually dried up.

A vice-president of the museum went to Europe at his own expense to locate and purchase European vehicles on the museum's behalf, since in the absence of U.S. cars this was felt to be a legitimate move to make. For the next few years a representative European collection was assembled and the track was laid. This latter task began in January 1969 and was complete by October when the first car ran.

Once the unusual fleet of diminutive trolleys began to run in the superbly groomed park, considerable interest was generated and eventually Mr. Chalk reversed his previous decision and let the cars come to National Capital after all, joining a small fleet of Washington, D.C., cars already owned by the museum. As time goes by, these latter are gradually being removed from off-site storage onto the museum site as space permits, to be restored when time and funds are available. Thus, in the fairly near future, both Washington and Baltimore will be able to boast operating trolley museums with collections largely devoted to cars of the museum's local city, from first to last. That is a very rare occurrence.

There are more than 1½ miles of track, running

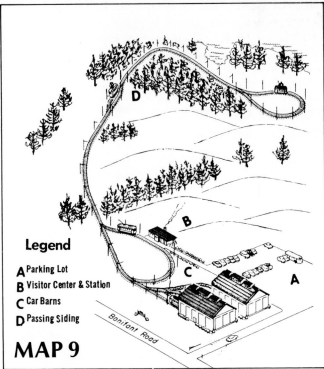

Legend

A Parking Lot
B Visitor Center & Station
C Car Barns
D Passing Siding

MAP 9

through beautifully manicured lawns and flower beds, through meadows and woodlands of great beauty. The whole operation has the air of a trolley park, operating as it does in a rural county park which insists on cleanliness and good landscaping at all times. These elements are of a very high standard at the National Capital Museum, so you will see no unnecessary poles and wires, no dirt or litter and no junk of any kind. The result is one of the most appealing trolley museums in North America, and a delight to visit.

The visitors' center is located at one side of the terminal area, built in the style of an old-time country railroad depot. Besides the obligatory gift shop and ticket counter, there is a large area devoted to small exhibit displays. The east wing of the center is an auditorium with regularly scheduled slide shows. A typical presentation of the late 1970s was a 10-minute show entitled *Trolley Car Heritage*.

On the outside of the center is a paved waiting area, surrounded by flower beds with blossoms of every color and hue. The unique brick carbarns give exactly the right touch. They are very similar to the small brick barns one might have seen anywhere in the country 60 years ago on a prosperous rural route. A visitor sitting in the barn area watching the cars come and go could not regard the place as being anything but idyllic.

NATIONAL CAPITAL TROLLEY MUSEUM. The attractively landscaped visitors' center is the hub of this museum's operations. The lead car is a rare pre-PCC Washington, D.C., streamliner of 1935, followed by a 1918 Washington car, #766. Behind is a little car from Austria, Graz #120.

Jim Walker

NATIONAL CAPITAL TROLLEY MUSEUM. Like many other museums in the eastern U.S., the Wheaton, Maryland, exhibit includes snow-fighting equipment, like *Capital Transit #07,* an 1899 McGuire product.

Robert H. Flack

Fleet No.	Principal Owner	Builder, Year	Remarks
City and Suburban Cars			
1	Capital Traction (DC)	Stephenson, 1872	ex-Horse Car, now Mobile Office
2	Hagerstown & Frederick (Maryland)	Brill, 1917	
120	Grazer Verkehrsberiebe (Austria)	Waggonfabrik Weitzer, 1909	
352	Johnstown Traction Co. (Penn.)	St. Louis, 1926	
522	Capital Traction (DC)	American, 1898	
678	Third Avenue (N.Y.)	TARS, 1939	
766	DC Transit	Kuhlman, 1918	
955	Dusseldorf (W. Germany)	Gebruder Schondorff, 1928	
1053	DC Transit	St. Louis, 1935	Pre-PCC
1101	DC Transit	St. Louis, 1937	PCC
5954	Berliner Verkehrsbetriebe (W. Germany)	, 1924	
6062	Wiener Stadtwerke (Vienna, Austria)	Waggonfabrik Simmering, 1910	
7802	Wiener Stadtwerke (Vienna, Austria)	Waggonfabrik Simmering, 1910	Trailer to 6062
Maintenance of Way Cars			
07	Capital Transit (DC)	McGuire, 1899	Snow Sweeper
026	DC Transit	Brill, 1905	Snow Sweeper
0509	DC Transit	American, 1899	Work Car

Michigan • Detroit

Detroit Citizens Railway. On Washington Boulevard and Jefferson Avenue in downtown Detroit, the line runs 1¼ miles between the Renaissance Center and Grand Circus Park. Owned and operated by Detroit Department of Transportation, 1301 E. Warren, Detroit, MI 48207. 2'11-7/16" gauge.

AS PART OF Detroit's attempt to rejuvenate its downtown, various cultural, recreational and tourist attractions were sought to round out the massive construction program of hotels, offices and shops. As a way of linking these areas, a young trolley enthusiast, then a part of Mayor Coleman Young's Merchants Assistance Program, hit on a very interesting thought. Why not link all the rejuvenated downtown areas with a vintage-style trolley line, which itself could be a point of focus tying together all the projects, and at the same time be a tourist attraction in its own right?

Alex Pollock's idea was one whose time had come, and as a city planner he was admirably prepared to cope with the problems of both funding and selling the idea. Michigan's Department of Highways and Transportation played a key role in providing money for an engineering feasibility study ($17,000) and also funded the major share of the installation ($625,000). In addition the Federal Urban Mass Transit Administration funded $422,000 and the City of Detroit another $350,000 to complete the project.

Cars were located in Lisbon, Portugal, by Paul Class of the Glenwood, Oregon, museum, and with the final hurdle crossed, work began on building the line in 1976, opening to the public on September 20 of that year. Eight cars were bought, though normally only two are in service at any one time. Two of the cars were bought simply to provide spares for the others. They were purchased in Lisbon for a very excellent reason; they were American-built cars, only slightly scaled down for European use and are otherwise identical to the quaint "dinky" trolleys immortalized in the *Toonerville Trolley* cartoons of Fontaine Fox.

A 12-minute service is provided and when not in use the cars are kept in a smart glass-walled carbarn at the Grand Circus Park end of the line. This tourist trolley line shares with Seattle and the Old Threshers' operation the distinction of providing genuine transportation services to the public on a regular basis.

A real gem, presently on loan to Detroit for five years, is a beautifully restored open-top British double-deck car from the long-closed Burton & Ashby Light Railway. An extension from Cobo Hall to the Renaissance Center was opened by this car in mid-1980 at the time of the Republican Party's National Convention. It was a great hit and this car now normally serves the extension.

Winter operation was a problem in the past since the cars, having been built for Lisbon's mild climate, were not able to keep the wild winters of Michigan at bay. A further Libson car has recently been purchased and rebuilt by John R. Stevens & Associates to stand the winter, and this fully overhauled, winterised car will bear the brunt of year-round operation for some years without need of further attention.

Mention should be made also of the Michigan Transit Museum, an organisation which had a great deal to do with the original concept of operating old-time trolleys in Detroit. Though presently without a permanent site of its own, the group is actively involved in the preservation of Detroit Street Railway's last two operational work cars, now housed at the department's Shoemaker carhouse.

In addition, this group has a Detroit Birney carbody, some Chicago rapid transit cars and a few pieces of railroad equipment. They are a classic example of an amateur-founded museum in its earliest formative stages and typical of the early years of almost all the museums discussed in this book. They can be reached at P.O. Box 12, Fraser, MI 48026.

DETROIT CITIZENS' RAILWAY. A car destined for the downtown Detroit line is shown being unloaded upon its arrival in the USA from Portugal. *Paul V. Class*

DETROIT CITIZENS' RAILWAY. St. Louis Car Co.-built in 1898, this little car spent all its working life in Lisbon, Portugal. It is being trucked to the Glenwood, Oregon, museum for overhaul before onward dispatch to Detroit.

Paul V. Class

DETROIT CITIZENS' RAILWAY. One of the vintage Lisbon cars is hard at work on its downtown circuit, rolling along narrow-gauge rails to serve some of the convention and tourist-oriented areas along the riverfront.

Jim Walker

Fleet No.	Principal Owner	Builder, Year	Remarks
City and Suburban Cars			
1	(ex-Lisbon #405)	St. Louis, 1899	
2	(ex-Lisbon #436)	St. Louis, 1899	
3	(ex-Lisbon #412)	St. Louis, 1899	
4	(ex-Lisbon #517)	Carris, Santa Amaro, 1925	
5	(ex-Lisbon #523)	Carris, Santa Amaro, 1925	
6	(ex-Lisbon #427)	St. Louis, 1899	
14	Burton & Ashby	Brush, 1904	Open Top Double Deck Car
247	(ex-Lisbon #247)	Brill, 1901	Open Car

All the cars were built for Carris, the transit operator of Lisbon, Portugal. They were purchased for use in Detroit and are now painted in the colors of the Detroit Citizens' Railway. In addition, Lisbon cars #457 (St. Louis, 1899) and #529 (Carris, Santa Amaro, 1925) were bought for spare parts.

Minnesota • Minneapolis

Minnesota Transportation Museum. Como-Harriet Streetcar Line. The museum is at 42nd and Queen Avenue South, at Lake Harriet, South Minneapolis. Owned and operated by the Minnesota Transportation Museum, P.O. Box 1300, Hopkins, MN 55343. Standard gauge.

THE ERA WHICH SAW the successful evolution of the operating trolley museum was also the era in which the traditional trolley finally vanished. So if today a group would want to establish a new trolley museum, they are faced with a totally different set of problems from those faced in the 1940s. Then, though suitable vehicles existed in abundance, there was usually no money, experience or home. The early struggles of many a group were as a result of the effort needed to overcome these handicaps.

Today, with over 40 years of experience on which to draw, those problems are less of a nightmare than formerly. However, locating cars has become far more of a problem.

It was already acute as early as 1963, so far as the newly formed Minnesota Transportation Museum was concerned. The site was there—indeed it was a natural, being the most scenic part of the old Twin Cities Rapid Transit Como-Harriet streetcar line. The experience was there, too, or at least could be drawn on from other museums. There was even a car, #1300 of 1908 vintage, a vehicle which had spent most of its working life on this line.

But you can't call yourself a trolley museum with only one car, as the MTM realised. So they neatly side-stepped the issue from the first by deciding to function not solely as a collector of trolleys, but rather as a comprehensive museum of Minnesota transport in all its forms, using the operating trolley line as the central focus of the proposed display. As a result, a collection of Minnesota's road and rail vehicles has been acquired, and wherever Minnesota trolleys are found, they are quickly snapped up.

Two derelict Duluth carbodies were found at one time, for example, and after years of effort, one has now been restored to operating condition and pristine appearance. Moreover, though the streamlined PCC car of the 1930s is already well represented in other museums, a few of Minneapolis' fleet of 300 PCC cars work to this day in Mexico City, in Newark, New Jersey, and in Shaker Heights, Ohio, after Minneapolis ceased trolley operations in 1954. Undoubtedly, at least one of these cars will be available to the museum in the near future.

Operation of #1300 was first undertaken in 1963 when, in a partially restored state, it ran in a St. Paul railroad yard with the assistance of a gasoline-motored generator hitched on the back. The interest in the car was intense, prompting the group to seek a permanent operating home for the car. In 1969 the group approached the Minneapolis Parks and Recreation Board, owner of an abandoned section of Twin Cities right-of-way between Lake Harriet and Lake Calhoun, four miles southwest of downtown Minneapolis. The Board was interested, and a partnership was arranged in which the group was permitted to use the present site for the car.

MINNESOTA TRANSPORTATION MUSEUM. The trolley line is only one facet of the organization. It also has a number of mainline rail-road pieces, including this *Dan Patch Line* pioneer gas-electric locomotive, at other locations.

Frank E. Sandberg

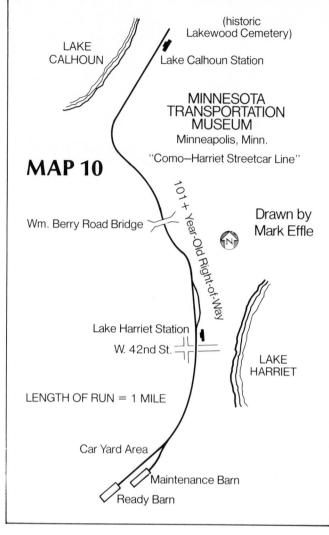

MAP 10

(historic Lakewood Cemetery)

LAKE CALHOUN

Lake Calhoun Station

MINNESOTA TRANSPORTATION MUSEUM

Minneapolis, Minn.

"Como—Harriet Streetcar Line"

101+ Year-Old Right-of-Way

Wm. Berry Road Bridge

Drawn by Mark Effle

N

Lake Harriet Station

W. 42nd St.

LAKE HARRIET

LENGTH OF RUN = 1 MILE

Car Yard Area

Maintenance Barn

Ready Barn

The enthusiasts were delighted to find over 300' of track still in place when they moved in, and by 1971 a further 1,200' had been added. August 1971 saw #1300 move its first revenue load, albeit still using the gas-motored generator. With the completion of a rectifier substation and the stringing of overhead wire in August 1973, #1300 started full electrical operation. The line was extended in August 1977 to just under a mile in length, upgraded and realigned to put it into top condition.

The city location has been of inestimable benefit. The year 1979 saw more than 50,000 passengers carried by just one car in an operating season closely matching that of the Seashore Museum. By contrast, Seashore's 1979 figure was its recent average of about 40,000, a reflection of its relative isolation, distance from a major city and that year's gasoline shortages. (The one-millionth recorded passenger rode the line during the summer of 1982.)

Normally a crew of three operates the line, changing shifts every three or four hours. Two stay aboard the car, the third stays on the platform at the 42nd Street end, sells tokens and flags the car across the line's single grade crossing.

The rest of the collection has not been neglected.

The restored Duluth car joined #1300 for the 1982 season. Current work at the Lake Como site includes the provision of turning loops at each end of the line and a further extension.

Steam railroad locomotives and cars have been acquired over the past few years as part of a project to create a live steam railroad museum at another local site. A complete restoration of the Dan Patch locomotive was completed in 1978; this was the first U.S.-built internal combustion locomotive and dates from 1913.

Fleet No.	Principal Owner	Builder, Year	Remarks
City and Suburban Cars			
78	Duluth Street Railway	Laclede, 1893	
265	Duluth Street Railway	Twin Cities, 1915	
1300	Twin Cities Rapid Transit	Twin Cities, 1908	
1496	Twin Cities Rapid Transit	Twin Cities, 1912	
Rapid Transit Cars			
4325	Chicago Transit Authority	Cincinnati, 1922	Elevated Car
4387	Chicago Transit Authority	Cincinnati, 1924	Elevated Car

MINNESOTA TRANSPORTATION MUSEUM. This museum's line is actually a portion of a former *Twin Cities Rapid Transit* route, the Como-Harriet line. Two cars now operate for visitors (#1300 is pictured at the Lake Harriet Station).
Frank E. Sandberg

Fleet No.	Principal Owner	Builder, Year	Remarks
Interurban Car			
10	Mesaba Electric Railway	Niles, 1913	Interurban
Motor Buses			
630	Twin Cities Rapid Transit	Mack, 1942	C-3
1399	Twin Cities Rapid Transit	GMC, 1954	TDH-5105
Steam Locomotives			
328	Northern Pacific	Alco, 1907	4-6-0
2156	Northern Pacific	Baldwin, 1909	4-6-2
Internal Combustion Locomotives			
61	Alter Corpn.	Plymouth, 1939	Diesel-Mechanical
100	Dan Patch Lines	GE, 1913	Gas-Electric
Steam Railroad Passenger Cars			
480	Great Northern	Pullman, 1917	Baggage
1084	Great Northern	Pullman, 1920	Solarium-Observation
1096	Great Northern	Pullman, 1946	Coach
1102	Northern Pacific	Pullman, 1914	Passenger/Baggage/RPO
1370	Northern Pacific	Pullman, 1915	Coach
2604	Chicago, Rock Island & Pacific	, 1927	Commuter Coach
Steam Railroad Freight Cars and Cabooses			
1091	General American Transportation		Tank Car
1653	Northern Pacific		Caboose
14287	Chicago, Burlington & Quincy		Caboose
14534	Chicago, Burlington & Quincy	, 1872	Caboose
37343	Union Refrigerator	GATX, 1948	Refrigerator
99014	Soo Line	, 1887	Caboose

All of the collection shown (except for Nos. 265 and 1300) were recently removed from the St. Paul railroad shop after it was closed.

Ohio • Olmsted Falls

Trolleyville USA. Located at the Columbia Park shopping center on Route 252, a short distance southwest of Cleveland. Owned and operated by the Gerald E. Brookins Museum of Electric Railways, Inc., 7100B Columbia Road, Olmsted Falls, OH 44138. The line is sometimes known as the Columbia Park and South Western. Standard gauge.

TRADITIONALLY, America has been the land of opportunity for those who wanted to take advantage of it. The ownership and operation of antique trolleys has been no exception—if you become successful enough in your life's calling to have sufficient money to indulge your hobby. Trolleyville USA is a case in point.

Columbia Park is a 130-acre parcel of land located in Olmsted Falls, owned by the family of the late Gerald E. Brookins, a successful businessman who passed away January 25, 1983. In the late 1950s he began to develop part of this property as a trailer park, including

a small shopping mall at the entrance. Soon after, he conceived the idea of building an electric trolley line through the trailer park as a service to the residents who were to be relieved of the long walk, and as a promotional venture.

He bought a batch of cars from the nearby Shaker Heights line where second-hand streamliners were going into service. Initially these cars were stored on a service track on display next to the shopping mall, but as the scheme progressed, track, poles and overhead wire were bought from Cleveland and building of the 1½-mile route began in 1961.

Professional labor was hired for the job (primarily retired transit employees) and the entire line was ready for operation at the start of 1962. At the same time a large batch of cars was purchased from the Chicago, Aurora and Elgin line, then recently closed, and after years of storage in Chicago, these began to arrive at Olmsted Falls in 1963. In that year the full service was begun.

The line was quickly provided with a museum build-

TROLLEYVILLE USA. Power for the streetcars. These motor-generator sets were purchased from the Connecticut Electric Railway Museum and were originally from the *Uncanoonuc Mountain Railway,* located at Goffstown, New Hampshire.

TROLLEYVILLE USA. A crew prepares to work on the overhead feeder system in front of the car-barn in June 1962. Pole at right carries feeder wires from the motor-generator sets inside.
BOTH: William E. Wood

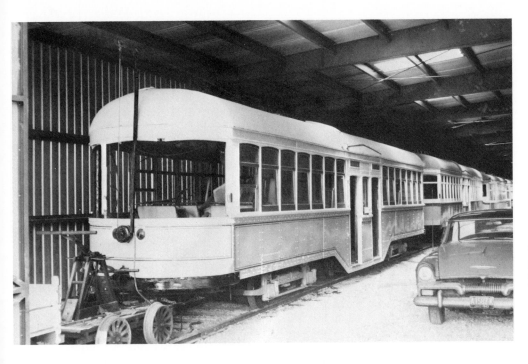

TROLLEYVILLE USA. One of the museum's 1200 series Cleveland cars was under restoration when this view was taken inside the all-metal barn in 1962. The center-entrance streetcars last served on the *Shaker Heights Rapid Transit.*
William E. Wood

ing and a carhouse, while the shopping mall provided a waiting room and ticket office. But it soon became clear that while the enterprise was a success, it was tourists who were doing most of the riding, not the residents and (as usual) the tourists wanted open cars to ride. In the mid-'60s a few open trolleys were still to be found. A vacation to Vera Cruz, Mexico, resulted in Mr. Brookins buying three U.S.-built open cars of which two came to Trolleyville. Since then more exotic cars have been imported, including a car from Fribourg, Switzerland, and a double-deck Blackpool Standard car from England (the latter unhappily is locked away in a small shed at present and out of public view).

This is a well-run tourist trolley line. It maintains its vehicles in excellent condition with the help of a dedicated, full-time, wage-earning staff. Because the original concept of Trolleyville was one of transport

service, the early purchases of seemingly identical cars were an attempt to provide some form of standardisation. But, because Mr. Brookins was a man who knew his traction history, the cars are of considerable historical interest also since they remain largely unduplicated elsewhere. This neat, clean and tidy operation is a model.

In more recent times, Trolleyville has begun to acquire single cars of historical interest wherever they can be found, and in whatever condition. With its facilities and staff, there has been little problem making many of these acquisitions fit for service and consequently Trolleyville today has a representative selection of trolleys and interurbans which either ran or were built in the state of Ohio. Relations with the local traction historical groups are good and cooperation is extensive. This is a most rewarding place to visit.

Fleet No.	Principal Owner	Builder, Year	Remarks
City and Suburban Cars			
4	Fribourg, Switzerland	, 1897	
9	Vera Cruz, Mexico	Brill, 1908	10-bench Open Car
19	Vera Cruz, Mexico	Brill, 1908	10-bench Open Car
147	Blackpool Corporation, England	Blackpool Corpn., 1924	Double Deck
585	Community Traction & Light (Toledo, Ohio)	American, 1911	
1218	Shaker Heights RT, Ohio	Kuhlman, 1913	Center Entrance
1225	Shaker Heights RT, Ohio	Kuhlman, 1913	Center Entrance
2227	Cincinnati Street Railway	Cincinnati, 1915	
2319	Cleveland Railway	Kuhlman, 1916	Trailer
4145	Pittsburgh Railway	Pressed Steel, 1911	
Interurban Cars			
36	Chicago, Aurora & Elgin	Stephenson, 1902	Interurban
40	Fostoria & Fremont	Colman, 1923	Combine
83	Lorain & Cleveland Electric Railway	Brill, 1898	Interurban
302	Aurora, Elgin & Fox River	St. Louis, 1924	Lightweight

Fleet No.	Principal Owner	Builder, Year	Remarks
303	Aurora, Elgin & Fox River	St. Louis, 1924	Lightweight
303	Chicago, Aurora & Elgin	Niles, 1906	Interurban
304	Aurora, Elgin & Fox River	St. Louis, 1924	Lightweight
306	Aurora, Elgin & Fox River	St. Louis, 1924	Lightweight
319	Chicago, Aurora & Elgin	Jewett, 1909	Interurban
409	Chicago, Aurora & Elgin	Pullman, 1923	Interurban
451	Chicago, Aurora & Elgin	St. Louis, 1945	Interurban
453	Chicago, Aurora & Elgin	St. Louis, 1945	Interurban
458	Chicago, Aurora & Elgin	St. Louis, 1945	Interurban
460	Chicago, Aurora & Elgin	St. Louis, 1945	Interurban
	Toledo Railway & Light	Toledo Rlwy & Lt., 1906	Private Car
100	Iowa Southern	American, 1914	Box Motor (?)
101	Iowa Southern	American, 1915	Box Motor (?)

Maintenance of Way Equipment

1	Iowa Southern	, 1896	Line Car

Interurban and Steam Railroad Freight Cars and Cabooses

102	Iowa Southern		Caboose
518021	Norfolk & Western RR	N&W, 1923	Caboose

Ohio • Worthington

Ohio Railway Museum. On Proprietor's Road, off Ohio 161, one mile west of I-71 in Worthington, a suburb of Columbus, Ohio. Owned and operated by the Ohio Railway Museum, P.O. Box 171, Worthington, OH 43085. Standard gauge.

THE ORIGINS OF this museum date to 1945 and the founding of the Central Ohio Railfans' Association, a social group interested in both trolley cars and railroads. In 1946, the Eastern Ohio chapter of the National Railroad Historical Society donated a car to the fledgling group and things got underway. One member owned property at the present museum site, and after lengthy negotiations the group first leased and then purchased the site, moving in during 1948 and laying down track shortly thereafter.

In 1950 the group was formally incorporated as a not-for-profit corporation dedicated to building and operating a museum for old railroad and trolley equipment which would be open to the public. Electric operations began in 1952, a carbarn was erected in the same year and, by 1954, 2,000 feet of track was in service, with another 900 feet under construction.

Power was originally obtained from one of the exhibits, a gas-electric car of the Erie Railroad. However the museum set a precedent in the movement when in 1960 it switched over to commercially supplied power, converting to trolley voltage with its own motor-generator set. Most museums have abandoned the bulky and temperamental gasoline or diesel-powered generators of early days to use commercial power through MG sets, rotary-converters or solid-state rectifiers, but Worthington was the first.

In the early years this was one of the few museums to collect interurban cars. This was due in part to the historic right-of-way, a part of the Columbus, Delaware and Marion's Worthington cut-off, built in 1923 (and closed in 1933) to provide speedier service by avoiding Worthington's crowded streets. The line had crossed

OHIO RAILWAY MUSEUM. This 1949 double-end PCC car of the *Illinois Terminal Railroad,* seen here crossing the bridge over Highway 161, was for some years on loan to the Shaker Heights, Ohio, Rapid Transit and used in daily service.
Ohio Railway Museum

OHIO RAILWAY MUSEUM. A beautifully restored Kuhlman-built 1926 city car of Columbus, Ohio, #703 was resurrected from a carbody by museum forces.

Ohio Railway Museum

OHIO RAILWAY MUSEUM. PCC car #450 is seen coming off the Route 161 bridge and is about to pass *Columbus, Delaware & Marion* interurban parlor car #501. The latter was a carbody only, superbly restored to operating condition, and is one of the few vehicles in the whole trolley movement still to be seen on its home tracks, since the ORM right-of-way is a small portion of what was in earlier days the Worthington cutoff of the CD&M.

Ohio Railway Museum

Ohio 161 on a trestle, which was long gone by the time the museum took possession of the site.

Negotiations with the local authorities went on for years over the replacement of this trestle and finally permission was obtained to erect a substantial replacement bridge, able to bear the weight of steam locomotives and heavy interurban cars. The bridge, too, opened up a considerable amount of new right-of-way on which to ultimately lay tracks and give the interurban cars space to "open up." At present the line is two miles long and services begin at the neatly kept station building, housing ticket offices, the dispatcher's office and a well-stocked gift shop.

The car collection is regional, specializing in the midwest. Restoration is done at the museum, two of the most interesting examples being interurban cars of local origin. Other interurban equipment comes from Ohio operators, while there are city cars from places as far apart as Detroit and Kansas City.

From the first, this museum has looked on itself as a rail transportation museum rather than simply a trolley museum. Much railroad equipment has been bought, along with the trolleys and interurbans, and steam trains are run regularly, intermingled with the trolleys.

OHIO RAILWAY MUSEUM. Though mentioned in the text, it is not until one sees the impressive bridge built over Ohio 161 that it can be understood how massive an undertaking it was and how substantial is the resulting structure. *Ohio Railway Museum*

OHIO RAILWAY MUSEUM. On a snowy day, *Chicago, North Shore & Milwaukee #154*, is posed towards the south end of the line. The ex-New York Central railroad is seen in the background, while the pole for the overhead line also carries an interurban signal unit. *Ohio Railway Museum*

Fleet No.	Principal Owner	Builder, Year	Remarks
City and Suburban Cars			
450	Illinois Terminal	St. Louis, 1949	PCC, Double End
472	Metropolitan St. Ry. (Kansas City)	Brownell, 1900	
703	Columbus Ry. Power & Light	Kuhlman, 1926	
1545	Kansas City Public Service	American, 1919	Birney Safety
3876	Detroit Dept. of Street Rys.	St. Louis, 1931	Peter Witt
Interurban Cars			
21	Ohio Public Service	Niles, 1905	Combine
41	Ohio Public Service	Kuhlman, 1924	Lightweight
119	Cincinnati & Lake Erie	Cincinnati, 1930	High Speed Lightweight

Fleet No.	Principal Owner	Builder, Year	Remarks
154	Chicago, North Shore & Milwaukee	Brill, 1915	Interurban
501	Columbus, Delaware & Marion	ACF, 1926	Parlor Car
Rapid Transit Cars			
4441	Chicago Transit Authority	Cincinnati, 1924	Elevated Car
4449	Chicago Transit Authority	Cincinnati, 1924	Elevated Car
Maintenance of Way Cars and Equipment			
C-2	Toronto Transportation Commission	TTC, 1924	Crane
C-124	Philadelphia Rapid Transit	Brill, 1924	Snow Sweeper
7763	Eastern Michigan	Detroit United, 1924	Line Car
Electric Locomotives			
2	Columbus Ry., Power & Light	CPR&L, 1926	Steeple Cab
7	Cornwall St. Ry., Power & Light	Baldwin/WH, 1922	
067	Columbus Ry., Power & Light	CRP&L, 1924	Center Cab Flat Car
Steam Locomotives			
1	Marble Cliff Quarries, Columbus	Vulcan, 1924	0-4-0T
578	Norfolk & Western RR	Alco, 1910	4-6-2
Internal Combustion Car			
5012	Erie RR	EMC, 1931	Gas-Electric Car
Steam Railroad Passenger Cars			
1511	Norfolk & Western RR	Harlan & Hollingsworth (?), 1918	Combine
4080	Southern		Baggage
7530	Pennsylvania RR	PRR, 1928	Business Car *Williamsport*
9510	Pennsylvania RR	PRR, 1926	RPO
	Pennsylvania RR	Pullman, 1929	Sleeper *John Greenleaf Whittier*
	Pennsylvania RR	Pullman, 1925	Sleeper *Times Square*
Interurban and Steam Railroad Freight Cars and Cabooses			
1003	Columbus, Delaware & Marion	Toledo & Ohio Central RR, 1898	Flat Car
02208	Baltimore & Ohio RR	B&O, 1915	Caboose
8010	North American Car	North American, 1927	Box Car
982131	Pennsylvania Railroad	PRR, 1906	Caboose

Oregon • Glenwood

The Trolley Park. Located at Glenwood, 39 miles west of Portland on Route 6. Owned and operated by the Oregon Electric Railway Historical Society, Star Route 1318, Glenwood, OR 97120. Standard gauge.

THOUGH WHAT IS acknowledged to be America's first electric interurban was built in the Portland area back in the 1890s, the Pacific Northwest had few trolley towns. Those systems which flourished were concentrated around Seattle, Spokane, Yakima, Tacoma and Portland. But those who regretted the trolley's disappearance were equally as dedicated to the museum as their eastern counterparts. The OERHS was established in 1957 to cater to those who deplored the gradual closure of Portland's trolley system.

The present site was located, tracks laid, wires strung, power connected and cars running. That should have been that. But it was at this point Glenwood's experience began to diverge markedly from the other museums. It was the first to notice visitor preference for riding open cars in the mild Oregon climate, and the relative indifference to restoration and museum display.

A lot of this indifference had to do with the museum's location. Those who made the journey to Glenwood were as much there for a day out in the country and a picnic in Oregon's timber lands as they were to ride trolleys. But to make so long a trip to the museum only for a short visit seemed to many a waste of effort, the more so since the ocean was but 30 miles further on. Thus the museum was being passed by.

If Glenwood was to survive, it had to start catering

THE TROLLEY PARK. Standing in front of one of the museum's rustic buildings is *British Columbia Electric Railway #1304, rebuilt* by that company in the 1940s after a fire virtually destroyed its frame. *Mark Effle*

more to its public's tastes. As simple survival is top of any museum's priority list, some imagination had to be exercised. The concept of a tourist trolley line had not yet been formulated and the task was difficult. Where do we go from here, now the cars are running, was the basic question and the answer was not easily found.

But over the years Glenwood has found the answer lay in the physical beauty of its location and has gradually converted itself into a "trolley park," a lovely place where visitors can be catered to for a day, or for an overnight camping stay, in which the operating trolley line is but one attraction among many. Implementation has not been easy but the site now boasts campgrounds, creeks, fishing, swimming and quiet outdoor relaxation as key elements of the park. It has become a place where kids and their parents can go their separate ways to "do their own thing" in safety, and be all guaranteed a good time.

That's fine for the summer and Glenwood's principal success has been in the summer, attracting day trippers from Portland and camping families from further afield. But imagination has not been confined to making the summer months worthwhile. The site was originally owned by a logging railroad which had built some very substantial barns, which still survive.

Over the years, these barns have been converted into a fine set of winterized trolley shops. New

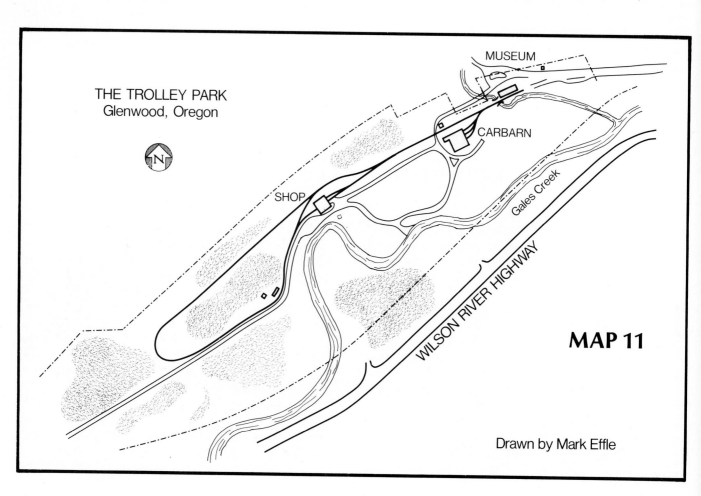

THE TROLLEY PARK
Glenwood, Oregon

MUSEUM

CARBARN

SHOP

Gales Creek

WILSON RIVER HIGHWAY

MAP 11

Drawn by Mark Effle

concrete floors, pits and heating were installed and the place has been crammed with elderly woodworking machinery originally built to repair wooden-bodied trolley cars. These were bought from Portland's bus operator in the '70s when new OSHA regulations made the machines obsolete there.

These facilities have been used on a number of long-term winter work projects which, among other things, are designed to bring a little extra revenue to the OERHS. In the main these have been trolley car restorations, both for Glenwood and for private customers. One of the more interesting private orders has been the restoration of a number of derelict Birney safety car-

bodies of the 1920s (ironically *metal-bodied* cars) for use as decorative centerpieces in the nationwide *Old Spaghetti Factory* restaurant chain.

Paul Class of this museum was deeply involved in the ARM bulk purchase of open cars from South America in 1965, a spin-off from Glenwood's desperate search for open cars which in the early '60s had led them to import trolleys from Australia and Britain. The museum shops have also hosted many cars from Portugal and Australia, destined for various streetcar revival projects including those in Yakima, Seattle and Detroit, and other more tentative projects in Portland and Aspen.

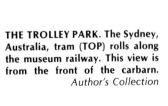

THE TROLLEY PARK. The Sydney, Australia, tram (TOP) rolls along the museum railway. This view is from the front of the carbarn.
Author's Collection

THE TROLLEY PARK. The site of the Glenwood museum is one of great peace and tranquility. Portland car #4012 is seen passing the site of what today is the picnic grounds, shortly after completion of the loop in 1978. *A.D. Young*

THE MUSEUMS • 123

Glenwood's tracks have been completely relocated in the last ten years and a large new turning loop has been added. Landscaping has begun and the remainder of the barns are being rehabilitated. A new feature recently added is an interpretive exhibition on the trolley's impact on American life. This is located at the entrance inside the station building. Many of the streetcars under restoration are displayed in appropriate shop and barn settings and in the midst of this cars continue to run every summer.

For Portland residents, there are a reassuring number of local cars to be seen along with vehicles from Vancouver and elsewhere. For the visitor from further afield, the cars provide an interesting museum display against an incomparable trolley park setting.

The year 1983 will see Glenwood's 20th year under wire. Using a powerplant from a U.S. Navy submarine, Glenwood's first car ran June 18, 1963. The public was admitted from September 1 and the place has never looked back.

Fleet No.	Principal Owner	Builder, Year	Remarks
City and Suburban Cars			
48	Blackpool Corporation, England	Blackpool Corporation, 1928	Double Deck
503	Portland Ry., Light & Power	Brill, 1902	Semi-Convertible
506	Portland Ry., Light & Power	Brill, 1902	Semi-Convertible
1187	Sydney, Australia	Meadowbank, 1912	Compartment
4012	Portland Traction	Brill, 1932	Master Unit
1159	Municipal Ry. of San Francisco	St. Louis, 1946	PCC (ex-St. Louis)
Interurban Car			
1304	British Columbia Electric Ry.	BCER, 1946	Interurban
Maintenance of Way Car			
1455	Portland Ry., Light & Power	McGuire, 1895	Snow Sweeper

Pennsylvania • Rockhill Furnace

Shade Gap Electric Railway. The trolley station is adjacent to the terminal of the East Broad Top RR at Rockhill Furnace, PA. Access via Fort Littleton exit of Pennsylvania Turnpike, and north on Route 522 to Rockhill Furnace via Orbisonia. The Shade Gap Electric Railway is owned and operated by Railways to Yesterday, 328 North 28th Street, Allentown, PA 18104. Standard gauge.

FONTAINE FOX'S cartoon strip, "The Toonerville Trolley that meets all the trains" was a much loved and widely syndicated feature, whose success was due in no small part to the cheerful antiquity and happily appalling state of the little trolley, a symbol of all the public felt to be wrong with transit in the 1920s. Without wanting to duplicate the Toonerville Trolley's dilapidated state, the Shade Gap Electric Railway is a wonderful example of a Toonerville operation, since it

has Toonerville-style cars which do, indeed, meet all the trains, in this case the narrow-gauge steam passenger trains of the East Broad Top Railway, a registered U.S. historic landmark.

Rockhill Furnace and nearby Orbisonia have a combined population of only 1,000, and lie in one of the most isolated sections of the Alleghenies. But coal is in the area, and coal is what prompted the construction of the East Broad Top RR and Coke Co. in the 19th century. Closed in 1956, it was reopened in part as a tourist line in 1960.

In that year, the trolleys ran for the last time in Johnstown, Pa., and with their passing died the very last U.S. small-town trolley system. Louis Buehler bought one of the old cars, and with the help of Tolbert Prowell a lease was negotiated with the East Broad Top RR, under which the railroad would lay both standard and narrow-gauge track over a portion of the still-closed Shade Gap branch.

SHADE GAP ELECTRIC RAILWAY. Although yet to be fully restored, ex-Rio de Janeiro #1875, a Brill-built open car which came back to the U.S. as part of the A.R.M. mass purchase in 1965, has always been mechanically sound and thus able to earn its keep at the Shade Gap museum. *A.D. Young*

The work was begun in 1961 and by October 13, 1962, 1,800 feet of track was ready for use. Wiring began a week previously, using a "new" never-before-used roll of trolley wire bought in 1917 by Ohio's Lake Shore Electric Railway and sold by them on closure in 1938 to Mr. N. Kovalchick, a metal dealer who dismantled the LSE and who by 1961 was owner of the East Broad Top. On October 13, Mr. Prowell operated the first electric car on the Shade Gap line.

Over the next few years the track was further extended and more cars purchased. Originally only one car was to have run in connection with the EBT trains, and no museum was contemplated. But the collecting bug bites deep and since 1961 quite a range of vehicles has arrived at Shade Gap, mainly from mid-Atlantic states operators or from companies which had the right kind of "Toonerville" image cars, in either open or closed versions. At Shade Gap, the open cars are U.S.-built, part of the ARM mass purchase from Brazil. The older closed cars include U.S.-built vehicles from Portugal. The most spectacular recent purchase has been of a complete *Electroliner* from its most recent owner, the Southeast Pennsylvania Transit Authority.

The trolley terminal is adjacent to the steam railroad's impressive station and forms part of the steam train's reversing triangle. There is an awe-inspiring quantity of mixed-gauge track, which extends about a third of the way along the electrified Shade Gap branch. Extensions are planned, there is a carbarn and a gift shop and more barns are planned so the whole fleet can go under cover and more cars, stored off the site, can be brought in.

Hurricane "Agnes" hit the museum in summer 1972, severely affecting operations when a flooding creek washed out a large section of track. This same hurricane totally wiped out the museum at Magee, Pa., and for a while there was some doubt if Shade Gap would survive. With difficulty the washed-out sections were restored to service; an act of faith on behalf of the museum's leadership that has been amply repaid since then.

While the trolley certainly does meet all the trains, the trolley service is much more frequent than that of the railroad and this small museum, once merely an adjunct to it, has taken on a vigorous life of its own. Part of its regularly scheduled year of activities has been an unusual and thrilling winter spectacular held in mid-February, featuring operating snowplows and winter rides in both open and closed cars. More recent years have seen this event moved into spring.

SHADE GAP ELECTRIC RAILWAY. Oporto, Portugal, #249 at East Broad Top Junction. Built by Brill in 1904, it served Oporto until 1972, when it was acquired by the museum. *Louis J.G. Buehler*

SHADE GAP ELECTRIC RAILWAY. Mixed freight and passenger train pulled by East Broad Top #12 and #14 rolls along on 3-foot gauge tracks past *Chicago, Aurora & Elgin* #315 during the 1977 Winter Spectacular at Orbisonia. *P.W. Laepple*

Fleet No.	Principal Owner	Builder, Year	Remarks
City and Suburban Cars			
13	Philadelphia & Suburban (Red Arrow)	St. Louis, 1949	PCC-style Double-end
23	Philadelphia & Suburban (Red Arrow)	St. Louis, 1949	PCC-style Double-end
163	York Railways (Penna.)	Cincinnati, 1924?	Lightweight Curveside
172	Oporto, Portugal	Brill, 1905	Semi-Convertible
249	Oporto, Portugal	Brill, 1904	Semi-Convertible
311	Johnstown Traction Co. (Penna.)	Wason, 1922	Double Truck Birney Safety
322	Rio de Janeiro Tramway, Light & Power	Brill, 1908	12-bench Open
362	Johnstown Traction Co. (Penna.)	St. Louis, 1927	Lightweight
1430	D.C. Transit/Capital Transit	St. Louis, 1944	PCC
1875	Rio de Janeiro Tramway, Light & Power	Brill, 1915	13-bench Open
Interurban Cars			
315	Chicago, Aurora & Elgin	Kuhlman, 1909	
802	Philadelphia Suburban/North Shore	St. Louis, 1941	Electroliner
Maintenance of Way Cars			
09	D.C. Transit	McGuire, 1898	Snow Sweeper
026	D.C. Transit	Brill, 1905	Snow Sweeper
64	Oporto, Portugal	Brill, 1904	Twin Cab Flat
107	Scranton, Penna.		Snow Sweeper
Internal Combustion Locomotive			
4	Mack Trucks		Gas-Electric Switcher
Trolley Coaches			
623	Wilmington, Delaware	Brill, 1939	40SMT
710	Johnstown Traction Co. (Penna.)	Brill, 1942	40SMT

Pennsylvania • Washington

Arden Trolley Museum. Entrance two miles north of Washington, Pa., on North Main Street extension. Owned and operated by the Pennsylvania Railway Museum Association, P.O. Box 832, Pittsburgh, PA 15230. 5'2½" gauge.

THE GAUGE OF THE TRACK at this compact regional museum of transport was almost universal in western Pennsylvania, in Philadelphia and on many of the state's interurbans. It was rarely used elsewhere. It is said that the hostility of the railroads toward the interurban and the rural trolley in the state led to the passage of legislation ensuring that the interurban trolley and local systems would have a gauge incompatible with direct interchange between railroad and trolley. Certainly the widespread use of the 5'2½" gauge prevented much easy freight interchange with the railroads at a time when both could have benefitted; but that was in later years when the interurban was on the decline. In the early years, the incompatibility of gauge seemed less important and the use of

this singular gauge at the museum is due entirely to the proximity of Pittsburgh and the continued existence of much historically interesting rolling stock from the region. That dictated the character of the museum from the outset.

The idea of a wide-gauge trolley museum to serve the Pittsburgh region is almost as old as the movement itself, for it was in 1940 a local group was formed to buy an elderly Pittsburgh trailer car. But, unlike the contemporary Seashore and Warehouse Point groups, the Pittsburgh group did not survive the war. Since no suitable site could be found and the car itself was gradually vandalized in the meanwhile, the group was eventually compelled to sell the car for scrap in 1944.

From that sad experience the Pittsburgh Electric Railway Club hoped to profit. In 1949 it, too, acquired an historic Pittsburgh city car, but once again the club seemed doomed to repeat its predecessors' experience when years were consumed in a futile search for an appropriate site. Matters came to a head in 1952 after the closure of the wide-gauge West Penn Railway,

dismantled by Pittsburgh Railways. This left the museum without traction current until their own electrical operations were ready to begin in 1962.

But a good start had been made. By 1955, 2,100 feet of track was the museum's and the first carbarn was completed by 1960. More cars were purchased, principally from lines in Western Pennsylvania and from New Orleans, the only major operator outside the state to share the unique gauge. New Orleans #832, the car chosen for the Arden collection has an even greater distinction, having achieved international fame when it appeared in a *Life* magazine article about the movie version of Tennessee Williams' play, *A Streetcar Named Desire*.

ARDEN TROLLEY MUSEUM. Pittsburgh #4398 and New Orleans #832 are among the workhorses of the operating fleet. They are shown here being spruced up for another heavy day's service.
Arden Trolley Museum

possibly the only interurban network to succumb to the impact of television and the change in riding habits wrought thereby. A car from that system had been purchased and it now became imperative to find a site, since the West Penn itself seemed bereft of anything suitable. But it was not until late 1953 that it was finally found. That site is the present one, which became available after the Pittsburgh Railways interurban route to Washington, Pa., was cut back to its present-day Drake terminal point on the Allegheny county line. It is a straight and almost level stretch, with a long passing siding, some two miles north of Washington, Pa., and the first three cars arrived from Pittsburgh under their own power after a temporary sojourn in Ingram carhouse. This move was completed in February 1954, and it was the last made on the Washington line as a complete entity, for the route was then

The present line gives a 20-minute round trip and ambitious extension plans for both track and facilities, first mooted in the early 1970s, are now coming to fruition. The well-equipped Reynolds Galbraith car shop was one of the first projects to be completed as part of these plans, being dedicated in August 1976. Track work is now underway on another extension of 5/8ths of a mile, utilizing the roadbed of an old coal mine spur. This will loop near the village of Arden Mines and is being funded by a grant from the Pittsburgh History and Landmarks Commission.

What little remains of the once-giant Pittsburgh trolley system's rolling stock consists of streamline PCC cars, of which there are already a number of representatives at this (and other) museums. Reconstruction of what's left of the Pittsburgh system is well underway and it will shortly metamorphasize as a brand-new

ARDEN TROLLEY MUSEUM. Two volunteers affix siding to the Reynolds Galbraith car shop in 1976. *Arden Trolley Museum*

ARDEN TROLLEY MUSEUM. The Reynolds Galbraith car shop under construction in 1976. It is a 40' by 160' pole structure.
Arden Trolley Museum

Light Rail system, complete with articulated cars built in West Germany. Since all Pittsburgh's old-time trolleys (or representative samples of them) are now at this museum, within an hour's drive of the city, it is in a unique position to cater to large numbers of local visitors, and advertising by the museum is done regularly in the metropolitan area. A Pittsburgh car returned to the city from the museum during the Bicentennial weekend of 1976 and carried over 5,000 riders on a downtown loop route at an old-time fare of 10 cents, thereby generating much publicity and goodwill for the museum. Other special attractions held at the museum are part of the annual Trolley Fair and include old trolley movies, model railroads, art and craft displays, a flea market and, occasionally, vintage automobiles.

During the 1970s a standard gauge railroad siding was acquired, running parallel to the trolley right-of-way. This was done to enable the museum to house the nucleus of a railroad collection (almost all of it from Pennsylvania) and evolve into a comprehensive regional museum of transportation, rather than just a trolley museum specializing in Pittsburgh and the Coke region. But, of late, the emphasis has shifted back to the trolley with a bulk acquisition of cars from Philadelphia's former Red Arrow Lines. These cars were replaced in late 1982 by new Japanese-built Light Rail cars. The acquisition is the culmination of a long-held dream of owning a representative sample of every type of car that ever ran on the Red Arrow suburban trolley system in the 1950s. It is obvious, therefore, that this delightful little museum is quickly becoming a significant regional museum of Pennsylvania rail transport.

ARDEN TROLLEY MUSEUM. The restoration of Pittsburgh #4398 was among the very few that have been financed outside the trolley museum movement. In this case, a grant from the Pittsburgh History and Landmarks Foundation was bringing the car back to pristine condition. It was displayed at Station Square in downtown for a time after completion.
Arden Trolley Museum

ARDEN TROLLEY MUSEUM. Not the least of the desirable skills at a trolley museum is that of welding. Member Brad Lester is about to commence work.

Arden Trolley Museum

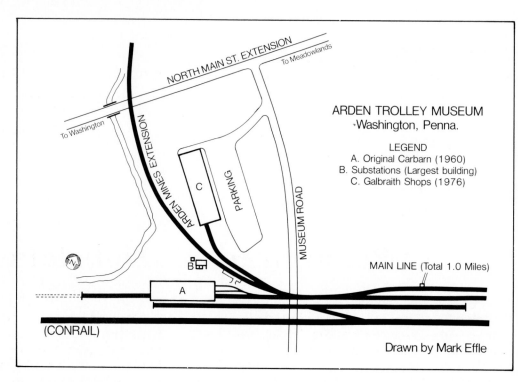

MAP 12

ARDEN TROLLEY MUSEUM
·Washington, Penna.

LEGEND
A. Original Carbarn (1960)
B. Substations (Largest building)
C. Galbraith Shops (1976)

NORTH MAIN ST. EXTENSION

To Meadowlands

To Washington

ARDEN MINES EXTENSION

PARKING

MUSEUM ROAD

MAIN LINE (Total 1.0 Miles)

(CONRAIL)

Drawn by Mark Effle

MAP 13

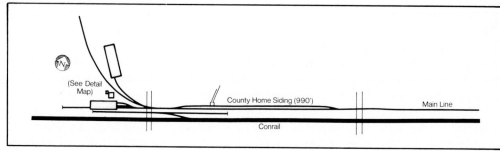

(See Detail Map)

County Home Siding (990')

Main Line

Conrail

Fleet No.	Principal Owner	Builder, Year	Remarks
Horse Car			
	Pgh., Allegheny & Manchester	Stephenson, 1893 ?	
City and Suburban Cars			
M-1	Pittsburgh Railways	Pullman, 1894	Pay Car
5	Red Arrow (Phila. Suburban)	Brill, 1941	Brilliner
14	Red Arrow (Phila. Suburban)	St. Louis, 1949	PCC-style Suburban
66	Red Arrow (Phila. Suburban)	Brill, 1925	Center-Entrance Suburban
78	Red Arrow (Phila. Suburban)	Brill, 1932	Master Unit Suburban
350	Johnstown Traction Co.	St. Louis, 1926	Lightweight
832	New Orleans Public Service	Perley Thomas, 1922	
1138	Pittsburgh Railways	St. Louis, 1937	PCC
1467	Pittsburgh Railways	St. Louis, 1941	PCC
3487	Pittsburgh Railways	St. Louis, 1905	High-Floor
3756	Pittsburgh Railways	Osgood Bradley, 1925	Low-Floor
4140	Pittsburgh Railways	Pressed Steel, 1911	High-Floor (M-200)
4398	Pittsburgh Railways	St. Louis, 1917	Low-Floor
5326	Philadelphia Transp. Co.	Brill, 1923	Lightweight
Interurban Cars			
274	Monongahela-West Penn	Jewett, 1918	Steel
722	West Penn Railways Co.	West Penn, 1921	Center-Entrance
832	West Penn Railways Co.	Cincinnati, 1930	Lightweight Curveside
Electric Locomotives			
1	West Penn Railways Co.	West Penn, 1916	Box Cab
3000	Monongahela-West Penn	Baldwin-West, 1921	Steeple Cab
Maintenance of Way Cars			
M-37	Pittsburgh Railways	McGuire, 1896	Snow Sweeper
M-56	Pittsburgh Railways/Beaver Valley	McGuire-Cummings, 1918	Sweeper
M-454	Pittsburgh Railways (ex-4115)	Pressed Steel, 1911	Work Car
T-16	Philadelphia Rapid Transit	Brill, 1913	Milk Car
2	Philadelphia Rapid Transit (C-125)	Brill, 1923	Line Car
3618	Boston Elevated Railways	Differential, 1927	Center Dump

Pennsylvania • Philadelphia

Waterfront Trolley. Located on Delaware Avenue, between the Benjamin Franklin Bridge and Penn's Landing. Standard gauge.

SINCE PHILADELPHIA remains one of the most comprehensively covered cities in the country so far as trolley services are concerned, it comes as a bit of a surprise that Philadelphia should be the locale of one of the newest tourist lines in the country. That, however, should only be a surprise momentarily. Philadelphia, after years of waiting and planning, has finally acquired a thoroughly modernized Light Rail system complete with a large fleet of new cars.

That has been complemented by a rejuvenated Light Rail system in the suburbs over the tracks of the former Red Arrow lines, together with a total revamp of 150 PCC cars and the trolley bus services. Moreover, the heavy subway system, too, is getting its share of new cars and thus the somewhat neglected and elderly Philadelphia electric transit system has taken a new lease on life.

The city of Philadelphia, noting the success of the Detroit operation described earlier in this book in rejuvenating the Washington Boulevard area, considered that the same success might attend its own waterfront project if a tourist trolley line were to be installed. The Buckingham Valley Trolley Association, temporarily without a home, was invited to run the line.

Immediate sponsors of the Delaware Avenue operation are known as Century VI, an organization set up to mark the city's 300th anniversary and in charge of the Penn's Landing project. It had been intended at first to run a steam train on the line, but the existing tracks of the Philadelphia Belt Line RR between Arch Street and Fitzwater Street were too rickety to allow for that, so a grant of $75,000 was offered by the city and Fidelity Bank jointly to turn the line into a tourist trolley operation. The money was spent on poles, overhead and converting a warehouse on Pier Five to be used as a carbarn.

The opening date was September 5, 1982, but operation has normally been confined to weekends up to the late Fall and tentatively scheduled from Easter to November in 1983. Originally a one-year operation was envisaged, but it is believed that the operation will now be permanent. Plans for 1983 include the possibility of running an open car originally from Wildwood, New Jersey's, Five Mile Beach line.

Fleet No.	Principal Owner	Builder, Year	Remarks
City and Suburban Cars			
9	Red Arrow Lines/SEPTA	Brill, 1941	Brilliner
15	Red Arrow Lines/SEPTA	St. Louis, 1949	PCC-style Double-end
26	Red Arrow Lines/SEPTA	Brill, 1918	Hog Island Car
76	Red Arrow Lines/SEPTA	Brill, 1932	Master Unit
80	Red Arrow Lines/SEPTA	Brill, 1932	Master Unit
120	Wilmington, Del./SEPTA	Brill, 1900	Rail Grinder
5205	Phila. Rapid Transit/SEPTA	Brill, 1923	
Interurban Car			
46	Philadelphia & Western/SEPTA	Brill, 1907	

Tennessee • Chattanooga

Chattanooga Choo Choo and Terminal Station. Located at 1400 Market Street, TN 37402, in the old railway terminal. Standard gauge.

CHATTANOOGA CHOO CHOO is an imaginative and dramatically spectacular redevelopment of Chattanooga's old Southern Railway Terminal. It comprises specialty shops and stores, restaurants, hotels, an ice rink and a magnificent model railway. The trolley line, a central focus for this complex, was established during 1973, the first trip being made on May 29.

Since then, the original quarter-mile-long trolley line has been extended a number of times to keep pace with the development. It reached the convention center in 1977, serving the station complex, the Choo Choo Hilton, ice rink and parking lot. It is an enormously busy line, the bulk of car service being provided by a nicely kept New Orleans car #952 in an inaccurate but pleasing yellow color. An open car, originally part of the mass purchase from Brazil in 1965, was acquired from the Warehouse Point museum recently, and entered service in 1980. A third car, New Orleans #959 has been bought from the neighboring Tennessee Valley Railroad museum, and it is hoped that it will be in service in 1984.

A further extension to the trolley line was made during 1981, and it now loops around the side of the Choo Choo restaurant. Choo Choo can boast a splendid array of railroad passenger cars, permanently stationed as a part of the hotel complex, providing eating, drinking and sleeping space for the thousands of tourists. The trolley, of course, meets all the trains. . . .

CHATTANOOGA CHOO CHOO. Ex-New Orleans car #952 rounds a curve in front of the concert and convention center. This building was formerly the Chattanooga freight house of the *Central of Georgia Railroad.*
David Steinberg

CHATTANOOGA CHOO CHOO. The trolley line at the Chattanooga Choo Choo complex serves the railroad station, the main section of which can be seen in the background. The various railroad coaches in the photograph are part of the Choo Choo Inn Hilton accommodations and are each divided into two rooms. A number of cars are also fitted out as lounges or bars. *David Steinberg*

Fleet No.	Principal Owner	Builder, Year	Remarks
City and Suburban Cars			
952	New Orleans Public Service	Perley Thomas, 1924	
959	New Orleans Public Service	Perley Thomas, 1924	
	Rio de Janeiro Tramway, Light & Power	St. Louis, 1912	12-bench Open

Texas • San Antonio

San Antonio Museum Association. Platform beside San Antonio Art Museum (old Lone Star Brewery), 300 W. Jones Ave., San Antonio, TX 78209. Standard gauge.

WHEN SAN ANTONIO'S streetcar system came to its end in 1933, track and wire were built into the grounds of the Witte museum, and San Antonio Public Service #300, a 1913 product of the American

Car Co., was rolled onto a specially built section of track. Then the connection was broken and the car remained on outside display until 1981.

By that time it had become what is commonly known as a "basket case," robbed of its motors, compressor and resistance grids during World War II; its body had become extremely shaky. Members of the San Antonio Museum Association, founded in 1926 to support such institutions as the Witte Museum, took up the cause and raised enough funds for a restoration. Rod Varney, a well-known electric railway historian, undertook to supervise the work, insisting that the body rebuilding be proper and authentic. The trucks, now devoid of motors and built to San Antonio's odd four-foot gauge, were found to be of no use if the car was to be operable, so a set of New Orleans Public Service trucks, with motors, were acquired. Railroad profile wheels were purchased and the trucks were re-gauged (from 5'2½" gauge) so the car could be used on open railroad track without difficulty. Most fortunately another body (#311) was located, still in use as a residence, and in far superior structural condition, so it was combined with small parts off the original #300 to become the "new" #300.

The restoration, completed in 1982, is high quality, and the car now daily roams over the electrified tracks

SAN ANTONIO MUSEUM ASSOCIATION. It took two old streetcar bodies to make one like-new streetcar #300. The thoroughness of the restorers is in these views of the Association's car. It carries passengers along the electrified freight trackage which serves the Pearl Brewery.
Both: Collection of John K. Kight

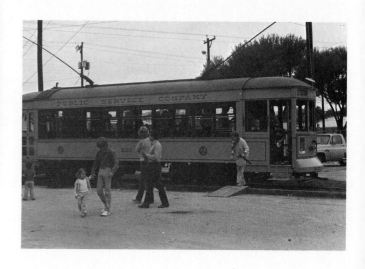

of the Pearl Brewery, usually on an hourly headway, serving the Art Museum (the old Lone Star Brewery), the Pearl Brewery, and the Jersey Lily Saloon. It is at present stored outdoors. Purchase of a ticket to any of the Association's three museums (Witte Museum, Art Museum or Transportation Museum at the Hemisphere Grounds) includes free rides on the car. While on the line, one can also see the Pearl Brewery's two vintage electric locomotives, still used to bring cars from the S.P. interchange.

SAN ANTONIO MUSEUM ASSO- CIATION. Visitors can often wit- ness electric locomotives switch- ing box cars at the Pearl Brewery.
*Texas Division,
Electric Railroaders' Association*

Washington • Seattle

The Waterfront Streetcar. Located on Alaskan Way and running from S. Main Street at Pier 48 to Broad Street at Pier 70. Owned and operated by Metro Transit of Seattle. Standard gauge.

THE LAST SEATTLE trolley car ran in 1940. Since then the city has relied on bus and trolley coach transit, apart from the unique Alweg monorail installed for the 1962 Fair. So it is quite unusual that, after a lapse of more than 40 years, Seattle has a batch of trolley cars once again running in public service. Even more odd is the fact that the cars are nearly as old as the vehicles scrapped way back in 1940!

The cars are back in Seattle as a result of the faith of Seattle City Councilman George Benson. He saw an operating vintage trolley line as providing the firm foundation on which to base a successful restoration of the city's historic waterfront district. Home of the original *Skid Row*, the Seattle waterfront has been greatly rejuvenated since the streetcar idea was first aired in 1974 and the Kingdome has already become a major focal point at the south end of the area.

What Councilman Benson felt was needed, how- ever, was not merely a focal point but an anchoring element which could knit together the disparate strands of a multi-block historic district and give to it a distinctive character.

To gauge response to the idea he arranged to borrow a Lisbon car already in the U.S. for another project. The car was displayed in Seattle for some weeks, the response was positive and the machinery was set in motion. Though progress was slow, it would have been far slower still had not the physical right-of-way already been in place. The Burlington Northern Railroad owned the present 1½-mile line which served the various piers. The present trend to roll-on roll-off containerized trucks has reduced railborne traffic to and from the docks and the railroad therefore was will- ing to let the city have use of the line.

Much of the time since 1974 has been used to com- plete the various obligatory studies, to prove the feasi- bility of the project, and to arrange funding. The line would have been open some years ago had not the city decided on an unprecedented total modernization and extension of its trolley coach network. Not until that was completed, in 1980, was the city able to turn its attention to equipping the streetcar line.

As with many other projects of this nature, Paul Class of Glenwood was appointed consultant. Since one of the major design parameters merely called for robust old-looking trolleys rather than insisting on something uniquely American, Mr. Class hit on the idea of buying elderly cars from Melbourne, Australia. These cars were in sound condition, and being with- drawn from daily service in their native city only because brand-new trolley cars were available to replace them.

So, three cars were duly shipped from Melbourne to

THE WATERFRONT STREETCAR.
The authentic atmosphere of a 1980s city (in this case a monumental double-deck freeway) is the backdrop to Seattle's tourist trolley line. *Michael Voris*

THE WATERFRONT STREETCAR.
One of the ex-Melbourne, Australia, trams is loading passengers at the Madison station.
Michael Voris

the U.S. at various times during 1978, finding their way to the Glenwood museum for reassembly and road testing, before proceeding onwards to Seattle. A fourth car, bought originally as a source for spares, arrived in 1980.

This line is an ambitious undertaking even for so experienced an undertaking as Seattle Metro. It is the first line to use Australian cars in this country. It is the first trolley line conceived of as an anchor to an historic district actually to have begun public service. It is

the first tourist trolley line in the U.S. to run as an integral part of a city's overall transit service. Moreover, the environment of the line is wholly urban and the trolleys fit perfectly in the scene—except, perhaps, in the eyes of the trolley purists.

The line opened on May 29, 1982, and was an immediate success. The cars operate every 15 minutes year-round and serve seven stops en route. The service is part of Seattle Transit and all Metro passes and transfers are honored. A direct connection with Metro route #11 is maintained at the Madison Street car stop. The line itself is known as Metro route #99.

Since the cars are of center-entrance design, it has been necessary to provide step-high platforms with associated shelters all along the line of route. Though of single-track layout throughout, there is a turnout about halfway along the line, at Pier 58. The carbarn is at the Broad Street end of the route and at that point current is fed to the overhead, via the usual solid-state rectifier apparatus. Route #99 serves the docks, Waterfront Park, parts of the lower downtown area, the Aquarium, the Kingdome and Pioneer Square. Its future looks very promising and it is likely that this kind of "vintage" trolley line will be the first of many.

The visitor to Seattle might also want to inspect Seattle cable car #13. This is an 1886 vehicle presently on static display in the Museum of History and Industry in Seattle. The presentation is a good example of how the success of the living trolley museum has influenced even the previously unimaginative static displays in more orthodox museums.

Seattle's last cable line on Yesler closed in August 1940. George W. Hilton, biographer of the cable car industry, has rightly commented that had the line survived World War Two, it would have been as great a tourist attraction for Seattle as the San Francisco cable cars have been to the Bay Area. But then there would have been no need for the waterfront trolley. . . .

Fleet No.	Principal Owner	Builder, Year
City and Suburban Cars		
272	Melbourne & Metropolitan Tramways Board, Australia	James Moore, 1925
482	Melbourne & Metropolitan Tramways Board, Australia	M&MTB, 1928
512	Melbourne & Metropolitan Tramways Board, Australia	M&MTB, 1929
518	Melbourne & Metropolitan Tramways Board, Australia	M&MTB, 1929

Washington • Yakima

Yakima Interurban Trolley Lines. Located in and around the city of Yakima, P.O. Box 124, Yakima, WA 98907. Standard gauge.

URBAN TROLLEY SERVICE in Yakima closed in February 1947, having been maintained on the tracks of a larger electric freight network built primarily to serve the apple-growing region around the city. Freight services continue to operate, however, to this day, thereby prompting a most fascinating revival.

In 1973, with the experience of the trolley museums in mind, the city of Yakima felt that the introduction of a passenger trolley service on the tracks within the city limits would be a tourist attraction, especially as a couple of the cars which closed down passenger service in 1947 still existed.

While terms could not be reached with the owners of these cars, the Union Pacific Railroad (parent company of Yakima Valley Transportation, the owner of the electric freight lines over which the city trolleys had run) became interested in the idea. When it proved impossible to locate suitable trolleys in the U.S. it was

decided to hire consultants. Paul Class of Glenwood was the successful candidate and the Yakima trolleys were the first of his successful tourist trolley line projects to go into service. He advised the city that cars still running in Oporto, Portugal, were almost identical to those run in Yakima from 1907 to 1930.

His advice was taken and the two trolleys arrived safely in Yakima at the end of 1974, despite their having been shipped at the height of the Portugese Revolution of that year! Cars #1776 and #1976 first ran for the public at the end of October 1974, and the net result has been the same as that experienced at the museums; people are happy to ride the old cars and do so in large numbers. Chartering was at a very high level for many years after the start of service and many special city events have been built around the trolleys.

Financial backing came from the city and county governments of Yakima, the various freight customers of the still-flourishing YVT and the Washington State Bicentennial Commission. There are three long lines out of town, which include many blocks of street trackage within the city limits.

Wisconsin • East Troy

East Troy Trolley Museum. Cars leave from 2002 North Church Street, East Troy. East Troy is on Wisconsin Highway 15 about 30 miles southwest of Milwaukee. Owned and operated by the East Troy Trolley Museum, P..O Box 726, East Troy, WI 53120. Standard gauge.

EAST TROY TROLLEY MUSEUM. Beulah Lake loop on the former Milwaukee Transport line, with an ex-Chicago, North Shore & Mil- **waukee car awaiting the passage of the northbound car. A typical interurban scene.** *A.D. Young*

L IKE SO MANY OTHERS, this museum uses the right-of-way of an old interurban line. But in this case there is a profound difference, since the line remains in regular use independently of the museum. Owned by the village of East Troy, it is used by the village to maintain carload freight service between the industrial enterprises of the village and the Soo line interchange at Mukwonago.

The East Troy line started life as an interurban division of John I. Beggs' Milwaukee Electric Railway and Light Company, the operator of Milwaukee's city streetcars. The 36-mile Milwaukee–Hales Corners–Mukwonago–East Troy division opened December 13, 1907, and led an uneventful life until cut back from East Troy to Hales Corners in 1939.

This left the village in a predicament, for the rail link to the Soo was needed to serve the various on-line customers in the village. To keep the customers in the village, East Troy took the unusual step of buying the line from the village back to the Soo line at Mukwonago, together with some cars and equipment, and operating the freight service themselves. They have done so ever since.

After the village bought a diesel locomotive in 1970, their need for an electrified line ceased. It was at this point the village was successfully approached by the Wisconsin Electric Railway Historical Society, an old, established car collecting group which needed a home. While the society had its roots among other groups in the Chicago and Milwaukee areas, by 1970 it had a well-defined interurban character, and the East Troy line seemed an ideal place to be. A lease was signed, the first museum vehicle operated into East Troy in April 1972, and the project was open to the public by June.

The one really unique feature of the museum is the length of track available. It is the only museum in the country collecting interurban cars with more than a couple of miles on which to run them (although others are catching up fast). Over five miles of track separate East Troy from the museum's trolley park and storage area at Phantom Woods, by far the longest museum run in existence. Moreover, there are no problems here

EAST TROY TROLLEY MUSEUM.
Santa's Express. North Shore #757
loads in East Troy. The 1909-built
brick depot-substation is at left.
Rod Robinson

about re-creating an authentic setting; this is an inter-urban museum and the setting *is* authentic. It is a pleasant run from a typical midwest farming village through pastoral countryside and woods, mostly by the side of the road, but at other times on its own cross-country right-of-way.

While the trolley park, crammed with vehicles await-ing restoration and close by a farm store selling cheese and dairy products (for those more interested in Wis-consin's more traditional claims to fame), is quite an attraction in its own right, the East Troy terminal has more formalized displays. It is a genuine country inter-urban terminal point, and the museum is fortunate enough to have use of the line's powerhouse as a sta-tion waiting area, shop, small relics display area and general point of focus for the line.

The ticket office and the associated dispatcher's office are furnished in much the style one would have seen around 1910, and the whole place has a period flavor to it that would be hard to re-create in a more usual museum setting. Moreover, its collection of cars is largely from the Chicago/Milwaukee area, thus mak-ing it a regional electric railway museum of great potential.

EAST TROY TROLLEY MUSEUM.
Phantom Woods yard is at the
north end of the line. North Shore
#757 and #763 are seen; one of the
museum's trolley buses is at the
right edge.   *Rod Robinson*

Fleet No.	Principal Owner	Builder, Year	Remarks
City and Suburban Cars			
17	Milwaukee City Railroad		Horse Car
Interurban Cars			
M1	Milwaukee Electric	TMERL, 1917	Box Motor
228	Chicago, North Shore & Milwaukee	Cincinnati, 1922	Box Motor
250	Chicago, North Shore & Milwaukee	Jewett, 1917	Combine
411	Chicago, North Shore & Milwaukee	Cincinnati, 1923	Interurban
715	Chicago, North Shore & Milwaukee	Cincinnati, 1926	Interurban
757	Chicago, North Shore & Milwaukee	Standard, 1929	Interurban
763	Chicago, North Shore & Milwaukee	Standard, 1929	Interurban
Maintenance of Way Cars and Equipment			
D5	Milwaukee Electric	TMERL, 1909	Snowplow
D7	Milwaukee Electric	TMERL, 1906	Snowplow
12	Milwaukee Electric	TMERL, 1926	Substation
D13	Milwaukee Electric	Differential, 1917	Differential Dump Car
D15	Milwaukee Electric	Differential, 1921	Differential Dump Car
D16	Milwaukee Electric	Brown, 1923	Crane
D22	Milwaukee Electric	TMERL, 1907	Line Car
D23	Milwaukee Electric	TMERL, 1907	Line Car
M37	Milwaukee Electric	TMERL, 1931	Container Car
B48	Milwaukee Electric	TMERL, 1926	Sweeper
Electric Locomotives			
L3	Milwaukee Electric	TMERL, 1920	Steeple Cab
L4	Milwaukee Electric	TMERL, 1920	Steeple Cab
L5	Milwaukee Electric	TMERL, 1926	Steeple Cab
L6	Milwaukee Electric	TMERL, 1929	Crane
L7	Milwaukee Electric	TMERL, 1931	Steeple Cab
L8	Milwaukee Electric	TMERL, 1935	Steeple Cab
L9	Milwaukee Electric	TMERL, 1944	Steeple Cab
L10	Milwaukee Electric	TMERL, 1944	Steeple Cab
Rapid Transit Cars			
4258	Chicago Transit Authority	Cincinnati, 1922	Elevated Car
4420	Chicago Transit Authority	Cincinnati, 1924	Elevated Car
Interurban Freight Cars			
M26	Milwaukee Electric	St. Louis, 1903	Flat Car Idler
E58	Milwaukee Electric	TMERL, 1907	Flat Car

Alberta • Calgary

Heritage Park Pioneer Village. Located in Heritage Park, 1900 Heritage Park Drive S.W., Calgary, Alberta, T2V 2X3, Canada. Standard gauge.

CALGARY'S HERITAGE PARK is a re-creation of several different periods in Alberta's colorful past. It is located on a 60-acre city-owned peninsula, which juts onto a man-made lake, and the high Rockies can be seen in the west. The view of the modern city is almost blocked out, thus maintaining the illusion of having stepped back in time.

The park has two main areas—the settlement area which depicts the austere life of 19th-century trappers, settlers and Indians before the coming of the railway, and the old railroad town area, typical of the boom towns which sprang up in the wake of the Canadian Pacific's trek west in the 1880s.

But it is the streetcar operation which concerns us in

CALGARY HERITAGE PARK. Parts of Calgary streetcars were made into a double-end replica of a typical design, with arch windows and a unique front door arrangement; the originals were single-end. *Calgary Heritage Park*

CALGARY HERITAGE PARK. The entire trolley line is visible in this aerial photograph. The car sits at its terminal at 14th St., S.W. and Heritage Dr. The carbarn is at top right center.
Bow Valley Photographic Services Ltd.

this most unusual theme park. A great deal of effort has been spent on creating a replica of Calgary streetcar #14, using parts from the original #14, whose body had survived until the 1970s. With the whole unit mounted on trucks taken from Toronto snow sweepers, an excellent re-creation of the original was achieved, and put into service in 1975 to open the trolley line.

The streetcar takes you to Empire Station at the park entrance. But do not imagine that is the end of the matter. Once in the town section, a beautiful replica of a Winnipeg horse car is available for rides, the only regularly scheduled horse-car operation in North America other than at Disneyland/Disneyworld. A third car is Montreal observation car #3, similar to that at Warehouse Point, and borrowed from the Canadian Railroad Historical Association of Delson, Qeubec. The car

is also very similar to one which operated in Calgary until 1939. It shares service on the line with #14.

Heritage Park was one of the first Canadian Parks to attempt deliberately to use the living streetcar as just one part of a total historical re-creation. The idea for such a park was mooted early in the 1960s by the city commissioners, and a not-for-profit organization was formed to oversee construction, operation and development.

This outfit is still responsible for the park, delegating its authority to a permanent staff of some 30 management personnel and scads of summer helpers. The example and success of Heritage Park has spilled over to other Canadian cities and it seems as if almost every major Canadian urban area is to have or already has a park on these lines.

Ontario • Rockwood

Halton County Radial Railway. The museum entrance is on Campbellville Road, 8 miles north of interchange 38 on Highway 401 near Rockwood. Owned and operated by the Ontario Electric Railway Historical Society, Box 121, Scarborough "A," Ontario, M1K 5B9, Canada. 4'10-7/8" gauge.

CANADA'S FIRST operating trolley museum was established in late 1953, largely as a reaction to the disposal by the Toronto Transit Commission of one of its collection of historic trolleys. By January 1954 the car (#1326) was in the group's hands, a site was found, and the details of purchase terms settled by February.

The present site was chosen since it was a graded stretch of right-of-way of the former Toronto Suburban Company's Guelph interurban (radial) line. Enough

track was laid to accommodate a number of cars, a barn was built and track work continued, most of the job being done after 1962.

Electrification preliminaries commenced in 1964, but the job was long and complex, being delayed by further land purchases the group had to make. As a result, the first car to move under its own power did not do so until May 1971, when about half the present line was put into service. The remainder opened in 1972, the official opening date being June 25.

The entrance is large and welcoming, being dominated by a genuine Canadian station building, originally sited at nearby Rockwood, Ontario, on the former Grand Trunk Railway. A waiting room, ticket office and bookstore are here, and the car ride commences. The ride is through 1¼ miles of wooded route, perhaps one of the museum's greatest assets, particularly in the

fall when colors are at their most vivid.

Suddenly the end of the line appears in a clearing, the barns can be seen as well as other exhibits. For most passengers, the activity at this end makes for a welcome opportunity to get off the car and see something other than woodland. It is unusual for a museum to have attractions at both ends of the line, and thus let the visitors break a journey.

The collection is Canadian in character, and largely regional, since a majority of the cars ran in Ontario. Practically every type of car that ran in Toronto can be seen, including a replica of an 1893 open car built in 1933 to celebrate the centennial of the city's incorporation. Current plans call for the completion of a new gift shop complex to include showers, bathrooms and workers' meeting rooms.

With cash short these days, and a slight decline in visitors because of the gasoline situation, this building has been given priority over construction of the proposed new shop building and terminal loop, since the new facility is expected to attract charter and bus tour riders in quantity, and thus boost revenues.

Fleet No.	Principal Owner	Builder, Year	Remarks
City and Suburban Cars			
55	Toronto Civic Railways	Preston, 1915	
225	Guelph Radial Railways	Brill, 1922	Birney Safety
327	Toronto Railways Company	TTC, 1933	10-bench Open (Replica)
410	Toronto Transportation Commission	Ottawa, 1924	Suburban
416	Toronto Transportation Commission	Ottawa, 1924	Suburban
521	Hamilton Street Railway	National Steel Car, 1927	
1326	Toronto Transportation Commission	Toronto Rys. Co., 1910	
1704	Toronto Railways Co.	Toronto Rys. Co., 1913	Convertible
2424	Toronto Transportation Commission	Can Car & Fdy., 1921	Peter Witt (Large)
2786	Toronto Transportation Commission	Can Car & Fdy., 1922	Peter Witt (Small)
2890	Toronto Transportation Commission	Ottawa, 1923	Peter Witt (Large)
2894*	Toronto Transportation Commission	Ottawa, 1923	Peter Witt (Large)
4000	Toronto Transportation Commission	St. Louis/CCF, 1938	PCC
4426	Toronto Transportation Commission	St. Louis/CCF, 1949	PCC
4633	Toronto Transportation Commission	Pullman, 1946	PCC (ex-Cleveland)
4684	Toronto Transportation Commission	St. Louis, 1946	PCC (ex-Louisville)

*On loan to Toronto Transportation Commission

Fleet No.	Principal Owner	Builder, Year	Remarks
Interurban Cars			
3	London & Port Stanley	Jewett, 1915 ?	
8	London & Port Stanley	Jewett, 1915	
69	Niagara, St. Catherines & Toronto		
107	Montreal & Southern Counties	Ottawa, 1912	Combine
Maintenance of Way Cars			
45	Oshawa Railway	N, St. C & T. Shops, 1925	Line Car
C1	Toronto Transportation Commission	TRC, 1922	5-ton Crane
M4	Lake Erie & Northern		Bonder
M5			Trackmobile
M6	Lake Erie & Northern		Line Truck
RT-7	Toronto Transportation Commission	Preston, 1917	Rail Grinder (ex-Toronto Civic 53)
S37	Toronto Transportation Commission	Russell, 1920	Snow Sweeper
TP11	Toronto Transportation Commission	National Steel, 1945	Track Plow
W4	Toronto Transportation Commission	TRC, 1904	Construction Car
W28	Toronto Transportation Commission	Preston, 1917	Rail Grinder
Motor Bus			
20	Kitchener, Ontario	Ford, 1946	

HALTON COUNTY RADIAL RAIL-WAY. Rockwood Station, and display carbarn at right. (Left to right) *TTC #1326, Toronto Civic Ry. #55, Montreal & Southern Counties #107, and Toronto's first PCC, #4000.*   *R.J. Sandusky*

HALTON COUNTY RADIAL RAIL-WAY. A large number of these Russell-built snow sweepers were operated by Toronto until very recently. They had been purchased used from New York's *Third Avenue Railway System,* **who in turn has purchased them second-hand from the** *Eastern Massachusetts Street Railway.* **On the right is replica car #327, a 1933 vehicle built by TTC to reproduce an early electric car of the 1890s.**   *R.J. Sandusky*

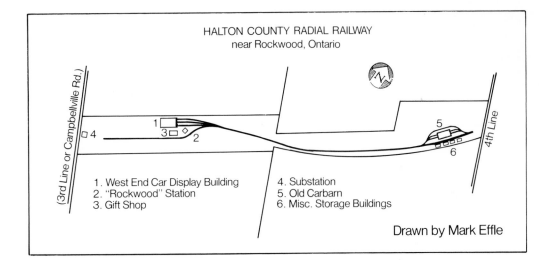

MAP 14

HALTON COUNTY RADIAL RAILWAY
near Rockwood, Ontario

(3rd Line or Campbellville Rd.)

4th Line

1. West End Car Display Building
2. "Rockwood" Station
3. Gift Shop

4. Substation
5. Old Carbarn
6. Misc. Storage Buildings

Drawn by Mark Effle

PART 3: Defunct, Static and Future Museum Projects

IT HAS UNHAPPILY been true that a number of promising projects have not made it. The most greatly to be regretted are those which actually got to the point of erecting wire and running cars. As noted earlier, the successful operation of cars is not always a guarantee of a happy ending and even with the hardest of work and the most determined of efforts, failure can still occur.

A good example of a group with mixed fortunes but which still has kept its head above water is that of the Buckingham Valley Trolley Association, formerly operating at a site in Buckingham, Pa. During the 1950s Philadelphia's trolley trackage was much reduced, almost to its current size. At the same time, a determined effort was made to rid the city of all non-PCC cars, that is to say all cars which were not modern lightweight streamliners.

A group of local enthusiasts purchased some of the cars being withdrawn, forming the Delaware Valley Railroad Association, and they leased a site at Tansboro, New Jersey, some two miles east of Berlin. Three hundred feet of Philadelphia gauge track was put in, together with some overhead and the line was given the name *Delaware Valley Short Line*. In the meantime, another group with a project hanging fire was the so-called *Trolley Museum of New York*. Open storage in a Staten Island railroad yard was not doing its cars much good and it joined forces with the Tansboro people, shipped the cars across and renamed the place *Trolley Valhalla*.

Unfortunately, the New York cars were of standard gauge, incompatible with the 5'2¼" of the Philadelphia cars and though Trolley Valhalla actually operated in the early 1970s, offering a half-mile round trip at the weekends, the New York cars never operated and little was able to be done at the leased site toward providing more permanent display facilities.

This problem was compounded by the building of the Philadelphia-Lindenwold rapid transit line east of the city, on the New Jersey side, since land values in the line's immediate vicinity began to rise abruptly. The owner of the leased site wanted to sell, found a buyer and Trolley Valhalla thus had to move. Another site

was located at Jobstown, N.J., on the Pennsylvania Railroad's former Kinkora-Birmingham branch and the whole move was undertaken in the years 1972 and 1973. Again, the Philadelphia wide gauge was used, and the New York group withdrew its cars, taking them instead to the Morristown steam railway, a tourist line which hoped to run a Toonerville service in connection with its trains. Nothing came of that either, and in 1977 all were moved back to Coney Island shops of the New York subway. Two cars have been restored in that location already and are planned to be a part of the New York subway museum, which will be described later in this chapter.

In the meantime, the Jobstown site was filling up with Philadelphia cars and the remaining group thought it had found a permanent home. Operations were started in 1973 and that should have been that.

The New Hope and Ivyland Railway, a tourist steam line run over a part of a former Reading Railroad branch, wanted to diversify its operations and attract more visitors. This line had a disused branch south of the Buckingham station which seemed to be ideal for a Toonerville operation, and Trolley Valhalla was invited to come and operate cars on it. That led to a major split in the Trolley Valhalla group. Those members who remained continued to have cars at the site, but no rides have been offered in many years, and the outdoor storage of the cars has done little to enhance their appearance. There seems indeed to be a major question mark hanging over the Jobstown site and its cars, one that may be resolved by the opening of the Delaware Avenue line in Philadelphia, since the Wildwood, New Jersey, open car scheduled to run on that line in 1983 comes from Jobstown, and other Philadelphia cars may follow.

Those who left Trolley Valhalla to run cars on the New Hope & Ivyland coalesced into a new group known as the Buckingham Valley Trolley Association, and took with them a handful of standard gauge cars to which individual members held title. Still other Trolley Valhalla cars have been stored and restored elsewhere and one or two have turned up as museum pieces to be run occasionally on Philadelphia's wide gauge tracks. The new Buckingham Valley line was electrified in 1974 and service was provided every few minutes on 1½ miles of route by Red Arrow car #26, which now provides service on the Delaware Avenue line in Philadelphia.

The long-term plan of the Association was (and remains) the creation of a full-scale regional trolley museum based around a Philadelphia collection. As always, the incompatibility of the 5'2½" gauge of the city and suburban trolleys and the standard gauge of the sites chosen has led to indefinite delays in fulfilling this dream, but all did seem to be set fair at Buckingham Valley until 1979.

A dispute with the railway could not be resolved satisfactorily and the service was shut down for the 1980 season and never reopened. Certainly for the Buckingham Valley group the Delaware Avenue project has been most timely and one wishes them good luck on this, their fourth attempt (in one institutional form or another) to bring their dream to fruition.

Another unfortunate demise was that of the Magee Transportation Museum. Located in Bloomsburg, Pa., it was founded by H.L. Magee, the retired board chairman of the Magee Carpet Company. Not only did it create the fine Magee Shortway Electric Railway, the museum had a superb collection of fire engines, farm equipment, old autos and other vintage vehicles. On the trolley car side, the museum was impeccably laid out, with a neat, clean, cared-for appearance one still sees only in a few other places. The exhibits were housed in new custom-built buildings while there were a few historic structures which had been re-erected from original locations elsewhere, in the manner of Canadian museums such as Heritage Park. There was a large number of cars, some merely bodies awaiting restoration, but others fully and superbly restored by the museum's Ed Blossom, a one-time Branford museum man. He had already restored two beautiful South American open cars, while a nice Pittsburgh low floor car had been added as recently as 1971. Other bodies were to be dealt with as the years went on, for Mr. Blossom is an agonizingly meticulous and thorough man when it comes to restoring a trolley car.

But disaster struck on the night of June 21, 1972, when, after days of heavy rain, Hurricane "Agnes" hit the museum. The creek alongside the site rose rapidly and by noon of June 22, water began to enter the museum buildings. By late afternoon there was three feet of water in the barns and auto museum and no less than four feet in the station, the restored farmhouse and antique carriage building. Had that been all, doubtless the museum would have survived, since mud can be cleaned up, traction motors dried out and things gradually brought back to a respectable state—at a price. The Baltimore museum suffered the same fate the year before, and again in 1979, but has been able to reopen.

Magee, however, suffered the bad fortune of losing most of its track, too. Only 500 feet of the extensive trackage was spared. As for the rest, the cinder ballast was washed out, much of the fill on which the tracks rested was damaged or destroyed and nearly 1,000 feet of track near the shops was twisted and overturned. Other sections of the property were nearly as badly damaged and while cleaning went on throughout the rest of the summer, the museum remained closed, pending a decision as to its future course.

Mr. Magee in the meanwhile died on October 9, 1972, and while the family did suggest that the museum would be reopened in 1973, it was clear a new site would have to be chosen. In the end, reopening did not occur and the collection was scattered. It has been suggested that as a wholly private museum project, Magee was not eligible for the kind of assistance given the Baltimore Streetcar Museum, for example, by the City of Baltimore in its hour of need. It is certainly true that massive amounts of money would have been needed to reestablish Magee as it had been. As it was, this very fine museum was overwhelmed by its problems and after years of good service is irretrievably lost to us.

Mr. Blossom, however, subsequently became the nucleus around which the now disbanded Dushore Car Company established itself in the mid-1970s, doing superb restoration work under contract for various organizations. A typical group for whom work has been done was the Liberty Bell Jewett Society. This is a federation of people who for many years have been attempting to restore various city and interurban cars formerly belonging to the Lehigh Valley Transit

Ed Blossom at work on extensive body rehabilitation at the Magee museum in 1970.   J.H. Price

MAGEE MUSEUM. Two years before the disastrous flood, these two fine ex-Rio open cars are seen outside the Magee museum's car shop, in July 1970. Most of Magee's finely restored cars have found new homes elsewhere. These are at the Midwest Electric Railway at Mt. Pleasant, Iowa. *Ralph Forty*

MAGEE MUSEUM. *Pittsburgh Railway's* #4145 had just been restored at the Magee museum by Mr. Ed Blossom when pictured in April 1971. The car is currently to be seen at Trolleyville, USA, in Olmsted Falls, Ohio. *Ralph Forty*

MAGEE MUSEUM. The devastation caused by the 1972 hurricane and flood at the Magee display was horrible to behold. This uprooted section of track was opposite the car shop. *Ralph Forty*

Company. LVT ran in the Allentown-Bethlehem area of Pennsylvania and had a long-lived interurban service to Philadelphia via trackage rights over the still-operating Philadelphia & Western, now a part of SEPTA's Red Arrow division.

The Liberty Bell Jewett Society and Mr. Blossom were already connected through the Magee museum, since there were some of the group's Lehigh Valley Transit carbodies on the property. After Mr. Blossom finished the restoration of Pittsburgh car #4145 in 1971, it was intended he should begin on one of the Lehigh Valley cars at the museum premises.

In the aftermath of the hurricane damage and the closure of Magee, the Dushore Car Company was set up and restoration work began on one of the Lehigh cars. The Liberty Bell group intended to continue the car restorations, create a Lehigh Valley Transit archive and library and eventually create a living trolley museum in which Lehigh Valley Transit equipment

would play a large part. They can be contacted at P.O. Box 144, Topton, PA 19562.

Mr. Blossom's latest completed work is the Burton and Ashby double-deck car, presently running on Detroit's Citizens' Railway. It was largely undertaken at Topton, Pa., under the auspices of Rail Technical Services, Topton. This new organization with which Mr. Blossom is connected is headed by Bruce W. Thain, a New Yorker and a Branford stalwart, who was also involved with Mr. Blossom in the earlier Dushore enterprise.

RIVERTON, NEW YORK

A MORE CHEERFUL prospect is presented by a number of embryonic projects which are at present static, but which plan electrification over the next few years. One such example is presently underway at Riverton, just outside Rochester, N.Y. Known as the New York Museum of Transportation, its membership is composed of disparate elements from groups such as Magee and the National Railroad Historical Society. This latter nationwide organization of railfans began its existence at the same time as the Electric Railroaders Association, and shared ERA's love of trolleys, tempered somewhat by an even greater love for railroads.

There are well over 100 chapters today, many of which specialize in the adoption of railroad museum projects. We have already noted the Warehouse Point Museum. To a certain extent, the New York Museum of Transportation will share that background and, when finally complete, this little-known museum promises to be one of the nation's best.

Many Magee cars found their way here, specifically those with New York State antecedents. In addition, there are cars from Rochester, including a horse car, two unique interurbans and various other transportation artifacts. In the past Ed Blossom's services were frequently requested and received, but the museum has always striven to be self-sufficient and a most unusual activity illustrating that philosophy is their learning and teaching project.

This project encourages the membership to learn under expert guidance the old skills and crafts that will put a trolley or an antique steam locomotive back on the rails again. One task undertaken was the replacement of a highly deteriorated car by a replica, since the original was too far decayed to be rebuilt. The replica was completed by hitherto totally inexperienced people, whose considerable skills came solely as a result of the learning project. They now form the nucleus of a talented crew able to tackle other restoration projects without outside help.

The collection is to be a regional one, specializing in cars of New York State, plus railroads and autos. The museum is set up in a building on the corner of a state farm for juveniles near Riverton, specifically in the town of Rush on East River Road at Henrietta-Rush Town Line Road, about two miles south of exit 46 of the New York State Thruway.

Operating plans call for the laying of several miles of track southward to the Oatka depot of the National Railroad Historical Society, giving a scenic ride through the rolling hills and woods of the Genesee Valley. A picnic grove is planned midway on the line, and tracks are already laid to this point, using material donated by the City of Rochester from the old trolley subway. The museum's mailing address is P.O. Box 136, West Henrietta, NY 14586.

FORT COLLINS, COLORADO

A VERY DIFFERENT trolley project is underway in Fort Collins, Colorado. That town was unique in American Traction history in many ways. When the trolleys ceased operation in 1951, Fort Collins had the lowest fare in the nation, was the smallest municipality in the U.S. to still have a trolley system, was the last Birney car operator on the continent and the last trolley operator in the state of Colorado.

Most unusual was the operation of the system. With cars every 20 minutes from downtown to anywhere, safety switching and transfer problems in the downtown area might have become overwhelming. They were solved by the institution of an extraordinary ritual, when every 20 minutes the three cars on the three different lines met at the corner of College and Mountain Avenues and traded passengers! With all the passengers transferred to the correct cars, the three vehicles then solemnly took off on the lines they had come in on. Since this ritual lasted well into the postwar museum and railfan era, it was well known and extensively photographed.

Universally regretted after its demise, it was not until the general revival of the restoration spirit in Fort Collins that anyone felt the trolley could be reborn. After closure the six cars had been scattered all over the country. One is at the Henry Ford Museum in Dearborn, Michigan; another is in Minden, Nebraska's Pioneer Village and a third is in the Colorado Railroad Museum near Golden. All are on static display in institutions which do not plan museum streetcar operation and hence have not been covered in this book. A fourth car stayed in Library Park, next to the Fort Collins museum as the city's tribute to the trolley car era and it has been this car on which present activities center.

By 1977 the car was more than a little decrepit when the Fort Collins Junior Women's Club asked the city if it could restore the car and put it on display in the "old town" area of Fort Collins. Not only did the city agree, it even helped move the car back to the Howes Street trolley barn for restoration work to begin in comfortable quarters. A total restoration of the car is now underway from the wheels up. It has been estimated that the value of donated materials and labor that have gone into the car is in excess of $100,000. This figure is calculated mainly on the thousands of labor hours, all of which is donated by the volunteers, but it is a good example of the real value of the volunteer labor at any of the larger trolley museums with their scores of restored cars and miles of trackage.

With the project under way, more ambitious ideas began to bubble up. The streetcar had caught the imagination of so many in Fort Collins that it soon began to be suggested that the car should be restored to operating condition and run in good weather on evenings and weekends on one of the original routes to and from City Park along West Mountain Avenue. The idea won wide acceptance and those who planned to implement it formalized their existence by incorporating as the Fort Collins Municipal Railway Society. On

April 1, 1980, the City Council accepted the whole plan after long discussions within the community, which gave evidence of solid support.

In brief, the April 1 resolution approved a contract between Fort Collins and the Society, stipulating that the city would agree to operation of Fort Collins car #21 on West Mountain Avenue's median by the Society and that the Society will be responsible for the construction, operation and maintenance of the line. The contract between the two parties was finally signed on March 17, 1981, and a big feature (made much of in Council and in the local newspapers) was that the city was asked to provide no money of any sort. All money needed was to be raised through public solicitation of funds or materials and the group was well on its way.

The car was scheduled to be completed by the end of 1982, and the construction of the rail line is planned to be done block by block, with a block completed before the next one is started. This means that the total completion date for the project is not until 1985, but there should be enough track ready by 1983 for limited car operation to begin. This is important for the Society since farebox revenues are a crucial element in keeping the project self-sustaining.

In all, over 1¼ miles of track are envisaged, and operation on the historic West Mountain Avenue route will reorient attention back to the historic downtown area of the city. The Fort Collins Municipal Railway Society can be reached in care of Joan Seegmiller at 731 West Mountain Avenue, Fort Collins, CO 80521.

LOWELL, MASSACHUSETTS

A FASCINATING TOURIST trolley project is currently underway in Lowell, Massachusetts, as part of the Lowell National Historic Park. For some years a motorized trolley vehicle known as the *Whistler* has been in service for visitors, prompting the thought that a revival of real trolley operation might be welcomed. But rather than vaguely and unsystematically look for old cars that could be restored to operating condition without guidance, the Park has instead done what most professional mass transit planners do and has gone for advice to a professional consulting firm, in this case Louis G. Klauder and Associates of Philadelphia. Estimates were prepared and designs drawn up for the system and the type of trolley it was proposed to run.

What the park wanted and what Klauder was able to help them with has taken more than two years to implement and the job is still far from completion. In brief, the need was for a set of trolley cars compatible with Lowell's real cars (now all gone) and track gauge. That, of course, translates into trolley cars from the early 1900s. Moreover, since the cars were to run for summer visitors in an outdoor park, open cars were vital. We have seen earlier in this book how open cars have become so scarce as to be worth their weight in

gold, but the park authorities didn't know that, and were devastated when they realized it. What to do?

Well, why not *build* some new open car bodies, replicas of the real thing, but using trucks and electrical equipment which could be bought second-hand somewhere in the world? After all, since this wasn't to be a trolley museum, but a tourist trolley operation instead, none but the purist would object to slightly different trucks on what was otherwise an authentic-appearing replica.

So it was that in May of 1982 four car sets of trucks and equipment arrived at the Park Service maintenance facility on French Street extension in Lowell. Once again our old friends at the Melbourne and Metropolitan Tramways Board in Australia were the source of this robust and serviceable equipment, coming from withdrawn 1920s cars of the same type as may presently be ridden in Seattle. With the trucks in hand, drawings for the needed new bodies could be finalized and the job put out to bid.

As can be seen, this project is rather different from the usual in that it is one of the few where a wholly professional group with access to state and federal funds is proposing to build a trolley line. Here, as in the more usual amateur-sponsored museum, money is a problem, but only insofar as both groups have to wait some time until it becomes available. The big difference is that with grant money, the money does come through in a predictable interval of time, and usually in approximately the quantity required. Since the Park Service has more than enough people on the payroll, the job can then be completed very quickly and the labor force paid.

This is where a professional approach seems to pay off in terms of speed and efficiency. The Park approached Klauder and Associates with a good plan already in mind, encompassing the whole project, from definition to detail. From this, Klauder and Associates was able to prepare a financial estimate of $600,000 for line and overhead construction and $450,000 for the new carbodies. These are to be replicas of 1902 Brill 15-bench opens for the Eastern Massachussetts Street Railway which ran in and around the town.

Armed with these estimates and Klauder's advice, it became a relatively simple administrative matter for the Lowell Historic Preservation Commission (the body responsible for the overall direction of the park) to work out a timetable and budget and apply for funding.

This, therefore, is an ongoing project and as the funding becomes available, so will the project come to completion. Current estimates call for the carbodies to be begun at the end of 1983, with the hope they and the line can be completed in time for the 1984 season, but budget shortfalls might delay that plan a year or so. Incidentally, there are four sets of trucks for three bodies since one set is to be held for spares.

FORD EDMONTON

CLOSELY AKIN to Heritage Park Calgary is a project underway at the Fort Edmonton historical complex in Edmonton, Alberta. That Canadian city installed a superb new Light Rail system some years ago, using vehicles which by coincidence were of the same track gauge and similar voltage to those of the city's previous trolley system, which was closed down in 1951. Car #1 of 1908 had been kept as a museum piece in the intervening years by a private group and to help celebrate Edmonton's 75th birthday in 1979; it was restored to operating condition in the Light Rail shops by volunteer labor.

Coincidentally those shops, only temporarily occupied by the Light Rail operation until its own new buildings were ready, were in fact the main Cromdale shops of the original trolley installation. When completed, #1 was operated on test runs over the new Light Rail tracks in the shop area. It performed very well.

Edmonton's trolley tracks had been extended southwards over the new High Level bridge in 1913, running on each side of the Canadian Pacific Railroad tracks for the nearly one-mile length of the bridge. Though trolley service over the bridge ceased in 1951, the poles and right-of-way remain. On October 5, 1979, with a power generator in town, the car was transferred to the railroad tracks leading to the bridge and was run in public service across the bridge on October 6, 7, and 8—a most imaginative birthday present for the city. Additionally, on October 4, 1979, #1 was run on the Light Rail line down to the underground Churchill station.

With the celebrations over, the Edmonton Radial Railway Society was formed to operate #1 and other representative cars at Fort Edmonton, a still-taking-shape historical complex of impressive proportions, already open to the public in part during the season. The province of Alberta has granted $177,000 to allow work to begin on building a carbarn and depot track, both of which were substantially complete by the spring of 1982.

Amazingly no less than six Edmonton carbodies have been located and purchased, while negotiations are underway to acquire two more Edmonton cars so that eventually it is hoped that, with restoration, every car type that ever ran in the city will be represented in operating condition on the Fort Edmonton tracks. Car #1 arrived at Fort Edmonton in the summer of 1981 and is to be seen currently running in service over the already installed steam railroad, again powered by its portable generator, safely in tow.

It is hoped the tracks will be completed and overhead energized on 1905- and 1920-era streets in the complex by 1983. Restoration of the Edmonton carbodies is proceeding in an orderly fashion and when complete Edmonton will rival the Baltimore Streetcar Museum in its ability to tell the story of trolleys in its urban area. The Edmonton Radial Railway Society can be contacted through the Fort Edmonton Historical Society at Box 8645, Postal Station L, Edmonton, Alberta. Fort Edmonton is in southwest Edmonton at Fox Drive and the south end of the Quesnell Bridge (Whitemud Freeway).

DELSON, QUEBEC

THERE ARE TWO other fine Canadian museums with substantial trolley car collections, but regrettably their plans for operating them are somewhat more tentative than either Fort Collins or Fort Edmonton. The Canadian Railway Museum at Delson, in Quebec, possesses a vast collection of Canadian transport relics. It was established in 1961 at a time the Canadian steam locomotive was about to go out of service for the last time. The tremendous rush of sentiment that event engendered, from the highest government bodies to the ordinary citizen, resulted in a demand to see the country honor the departing giants in a suitable way.

The Canadian National Railroad Historical Association came up with an imaginative plan for a national rail transport museum to be financed by public institutions and private industry, but staffed and run by volunteers, much as the successful U.S. trolley and railroad museums were doing. By 1964 cash donations had already exceeded $150,000, a sum, it has been rightly observed, that many museums elsewhere could be said to have barely earned in their entire working lives up to that time.

This got the project off to a flying start. Ten acres of the present site were received as a donation and quickly covered with tracks and buildings, on which an extraordinary collection of railroad artifacts was placed. All the exhibits were donated and many were thoroughly restored by their donors before being handed over. It is of course the trolley collection which concerns us here. The collection was started by the Canadian Railroad Historical Society more than 30 years ago when it purchased an historic Montreal trolley for itself and sponsored the restoration of two others for the Montreal Transportation Commission.

In due course that body amassed an historic fleet of 12 Montreal cars and the whole group was passed on to the Canadian Railway Museum. A second main building was erected to house them in 1967-1968. One of the stepped sightseeing cars has since been loaned as an operating car to Heritage Park, Calgary. In addition to the Montreal cars, there are vehicles from Ottawa, London and Port Stanley, Montreal and Southern Counties, and the Quebec Railway Light & Power Company, all long-lived Canadian trolley and interurban operators.

A "belt line" of continuous single track runs around

the perimeter of the site and from the beginning has been slated as an operating electric trolley line. But over the years other priorities have taken precedence and indeed, in 1971, the museum donated an Ottawa car, originally intended to run the main service, to the National Museum of Science and Technology in Ottawa.

Since there are passenger movements on the track on a regularly scheduled basis by both diesel and steam trains, the possibility of electrifying the tracks is still alive. The museum entrance is in St. Constant on the south shore of the St. Lawrence River, just off Highway 132. It is about 10 miles from downtown Montreal and some 30 or so from the U.S. border. The museum can be reached at P.O. Box 148, St. Constant, Quebec J0L 1X0, Canada.

The aforementioned National Museum of Science and Technology has no plans at all to run its cars, since it is a more traditional museum than any so far covered in this book. It is included here largely because of its collection of Canadian trolleys. It is a Canadian government-operated educational project covering a wide range of subjects of which transport is but one. However, the trolley cars and steam locomotive displays are worth a visit if only to see how the non-operating approach of a traditional museum while highly informative to the visitor, misses that crucial element of movement, so much a part of the living trolley. The museum is located at St. Lawrence Boulevard and Russell Road in Ottawa's suburbs.

ST. LOUIS, MISSOURI

A LARGE, FASCINATING, but to date static museum is to be found in St. Louis. The National Museum of Transport began life in 1944 when the St. Louis Public Service Co., chronically short of space, threatened to scrap a mule car of the 1880s which it had in storage. A group was formed to preserve it and with other acquisitions in mind, acquired 44 acres of railroad land around a right-of-way recently abandoned by the Missouri Pacific Railroad in order to bypass two restricted single-line tunnels.

From the first, this was intended to be a complete museum of transportation and given the early date of its establishment it can be seen that it was the first of the amateur museums to actively pursue such a course. With the huge site available to it, trolley cars poured in, as did steam railroad locomotives, passenger and freight cars, automobiles and other exhibits.

But operation was never contemplated by the then-Board members and it has taken decades to get even a small proportion of the exhibits into good order. In fact, this priceless collection of transport artifacts quickly grew beyond the ability of the limited group of dedicated amateurs to fully cope. It is a good example of how easy it is to acquire exhibits, but how difficult it is to properly care for them when there are too few volunteers, too little money and too many exhibits.

No cover had ever been erected for the rail exhibits in the nearly 40 years of the museum's existence, nor anything more than a small gift shop and visitors' center established until very recent years. And yet, in two areas, this museum has been among the leaders in the trolley museum movement: the acquisition of a good library and archive collection (unfortunately never properly accessioned, nor opened to public use) and the institution of guided tours for visitors, where the exhibits and their relationship to each other are carefully explained. Moreover, its collection of St. Louis area trolleys and interurban cars is unique in the country and could, if properly displayed, rank the museum along with Baltimore in its ability to tell the story of the trolley in its area.

In recent times, the structure of the museum administration has been changed, with a transfer to the local county parks system. That body now runs the museum and provides labor for the restoration and upkeep of the exhibits. First priorities were to build a new visitors' center and parking area and the new *Barrett's Station* is as fine a building as any in the country. Now these projects are complete, and work is scheduled to begin on covering some of the exhibits.

When the county took over, it was decided to rearrange many of the exhibits on the site for better viewing and to that end one of the diesel locomotives in the collection was overhauled and put back into running order. Since then it has been in fairly regular use as the museum's switch locomotive and thus far has been responsible for the only powered movements on museum property in the NMT's history. The augmented work crews of St. Louis County Parks Department employees have done good work in making the exhibits presentable to the public, but years of neglect have taken their toll on even the largest locomotives and the clean appearance of recent years cannot mask that fact.

Even so, many of the exhibits are in reasonable condition and there are plans to have at least a couple of the steam locomotives made operable again by volunteer crews and other bodies. Those interested in the large trolley and traction collection will find little change as yet, though long-term plans do for the first time call for the operation of one or more trolleys on a proposed *intramural* line within the grounds.

That, however, is dependent on the county budget, which has been considerably cut of late. The museum can be reached at 3015 Barrett Station Road, St. Louis, MO 63122. It is some miles to the west of the city. On I-270 going southbound, use the Big Bend exit and continue about 1½ miles west to Barrett Station Road. On I-270 going northbound use the Dougherty Ferry Road exit and continue about 1½ miles west to the junction with Barrett Station Road, then south on Barrett Station Road for ½ mile.

SNOQUALMIE, WASHINGTON

A MUCH SMALLER transport museum with hopes of future trolley operation is that of the Puget Sound Railway Historical Association at Snoqualmie, Washington, in the foothills of the Cascade range. This operating museum railroad possesses some 10 trolley and interurban cars. For some years it has been the custom to operate a handful of the trolleys using a portable generator towed behind the car. The museum still hopes that by 1984 a part of the trackage can be wired and a permanent trolley service offered.

The museum can be found near the Snoqualmie Falls exit of I-90 or Washington 202, by traveling three miles west along Route 202 to the Association's restored ex-Seattle, Lake Shore and Eastern railroad depot of 1890 in the village of Snoqualmie. The address is 109 King Street, Snoqualmie, WA 98065.

NORTH PRAIRIE, WISCONSIN

A NEW PROJECT, uncompromisingly known as the North Prairie Electric Railway, is being created by the Wisconsin Trolley Museum, Inc., in North Prairie, Wisconsin. The group was formed in 1976 to preserve streetcars from Wisconsin but has quickly expanded its collection areas to include cars from adjacent states and is becoming a regional trolley museum. Not surprisingly, a new project of this nature has more than its share of problems in locating suitable streetcars for exhibit, and this is to be one of the first museums to face the problem squarely and deal with it by building a replica car.

Attacking the problem at its root, it is to be an open car, so that whatever else the museum may run, the all-important visitor will have one of the most popular types of cars to sample. The car being built is coming together from a collection of suitable parts accumulated over the years and will be a single-truck vehicle. At the same time work began on the open car in 1976, a restoration project was begun on a Birney safety car, La Crosse #12 and that, too, is in an advanced stage of completion. This is a welcome addition to any museum, for operating Birney cars are rare; yet are typical of small-town and rural trolley operations in the midwest 60 years ago.

For many years this project was without a suitable home, but in March 1981 a site was located at North Prairie, Wisconsin, and the old Milwaukee Road depot, plus adjoining land was bought. The depot is 27 miles west of Milwaukee on one of the oldest railroads in the state, the **Milwaukee and Mississippi,** first constructed in 1858. A carbarn was quickly erected and, in July 1981, both the open car and the Birney were moved in.

Later on that month the group acquired Duluth-Superior #253, which will be one of the first cars to operate under wire when electrical services start, presently planned for the 1984 season. Since then an additional car has been purchased, a Wisconsin Power and Light owned vehicle, Sheboygan #253, while #4420 (one of Chicago's ubiquitous Cincinnati-built elevated cars) completes the present rolling stock roster. The gift shop is already open and functioning and can be found at 132 Main Street in North Prairie, WI 53153.

SAN FRANCISCO, CALIFORNIA

W HILE CABLE-HAULED streetcars are not electric trolleys, they are even more antique and certainly as well loved by the general public. San Francisco's remaining three-route network, while an integral part of that city's public transit, is still a living, breathing museum of the streetcar. Though presently closed down for its first complete overhaul since the 1880s, the whole network will reopen on schedule during 1984 and in the meantime, the replacing diesel buses which manfully struggle with the incredible hills show just how important the cable cars were to the area, since they did not pollute. A fascinating adjunct to the cable car lines is the San Francisco cable car museum, which occupies the upper gallery of the powerhouse at Washington and Mason. Both the cable car system and the building were declared U.S. National Historic Landmarks back in the 1960s and, while the museum and the powerhouse are currently closed as part of the cable car renovation, it is expected that 1983 will see at least these attractions reopened as the work progresses. An intending visitor should check with the Municipal Railway by writing direct.

The National Historic Landmark designation prompted the Municipal Railway, in conjunction with members of the Pacific Coast chapter of the Railway and Locomotive Historical Society, to turn part of the cable car powerhouse into a public display area. In this mezzanine area, forming a large gallery overlooking the cable-winding equipment, are three full-size cable cars, nearly 60 models, documents and informative displays. A good-sized gift shop helps defray many of the running costs through its sales of merchandise and anyone riding the cable cars again after reopening should certainly not miss this intriguing little museum. The museum is at 1201 Mason Street, San Francisco, CA 94108.

FRENCH LICK, INDIANA

T HE TROLLEY MUSEUM movement now is beginning to intrigue some of the steam railroad operations with its possibilities. An example of this phenomenon is presently under development at the Indiana

Railroad Museum's **French Lick, West Baden & Southern Railway** in French Lick, Indiana. A famed resort area of old, French Lick was one of the few places in North America where at busy times one could see upwards of 50 railroad private cars being serviced and made ready for their owners (who would be experiencing the delights of the classic hotels in the vicinity). Both the Monon and the Southern Railroad terminated in the town and the ex-Monon depot is focal point for the activities on the line.

A round trip of 18 miles from the Monon depot is operated between April and November using steam power, and the museum itself possesses some 30 pieces of equipment with an active restoration program underway. One of those pieces is a Cincinnati and Lake Erie freight motor, #646, which runs trips utilizing an on-board diesel motor. This has prompted the more trolley-minded members of the museum to come up with a development project based around tourist trolleys. The plan is to electrify some 1½ miles of the available track around French Lick and to import trolleys from abroad to run the services. At the time of writing, material for electrification was being stockpiled and the full complement of poles, wires, electrical substations and the like were on hand. All that was missing were the cars, but it was hoped that the end of the 1983 season would see operations commence, with a full service to be run in 1984, possibly on a daily basis much as the tourist trolleys in other towns have been run up until now. Since French Lick's economy is primarily tourist based, the addition of a tourist trolley ride is something both the town and the hotels are enthusiastic about and the scheme promises to be of great interest. The museum can be contacted at P.O. Box 150, French Lick, IN 47432.

BROOKLYN, NEW YORK

AND FINALLY, since subway cars are an accepted part of many a trolley museum collection, one cannot ignore the superb subway museum operated by the New York MTA in the former Court Street subway station in Brooklyn. There are many very old New York subway cars in their original colors, the station is elderly but clean and well maintained and there are lots of fascinating small exhibits. In conjunction with the museum, a weekend *Nostalgia Special* is run on the subway, from the 57th Street/6th Avenue Station on Manhattan, non-stop to the museum. After a one-hour stop, the train continues on down to the Rockaways. This is a fine way to experience both the living subway, through its operating museum cars, and the subway's history, through the static interpretive display. Though not yet on exhibit, a few historic New York trolley cars are also on the property, being restored to operable condition, with the possibility of operation in the future somewhere in the New York area. The subway museum is two blocks south of Brooklyn Borough Hall at Boerum Place and Schermerhorn Street. Under the name *New York City Transit Exhibit,* the museum can be contacted via the New York City Transit Authority, 370 Jay Street, Brooklyn, NY 11201.

Index

This book was typeset in Optima

Typesetting by Roc-Pacific Typographics, Los Angeles

Printed by G.R. Huttner Lithographers, Burbank, California